Essays and Studies 2008

Series Editor: Peter Kitson

The English Association

The objects of the English Association are to promote the knowledge and appreciation of the English language and its literature, and to foster good practice in its teaching and learning at all levels.

The Association pursues these aims by creating opportunities of co-operation among all those interested in English; by furthering the recognition of English as essential in education; by discussing methods of English teaching; by holding lectures, conferences, and other meetings; by publishing journals, books, and leaflets; and by forming local branches.

Publications

The Year's Work in English Studies. An annual bibliography. Published by Blackwell.

The Year's Work in Critical and Cultural Theory. An annual bibliography. Published by Blackwell.

Essays and Studies. An annual volume of essays by various scholars assembled by the collector covering usually a wide range of subjects and authors from the medieval to the modern. Published by D. S. Brewer.

English. A journal of the Association, *English* is published three times a year by the Association.

The Use of English. A journal of the Association, *The Use of English* is published three times a year by the Association.

Newsletter. A *Newsletter* is published three times a year giving information about forthcoming publications, conferences, and other matters of interest.

Benefits of Membership

Institutional Membership

Full members receive copies of *The Year's Work in English Studies*, *Essays and Studies*, *English* (3 issues) and three *Newsletters*.

Ordinary Membership covers *English* (3 issues) and three *Newsletters*.

Schools Membership includes copies of each issue of *English* and *The Use of English*, one copy of *Essays and Studies*, three *Newsletters*, and preferential booking and rates for various conferences held by the Association.

Individual Membership

Individuals take out Basic Membership, which entitles them to buy all regular publications of the English Association at a discounted price, and attend Association gatherings.

For further details write to The Secretary, The English Association, The University of Leicester, University Road, Leicester, LE1 7RH.

Essays and Studies 2008

Literature and Science

Edited by
Sharon Ruston

for the English Association

D. S. BREWER

ESSAYS AND STUDIES 2008
IS VOLUME SIXTY-ONE IN THE NEW SERIES
OF ESSAYS AND STUDIES COLLECTED ON BEHALF OF
THE ENGLISH ASSOCIATION
ISSN 0071–1357

First published 2008
D. S. Brewer, Cambridge

D. S. Brewer is an imprint of Boydell & Brewer Ltd
PO Box 9, Woodbridge, Suffolk IP12 3DF, UK
and of Boydell & Brewer Inc.
668 Mt Hope Avenue, Rochester, NY 14620, USA
website: www.boydellandbrewer.com

ISBN 978-1-84384-178-4

A CIP catalogue record for this book is available
from the British Library

The Library of Congress has cataloged this serial publication:
Catalog card number 36–8431

The publisher has no responsibility for the persistence
or accuracy of URLs for external or third-party internet websites referred
to in this book, and does not guarantee that any content on such
websites is, or will remain, accurate or appropriate.

This publication is printed on acid-free paper

Printed in Great Britain by
CPI Antony Rowe, Chippenham, Wiltshire

Contents

Illustrations

Cover: William Blake, *Newton*, reproduced with the permission of The Tate Gallery, London.

Figures

Acknowledgements

The general editor of the Essays and Studies series, and President of the English Association, Professor Peter Kitson, has been a tremendous help throughout the process of this volume. It was his idea from the beginning and this seems appropriate, given his own particular contribution to the subject of Romantic-period literature and science. I would like to thank the contributors to this volume for their brilliant work, and help in meeting deadlines, and my partner, Jerome de Groot, for being wonderful.

Notes on Contributors

David Amigoni   is a Professor of Victorian Literature at Keele University. He is the author of books on Victorian biography and life writing, and the English novel, most recently his 2007 monograph, entitled *Colonies, Cults, and Evolution: Literature, Science, and Culture in Nineteenth-Century Writing*. He is editor of the *Journal of Victorian Culture*.

Brian Baker   is Lecturer in English at Lancaster University. He has published *Masculinity in Fiction and Film*, *Iain Sinclair*, and with John H. Cartwright, *Literature and Science: Social Impact and Interaction*. He has also published more widely on science fiction in the journals *Extrapolation*, *Foundation* and *Vector*.

Elaine Hobby   is Head of Department, and Professor of Seventeenth-Century Studies, in the English and Drama Department at Loughborough University, where she has worked since 1988. She is working on a history of the early-modern midwifery manual in English, 1540–1720.

Alice Jenkins   is a Senior Lecturer in the Department of English Literature at the University of Glasgow. Recent books include *Space and the 'March of Mind'. Literature and the Physical Sciences in Britain, 1815–1850* (2007) and *Michael Faraday's Mental Exercises: An Artisan Essay-Circle in Regency London* (2008). She is the Chair of the British Society for Literature and Science.

Katy Price   teaches English and Writing at Anglia Ruskin University and is Communications Officer for History of Science at the BA Festival of Science. She has published on William Empson's astronomy love poems in *Interdisciplinary Science Reviews* (2005) and *Versions of Empson*, ed. Matthew Bevis (2007).

Gillian Rudd   is a Senior Lecturer in the School of English at the University of Liverpool. She teaches and researches in the areas of late medieval English literature and nineteenth- and twentieth-century women's writing and has been developing an interest in eco-criticism since the late 1990s. She has published several articles and chapters on this theme, as well as a book: *Greenery: Ecocritcal Readings of Late Medi-*

eval English Literature (2007) and is currently engaged in a project taking an ecocritical approach to flowers in medieval literary texts, and in medieval illuminations and post-medieval illustrations of medieval works such as Chaucer's *Legend of Good Women*.

Sharon Ruston is a Senior Lecturer in English at Keele University. She has published *Shelley and Vitality* (2005), *Romanticism: An Introduction* (2007), and many articles on the relationships between Romantic-period literature, science and medicine.

Martin Willis is a Senior Lecturer in the Department of English at the University of Glamorgan and Co-Director of the Glamorgan Research Centre for Literature, Arts, and Science (RCLAS). He is the author of *Mesmerists, Monsters and Machines: Science Fiction and the Cultures of Science in the Nineteenth Century* (2006) and co-editor of *Victorian Literary Mesmerism* (2006), *Repositioning Victorian Sciences* (2006) and *Jack the Ripper: Media, Culture, History* (2007).

Introduction

SHARON RUSTON

WHEN INTERVIEWED by the *Times* in August 2007 V. S. Naipaul said that English literature departments in universities should be closed down. Naipaul claimed that universities should only teach science and that they should only 'deal in measurable truth' (Appleyard 2007). This is a striking case of a man best known as a novelist denying the validity of the professional literary critic. One might draw a parallel with C. P. Snow's Rede Lecture in 1959, in which he too objected to 'literary intellectuals' (Snow 2005, 4). Why is it that literary critics engender such feelings in the authors they study and discuss? And, why is it that the study of literature (as opposed to the study of other humanities subjects) has so often been positioned antagonistically against science?

Certainly Naipaul's work, unlike, say, Ian McEwan's, is not especially interested in exploring scientific matters or methods, or any possible common ground between science and literature. His objection with English literature academics is that by publishing their ideas they 'distort' our view of things. The ideas they present are not popular or widely held: 'They're just ideas in grubby little textbooks that are stuffed in students' bags.' Closing down English departments across the world would have an immediate impact: 'It would release a lot of manpower. They could go and work on the buses and things like that' (Appleyard 2007). These few lines reveal some often-heard criticisms of the English academic: they have an unrealistic sense of their own importance; their profession is enclosed, self-sustaining and separate from the outside world; they could be doing something more useful. To a literary critic, though, the wording of that phrase, the 'grubby little textbooks' that we write for students, is fascinating and suggestive. It smacks of a kind of Leavisite-elitism that was clearly revealed in that critic's vitriolic response to Snow, accusing him of a 'vulgarity of style', his novels of evincing 'nonentity' on every page (quoted in Snow 2005, xxxiv).

How much has changed since C. P. Snow's lecture, which gave us the phrase 'two cultures' to describe the 'gulf of mutual incomprehension' that existed between 'literary intellectuals' who did not know the

Second Law of Thermodynamics, and scientists, who, with 'the future in their bones', found Dickens 'the type-specimen of literary incomprehensibility' (Snow 2005, 4, 15, 10, 12)? The *Observer* recently tested three writers, two scientists and two broadcasters on their knowledge of science (including the fatal question asked by Snow, of course) and their answers were interpreted by the newspaper 'to confirm the arts/science divide'.[1] It also seems that the elitist, snobby attitude of literature scholars Snow suffered under is still perceived, and that literature is being written out of some possible future reconciliation between literature and science. John Brockman, creator of *Edge*, and proponent of the 'third culture', uses Snow's very same phrase to describe the opponents of scientists: 'Literary intellectuals are not communicating with scientists. Scientists are communicating directly with the general public' (Brockman, 1991). Scientists are writing themselves, and there is no need, it seems, of the literary.

The terms 'literature' and 'science' are of course hugely contested, and rather than rehearse some of these well-known arguments, it might be useful to consider these words in their adjectival form, especially since these are the terms often used by protagonists in these debates. The word 'scientist' itself is at times used anachronistically in this volume, given that its first coinage was in the 1830s and that natural philosophy was the dominant term until the professionalism of science in the nineteenth century. What are we describing when using the word 'scientific' or 'literary'? Thinking about this form of the word takes us to the very heart of their properties, to their characteristics. To describe something as scientific might mean to consider it demonstrable, empirically proven, methodical, objective, or systematic. Calling something or someone literary, on the other hand, carries with it a whole host of assumptions, that they are not simply literate but well-read in classical literature. Leavis, with his clear sense of 'great' literature, would presumably not consider everything printed to be literary. Perhaps the continuing sense that English academics study only the canon of traditional writing is the reason that we are denied the possibility of swelling the numbers of the new 'public academics' that Brockman celebrates (1991). In fact, Brockman's definition of science as 'public culture', is one that most English academics would recognize. He describes these new scientists as 'taking the place of the traditional intellectual in rendering visible the deeper meanings of our lives, redefining who and

---

[1] 'The Panel', accompanying Adams 2007.

what we are' (1991). It could be regarded that literature does exactly this, and that it is the job of the literary critic to discover, explain, even 'render visible' the deeper meanings we find in literature?

English can be seen as an amorphous discipline, one that it is difficult to define. In modern English departments, one can find the study of film, theory, performance, and much more, rather than solely the written word. What defines English might be the attention paid to the language used; literary criticism could be regarded as a method rather than an object of study. Many English academics have embraced the creation of a new discipline, cultural history, which is not necessarily limited to the printed text, and which has extended its purview to science as part of the culture of the past.

As far back as the debate between Matthew Arnold and T. H. Huxley in the 1880s the idea of what might be classed as literature was under debate. Arnold, responding to Huxley, wanted to be clear even then that by literature he did not mean simply *belle lettres*. In the title of his 1882 Rede Lecture, 'Literature and Science', he did not even mean English literature, but the classics. If you agreed with Arnold that the aim of culture was '*to know ourselves and the world*', and agreed that the means to this end was '*to know the best which has been thought and said in the world*', then one should read Euclid's *Elements* and Newton's *Principia* and learn about 'such men as Copernicus, Galileo, Newton, Darwin' (Arnold 1992, 458, 460). He continued with 'To know English *belle lettres* is not to know England', and accepted that 'In that best I certainly include what in modern times has been thought and said by the great observers and knowers of nature' (Arnold 1992, 461). It is perhaps important to note, though, that in his later discussion of classical literature he points out that some of the 'best' of the past has been written by men who 'had the most limited natural knowledge' (468). For Arnold, it is something else entirely that makes classical literature worthy of our study and, using a phrase that he repeats throughout 'Literature and Science', it is 'a suggestive power, capable of wonderfully helping us to relate the results of modern science to our need for conduct, our need for beauty' (468). The suggestiveness of literature, its ability to influence human conduct, seems primary for Arnold. His notion of 'culture', of course, was as a moral cure for the 'anarchy' he found in society.

In the same terms, and at around the same time, English as a university discipline was trying to justify its need to exist. E. A. Freeman, Regius Professor of History in Oxford, in 1887 objected to the creation of an English School at that university because 'we do not want … subjects which are merely light, elegant, interesting. As subjects for examination, we must have subjects in which it is possible to examine' (quoted in Moran 2006, 23). Implied here is the lack of 'measurable truth' that Naipaul finds in literary study, the idea that there is no right answer, or that all interpretations are subjective. Although Arnold did not support the establishment of English as a university subject his ideas were influential, particularly that of 'knowing' England through its literature. Joe Moran sees the turn away from so-called 'German' research and the promotion of literature 'as the prime purveyor of [English] national culture' by such figures as Arthur Quiller-Couch and I. A. Richards as part of the anti-German sentiment of the post-First World War period in the 1920s (2006, 38, 37).

Since its beginnings then, the academic discipline of English has debated, interrogated, questioned and challenged itself: its notion of what it is, what it is for, what is its value and worth, have constantly been questions it has asked of itself. These are questions that science has been less quick to ask itself and it is significant that the new science GCSEs being taught to students who are unlikely to continue with an education in science, which consider the 'social, political, economic and ethical dimensions of the subject' and equip students to 'evaluate science-related questions that they will encounter in real life', have been criticized for doing so. Asking such questions, according to a study that was published in March 2007, only encourages cynicism (Randerson 2007).

One possible definition of the discipline of English on which many now working in it may well agree, is that studying literature reveals the part that it plays in the formation of identities, such as, for example, national identity (it is, after all, called 'English'). One could argue that Naipaul has done well out of this aspect of the discipline, with the emergence of postcolonial criticism. Science has also been seen as playing a part in the formation of such identities. Huxley declared in the opening gambit of his debate with Arnold, on the occasion of a new science college opening in Birmingham in 1880, that 'modern *literatures*' should not speak for his age, the 'distinctive character' of which 'lies in the vast and constantly increasing part which is played by natural knowledge' (quoted in Arnold 1992, 460). C. P. Snow also regarded literary intellectuals as 'natural Luddites', who could not see the ameliorating benefits of the industrial revolution (Snow 2005, 22). In spite of having read Raymond Williams' work on the nineteenth-century novelists' complex engagement with the industrial revolution, Snow thought the class position of writers – 'The industrial revolution looked very different according to whether one saw it from above or below' – meant that they could not see the primal benefits afforded by the progress in science and technology (Snow 2005, 27).[2]

Huxley asked, what was the use of 'mere literary instruction and education' compared to 'sound, extensive, and practical scientific knowledge' (quoted in Arnold 1992, 458)? In the same manner, while Snow admits that 'Man doesn't live by bread alone', he pointed out that this 'is not a remark that one of us in the western world can casually address to most Asians, to most of our fellow beings, in the world as it now exists' (Snow 2005, 78–79). This utilitarian notion is one that Leavis reacted to, in his condemnation of, as Stefan Collini has put it, 'the "technologico-Benthamite" reduction of human experience to the quantifiable, the measurable, the manageable' (Snow 2005, xxxiii). It is a refrain that is still heard today; what is the point of literature? English students are never going to find a cure for cancer, but *Brave New World* presents a rather bleak view of a world with health but without culture.

In an attempt to articulate the *raison d'être* for literature and its critics, claims were made that many of us are now uncomfortable with: both science and literature have claimed to be the means by which to reach 'truth' in terms that religion had used in centuries previous. Arnold's insistence, for example, that literature could act as a moral guide and civilizing influence on our lives can seem like a recasting of the role religion once held. Even before religious doubt had gained its hold on British society, Wordsworth compared his projected poem *The Recluse* to a 'gothic church', and M. H. Abrams took this up in his 1971 book on Romantic poetry *Natural Supernaturalism*, finding secularized versions of traditional theological concepts in this and other writing of the period (Abrams 1973). If literature is the new religion ('spilt' or otherwise), then as John Cartwright has put it, 'literary critics become the new priests of culture' (Cartwright and Baker 2005, 270).[3]

Coleridge in his 1830 *On the Constitution of Church and State* imagined the formation of a 'clerisy', though he was not thinking here of literary critics, but more of, in Peter Allen's words, 'a permanently

---

[2] Stefan Collini tells us that Snow had read Williams' *Culture and Society*, which was published in 1958, the year before Snow's Rede lecture. Collini thinks that Snow's quotation of Coleridge, for example, comes from Williams' book, but in spite of this evidence finds that Williams' 'complex discussion of the literary responses to industrialism does not seem to have modified Snow's conviction that the champions of "culture" were all tainted with "Ludditism" ' (Snow 2005, xxxv, n. 25).

[3] T. E. Hulme famously described Romanticism as 'spilt religion' (1970, 58).

endowed learned class', or 'an intellectual establishment' (Allen 1989, 485). Coleridge imagined that these figures would 'preserve the stores, to guard the treasures, of past civilisation, and thus to bind the present with the past' (Coleridge 1976, 43). The elitism of such a position, and the responsibility for deciding which were the 'stores' and 'treasures' that should be preserved, is one that Leavis took upon himself but which current English academics have found more problematic. The increased diversity of both students and staff in English departments has decreased the stranglehold that the canon of literature once had on curricula. The equally pervasive influence of postmodernism has made us more wary of speaking in terms of absolute truths, and few people these days would regard literature as containing some special, mystical quality.

Abrams' borrowing of his title from Thomas Carlyle's *Sartor Resartus* is a further possible point of connection between the study of literature and science, which is the study of nature. The idea that one can find the miraculous or the wonderful in the material and the everyday is something both literature and science have claimed for themselves at different times. Often stemming from Darwin's final passage of *Origin of Species*, where he declares upon contemplating the entangled bank, 'there is a grandeur in this view of life', popular science writers have made it their career to enthuse the public with a sense of wonder at the natural world. Stephen Jay Gould's title *Wonderful Life* comes from Frank Capra's film *It's a Wonderful Life*. The wonder of both texts is primarily amazement at the historical concept of contingency, where seemingly insignificant events are understood to have radically and irrevocably led to the present. As Gould points out, this 'great theme of contingency in history' has been 'imposed' because of discoveries such as those made at the Burgess Shale 'upon a science uncomfortable with such concepts' (Gould 2000, 14).

The committed atheist Richard Dawkins, who describes himself, presumably, in his first chapter's title 'A deeply religious non believer', has also set himself to the task of reminding people of 'the sense of wonder in science' (Dawkins 2006; 1998, xii). Dawkins considers this sense to be 'a deep aesthetic passion to rank with the finest that music and poetry can deliver', and in his book *Unweaving the Rainbow: Science, Delusion and the Appetite for Wonder* is intent on proving that literature does not have a monopoly on inspiring feelings of awe (Dawkins 1998, xxii). From the other side of the fence (if there really is a fence) Emeritus Professor of English at Rutgers University George Levine's most recent book, *Darwin Loves You: Natural Selection and the Re-enchantment of the World*, takes for its title the commonplace (particularly in America) bumper-sticker 'Jesus Loves You' (Levine 2006). Clearly Levine wants to show that as much comfort can be drawn from the natural world as is from the spiritual one by those who believe in it. Levine's efforts are to disprove Max Weber's claim that science robs the world of meaning and value, and to emphasise that Darwin had this same sense of wonder in the world he saw before him.

Darwin has been one of the most suggestive scientists and science writers to fiction writers, poets, and literary critics. He has arguably been the most important scientist in the development of a new interest in the connections between literature and science. Nearly all of the essays in this collection refer to the work of Gillian Beer (author of *Darwin's Plots*) at some point and her work has been hugely influential: her insistence that the relationship between literature and science is one of 'interchange rather than origins and transformation rather than translation' can be seen throughout this volume (Beer 1990, 81). There have been a number of important critics on the cultural history of science, including, among others, Roy Porter, Simon Schaffer, John Gascoigne, Ludmilla Jordanova and Patricia Fara. The essays contained represent the possibilities of engagement between the two cultures, rather than a dismissal of the 'literary' in the invention of a 'third culture'. As Snow hoped: 'The clashing point of two subjects, two disciplines, two cultures – of two galaxies, so far as that goes – ought to produce creative chances' (Snow 2005, 16). These creative chances have been seen in much interesting work produced by such contemporary writers as Michael Frayn in *Copenhagen*, Tom Stoppard in *Arcadia*, Ian McEwan in *Saturday*, and the poetry of Daniel Abse, Deryn Rees-Jones and Helen Clare. In Britain alone, the creation of the British Society of Literature and Science in 2005, the Liverpool University Centre for Poetry and Science in the same year, and the fact of this volume testify to the developing interest in the connections and exchanges possible.

The essays contained in this volume could never have represented all of the historical periods of literature or science; neither the many genres of literature nor subjects of science; and not the multitude of possible methodologies that might be used in considering the relationship between the two. Yet in their multiplicity of text and methodology they demonstrate the complexity of literature, science, and the interfaces between them. Elaine Hobby's essay ' "Dreams and plain dotage": The Value of *The Birth of Mankind (1540–1654)*' makes a scientific text her subject, to which she applies the methods of literary criticism, and in fact all of the essays reveal this exercise to be primary to their purpose. All authors here approach the texts in question, whether scientific or literary or critical, with an attention that is alive to the way things are said alongside the meaning of what is said. In David Amigoni's essay ' "The luxury of storytelling": Science, Literature and Cultural Contest in Ian McEwan's Narrative Practice', Darwin's use of stories as a means of communicating science is lambasted by Joe Rose, a scientific journalist in McEwan's novel *Enduring Love*. Contrary to Rose's view, which pits 'the power and attractions of narrative' against 'judgement', theoretical underpinning, definition of terms, and demonstrable evidence, Amigoni finds that in McEwan's novels narrative continues to exert a power and an authority.

McEwan's *Saturday* more than any other recent novel perhaps dramatizes the clashing of two cultures, in the characters of Henry Perowne, a middle-aged, well-off brain surgeon, his famous poet father-in-law, Grammaticus, and his fledgling poet daughter, Daisy. The lack of comprehension, and barely concealed dislike, between Perowne and Grammaticus seems to confirm the completely different world views of the scientist and the literary intellectual; while Perowne has been criticised for his smugness, the poet is arrogant, pompous, inexplicably moody, and a drunk, seeming to confirm many widely held opinions of his type. Yet, in the novel, reciting Matthew Arnold's poem 'Dover Beach' aloud at a critical moment distracts the attention of a dangerous and unstable man who declares it 'beautiful' and indeed it is literature that saves the day (and then science that saves the man). As Amigoni discusses, this episode asks, what does literature do? What can it achieve? What is its proper place in the history of civilization?

In 'Evolution, Literary History and Science Fiction', Brian Baker takes as his subject literary critical modes, examining, for example Joseph Carroll's 'rhetoric' in making both evolutionary psychology and the humanist methods of practical criticism seem quite simply as though they are common-sense, or even 'correct'. Baker also considers Franco Moretti's use of 'quantitative modelling', itself a scientific method, to see how such a technique bears up under close scrutiny. Moretti is unable to adequately explain why when applying this method to the SF genre it fails to account for the longevity of this particular genre, its refusal to become extinct and to revive in similar but related forms. Baker's essay asks why it is that biological method (used to such different ends by such critics as Moretti and Carroll) are so influential in literary theory: 'The question we must ask is: why (biological) science, and why now?'

The application of 'literary and critical techniques to analyse such features as metaphor and tone' in Hobby's essay is coupled with reading the scientific text, in this case *The Birth of Mankind*, historically. Hobby considers the textual history of this book, which had appeared in many guises and languages. She argues that the book in the form in which she deals with it most tells us about the world it was received by, thus correcting some misunderstandings about early-modern life and relationships. Not only this, the book also proves that some of our now commonplace assumptions about gender, coming from Michel Foucault through Thomas Laqueur, are similarly unfounded. Instead *The Birth of Mankind* 'reimagines' the female body in surprising and complex ways, refusing to accept the mistaken assumptions of the past.

The use of science in the representation and even formation of gender stereotypes is at issue in a few of the essays included here. My own essay 'Natural Rights and Natural History in Anna Barbauld and Mary Wollstonecraft' looks at how both of these writers turned to science to find support for their conviction that there were natural rights, whether female or male, orthodox or dissenter. The idea of what was 'natural' to women was supported then, as it is still now, by the evidence drawn from the animal world. Wollstonecraft used such evidence to her own advantage, comparing woman in her civilized condition to a domestic animal who had been forced and trained into behaving in a way that is not natural. The women she sees around her are therefore merely unnatural versions of what they could be, with overly refined, delicate and unhealthy constitutions. Amigoni's essay similarly points out that McEwan's *Saturday* explores the competing claims of 'biological determinism and indeterminate, proliferating social and cultural meanings'.

While many essays deal with broadly biological sciences, Alice Jenkins and Katy Price write about the hard sciences, mathematics and physics respectively. Jenkins' essay 'George Eliot, Geometry and Gender' asks us to remember just how influential the study of Euclid was, taught as it was to many generations of pupils. She reveals his presence in the 'metaphors, structures and key words which shape an extraordinary number of Victorian literary, political and polemic writings'. Considering the novels of George Eliot specifically, geometry is used 'to suggest the fixedness' of such systems as gender difference. Certainly it seems that there were many men of the period who would have sympathized with poor Tom Tulliver in *Mill on the Floss*, who has such trouble with his lessons in Euclid. One of the 'Novel Possibilities' of Einstein's theories that is presented in Price's essay also involves the debunking of the 'hated Euclid' whom it is hoped 'may have been talking through his hat all these years about the parallel lines that never meet'. For Tom's sister, the precocious Maggie (as was the case too, it seems, for Marian Evans herself), learning Euclid promised but failed to bring the 'mascu-

line wisdom' that would help her find contentment and relieve her frus-
trations. Jenkins also discovers more about the nature of the teaching of
Euclid in such institutions as the Ladies College, and the reformist pedagogical aims of its mathematics teachers.

According to Jenkins Euclid was used as a 'mental exercise' to clear
and order the minds of adolescent boys; similarly physics is used to
'establish a tension between messy human passions and cold abstraction'
in Dorothy L. Sayers' *Documents in the Case*. Marital and other relationships are signified by characters' reactions to Einstein's theory of the
fourth dimension in Katy Price's essay 'On the Back of the Light Waves:
Novel Possibilities in the "Fourth Dimension" '. Price's essay uses a range
of contemporary popular writing about the subject, including essays in
Punch and reports in the *Times* that show the world was alive to the
comic possibilities of these theories. Price finds that what she calls the
'mixing up' of scientific and social themes enables discussion of both
rather than writing this off as simply 'bad science'. Almost all of the
essays deal with the representation of science as 'truth' whether the texts
they examine challenges this or not. One (female) character in Sayers'
The Documents in the Case declares poetry one of the 'only true realities
after all'. This character is not, however, a mouthpiece for Sayers herself.
Price finds that relativity is used both as a subject and a method in
Sayers' novel, and ultimately, as is also the case in 'Absolutely Elsewhere' there is a solution to the mystery.

Jill Rudd's essay 'From Popular Science to Contemplation: The
Clouds of *The Cloud of Unknowing*' also considers popular science
writing, this time from the medieval period. She finds evidence that the
clouds which feature in a fourteenth-century mystical treatise, *The Cloud
of Unknowing*, are not solely metaphorical (there to represent forgetting
and unknowing) but can be identified with discussions of clouds in contemporary books of science, such as *Sidrak and Bokkus* and *On the Properties of Things*. Such findings remind us that 'the blending of scientific
and literary modes recently advocated by Gould' has been going on for
far longer than the nineteenth century. The particular place of clouds in
literary texts, and their seemingly 'automatic' association with metaphor, gives them a special status, which, as seen in the recent work of
Richard Hamblyn 'make claims for meteorology as a literary form as
much as a science'.

Martin Willis's essay considers both gender and national identity in
his essay 'Le Fanu's "Carmilla", Ireland, and Diseased Vision'. As with
other essays in this collection, he points out that 'science never remains
unadulterated when it enters the public sphere, and that public under-

standings of science, as well as misunderstandings, are just as much a part of *science* as the theoretical and experimental work of the scientist'. Willis argues that in Le Fanu's gothic tale 'disease' is situated in the body of the Other, or, in the body that represents foreign-ness, in this case, the Irish and the female. Using medical theory from the period Willis reads and tests the story against competing ideas of how disease was caught and transmitted. He reminds us that science often works on the level of the imagination, where, in this case, the public cannot actually see the enemy ('the parasite or the dust mote'), which can only be seen by the use of the microscope and finds in the 'construction of a micro-scopic world' 'a process of myth-making'.

All of the essays in this collection testify to the idea that we can find in both literary and scientific texts common ground, common purpose and common means. Wordsworth in the opening to *The Recluse* declared that he would be writing 'On Man, on Nature, and on Human Life/ Musing in solitude'. Abrams also chose these lines with which to open his critical book *Natural Supernaturalism* (1971). Surely these are the subjects of both literature and science and the essays contained here find wonder and awe in all texts dealing with them. We should neither dismiss the literary from the scientific nor the scientific from the literary and I hope that, using Snow's phrase, this collection proves that from contemplation of the two, we can 'produce creative chances'.

Works Cited

Abrams, M. H., 1973 (1971). *Natural Supernaturalism: Tradition and Revolution in Romantic Literature*. New York: W. W. Norton.

Adams, Tim. 2007. 'The New Age of Ignorance'. *The Observer*, 1 July. http://observer.guardian.co.uk/review/story/0,,2115519,00.html <date accessed: 11 September 2007>

Allen, Peter, 1989. 'Morrow on Coleridge's Church and State', *Journal of the History of Ideas* 50: 3 (July–September): 485–89.

Arnold, Matthew, 1992. 'Literature and Science', in *Matthew Arnold: A Critical Edition of the Major Works*, ed. Miriam Allott and Robert H. Super. Oxford: Oxford University Press.

Beer, Gillian, 1990. 'Translation or Transformation? The Relations of Science and Literature', *Notes and Records of the Royal Society of London* 44: 81–99.

Brockman, John, 1991. 'About Edge', *Edge*. http://www.edge.org/about_edge.html <date accessed: 11 September 2007>

Cartwright, John and Brian Baker, 2005. *Literature and Science: Social Impact and Interaction*. California: ABC-CLIO.

Coleridge, S. T., 1976. *On the Constitution of the Church and State*, ed. John Colmer. *The Collected Works of Samuel Taylor Coleridge*, ed. Kathleen Coburn, vol. 10. New Jersey: Princeton.

Dawkins, Richard, 1998. *Unweaving the Rainbow*. Harmondsworth: Penguin.

Dawkins, Richard, 2006. *The God Delusion*. London: Black Swan.

Gould, Stephen, 2000. *Wonderful Life: The Burgess Shale and the Nature of History*. London: Vintage.

Hulme, T. E., 1970. 'Romanticism and Classicism', in *Romanticism: Points of View*, ed. R. F. Gleckner and G. E. Enscoe. New Jersey: Prentice-Hall: 55–65.

Levine, George, 2006. *Darwin Loves You: Natural Selection and the Re-enchantment of the World*. New Haven: Princeton University Press.

Moran, Joe, 2006. *Interdisciplinarity*. The New Critical Idiom. London: Routledge.

Randerson, James, 2007. 'New Science GCSE Fosters Cynicism Among Pupils, Says Study', *The Guardian*, 1 March.
http://education.guardian.co.uk/gcses/story/0,,2023788,00.html
<date accessed: 16 September 2007>

Snow, C. P., 2005 (1959). *The Two Cultures*. Introduction by Stefan Collini. Cambridge: Cambridge University Press.

From Popular Science to Contemplation:
The Clouds of The Cloud of Unknowing

GILLIAN RUDD

THIS ARTICLE deals with the clouds which give the medieval mystical treatise *The Cloud of Unknowing* its name. Rather than being solely metaphorical, the clouds of forgetting (beneath the contemplative) and unknowing (above and affected by light) have much in common with clouds as explained by contemporary books of popular science, such as *Sidrak and Bokkus* and John Trevisa's *On the Properties of Things*. This demonstrates how these medieval texts exemplify the blending of scientific and literary modes recently advocated by Gould (2003).[1] In general, these religious and scientific texts combine factual observation, deduction and religious interpretation with direct human response to the natural world to arrive at a whole understanding of the physical and metaphysical world. In this these works share common ground with current green thinking.[2] Broadly speaking, greens promote the value of the non-human in terms which do not require 'nature' to be subservient to, or have existence solely within, a human value-system.

Clouds appeal: witness the popularity of Richard Hamblyn's *The Invention of Clouds* (2001) and Gavin Pretor-Pinney's *The Cloudspotter's Guide* (2006). Both can be classed as 'popular science' since they address a general audience by providing hard scientific (meteorological) information alongside lighter matter: in Hamblyn's case biography, in Pretor-Pinney's joyous appreciation of natural phenomena.[3] Each attests

---

[1] In *The Hedgehog, the Fox and the Magister's Pox: Mending the Gap between Science and the Humanities* Stephen Jay Gould uses the adage *multa novit vulpes, verum echinus unum magnum* ('the fox knows many things, but the hedgehog one big thing') as a hook for his argument that sciences and humanities must blend strategies and rhetorics to create a needful wholeness (2003, 1–8).

[2] The terms 'green', 'ecological' and 'environmentalist' are almost exchangeable. A good introduction is Garrard (2004). I suggest how ecocriticism might be applied to medieval literature in *Greenery: Ecocritical Readings of Late Medieval English Literature* (2007).

[3] *Wikipedia* (itself arguably an example of the genre) defines popular science as writing by experts for non-experts. It is thus distinct from science journalism

the enduring appeal of clouds as fascinating but somehow ultimately unknowable, despite meteorology's careful categorization of their causes, forms and effects. These books highlight the science, but they also maintain the clouds of our imaginations both as white puffs ('our fluffy friends') and dark banks (cumulonimbus is 'the Darth Vader of clouds') (Pretor-Pinney 2006, 45). They also reinforce an association of clouds with metaphor which seems almost automatic and is perhaps linked to the habit of seeing shapes in clouds like Polonius (*Hamlet* 3.3.366–72) or Antony in *Antony and Cleopatra* (4.12.1–22). Hamblyn's subtitle, *How an Amateur Meteorologist Forged the Language of the Skies*, is in a similar vein while his prose asserts an explicit link between clouds and language in terms which make claims for meteorology as a literary form as much as a science:

> Yet meteorology is not an exact science. It is, rather, a search for narrative order among events governed not by laws alone but by the shapeless caprices of the atmosphere. Weather writes, erases, and rewrites itself upon the sky with the endless fluidity of language; and it is with language that we have sought throughout history to apprehend it. Since the sky has always been more real than measured, it has always been the province of words. (Hamblyn 2001, 17)

Hamblyn defies Frisinger's assertion that 'a distinction must be made between meteorology as a science and meteorology as a branch of knowledge', which implies that the difference between science and knowledge is largely a matter of making precise measurements, preferably using instruments (Frisinger 1977, 1). Frisinger credits Roger Bacon (c. 1220–1292), with establishing the importance of experimentation and proof for science, thus introducing what became the distinguishing factor between scientific knowledge and any other form of learning, particularly theology (47). However, as Frisinger acknowledges, one consequence of Bacon's empirical method was to remove knowledge from being the sole province of the educated cleric and place it within reach of the educated and intellectually curious layman. Significantly, clouds make few appearances in Frisinger's history. They seem to defy measurement, not least because of their evershifting form which makes clouds difficult to quantify or set easily within his notion of proper

(written by non-experts for non-experts) and from scholarly works (written by experts for their peers).

science. It is this shifting quality that intrigues observers and aligns clouds so closely with metaphor: simply, they evoke more than they actually are and look substantial, although we know they are vapor and so literally ungraspable. Hence they impel us to refer to other things in order to describe them.

The fourteenth-century English mystic treatise, *The Cloud of Unknowing*, takes its reader (who is addressed almost conversationally) through the stages necessary to achieve the highest level of contemplation achievable in this world. The method advocated are those of the *via negativa* (negative way) which seeks to achieve apprehension of the divine by rigorously setting aside the use of images, including similes, as ways to think about God, even when the point of such images is to show how far God outstrips the greatest thing humanly imaginable. As such, the treatise is normally placed within the affective tradition of PseudoDionysius, with particular debt to Richard of St Victor, some of whose works the anonymous *Cloud* author translated.[4] This tradition is undoubtedly important to *Cloud*, not least in providing the source for the eponymous image, namely the cloud that surrounds Moses on Mount Sinai (Exodus 24:15–18). Unsurprisingly, then, this background has been the dominant one for critical discussions of this treatise; Minnis (1982), Lees (1983), and Clark (1980) have all proved the relevance of the religious and scholastic context for *Cloud*, as have the editions by Hodgson (1944 and 1982) and Gallacher (1977). Meanwhile the work itself continues to be admired for its fluidity of language and dexterity of image, which led David Knowles in 1961 to describe the writer as 'the most subtle and incisive, as well as the most original spiritual writer in the English language', a description which Hodgson quotes with approval (Hodgson 1982, lvii). The difficult, the abstract, the abstruse are drawn together in this masterpiece in a way which is accessible without ever implying that the spiritual endeavor it outlines is easy to accomplish. Far from it, the author is adamant that contemplation is

---

4 For a useful discussion of the *Cloud*-author's corpus see the Introduction to *The Cloud of Unknowing and Related Treatises* (Hodgson 1982). John P. H. Clark's three-volume *'The Cloud of Unknowing': An Introduction* (1995) offers a comprehensive discussion of the texts' authorship and their intellectual milieu as religious works, but, in common with most commentators, places them firmly in the context of religious and scholarly, making no allusion to works of popular science. Although clouds feature in the author's other treatises as well, my essay deals only with the best known of the works, *The Cloud of Unknowing*.

work, requiring dedication and practice as well as right attitude and the grace of God. It is a frequently acknowledged irony that this text is now read widely by scholars and students who feel no personal calling to the contemplative life, despite a Prologue that specifically exhorts such people to leave the text alone.[5] Part of its success with this wider audience must lie with its 'genial and hospitable' tone (Gallacher 1977, 1) which draws in even those who have little interest in religious matters.

In the Introduction to his translation, Spearing points out how far the treatise is infused with the relations and rhythms of speech, and comments on how these lend additional effect to the central paradox of expressing the divine, inexpressible and non-bodily through a language which is human and bodily (Spearing 2001, xxvii–xliv). That paradox may also account for this text's latter-day popularity, as it reflects modern concerns with the approximate nature of language, and the power of text, but it also reflects the author's wish to convey abstract ideas in direct ways, often using the very images he elsewhere encourages us to relinquish.[6] Although such imagery is not confined to clouds, there is a clear analogy between Spearing's comment on the text's general language and the specific example of its eponymous cloud. Capable of being both wispy vapor and solid cover, clouds epitomize the attempt to combine the bodily and non-bodily, physical and ethereal. Much has been said about this contradiction, leading to the pleasing oxymoron 'concrete imagery' (peculiarly appropriate for clouds), but it is also important to note the author's easy incorporation of contemporary science within his text.[7] Thus, when speaking of the fleeting moment typical of a first successful experience of contemplation, the author uses the word 'athomus' and then explains:

[5] Although the main text of *Cloud* addresses an anonymous disciple, a wider audience is harangued to read the whole text with due attention both in the Prologue and in the final chapters, where the author expressly declares that 'Fleschly iangelers, glosers & blamers, roukers & rouners, & alle maner of pynchers' (Hodgson 1982, 73) (worldly chatterers, flatterers, disparagers, telltales and gossips and all kinds of scandalmongerers) should not touch his book.
[6] As Spearing says, the use of the term 'this work' ('þis werk') throughout the treatise can refer to both the spiritual endeavour and the text itself (2001, xxxvi). See also Nike Kocijanèiè Pokorn's deconstructionist article 'The Language and Discourse of *The Cloud of Unknowing*' (1997).
[7] The term is Spearing's (2001, xxxii) but comments in the same vein feature in all editions and translations, as well as in influential studies of the work, not least John Burrow's 'Fantasy and Language in *The Cloud of Unknowing*' (1977).

þe whiche athomus, by þe diffinicion of trewe philisophres in þe sciens of astronomye, is þe leest partie of tyme; & it is so litil þat, for þe littilnes of it, it is undepartable & neiзhonde incomprehensible.

(Hodgson 1982, 10)

Editorial notes tell us that this 'least part of time' is 15/94ths of a second, but the *Cloud*-author is content with its indivisibility and the fact that it has been defined through the precise measurement associated with 'the science of astronomy'.[8]

So *Cloud*, which expresses its theology in 'simple everyday terms, deliberately avoiding all learned terminology' (Hodgson 1944, lvii), shares its style with medieval books of knowledge and latter day popular science.[9] All seek to distil complex and often convoluted scholarly knowledge into appealing and evocative terms which both satisfy curiosity and inspire further investigation. Latter-day practitioners include John Gribben, who describes *Deep Simplicity* as 'an attempt to take the obvious step of trying to explain chaos and complexity the simple way, from the bottom up – for everybody' (Gribben 2005, 3); Dawkins, who declares 'one of my aims in the book is to convey something of the sheer wonder of biological complexity to those whose eyes have not been opened to it. But having built up the mystery, my other main aim is to remove it again by explaining the solution' (Dawkins 1986, ix), and Bryson, who states that the idea behind *A Short History of Nearly Everything* 'was to see if it isn't possible to understand and appreciate – marvel at, enjoy even – the wonder and accomplishments of science at a level that isn't too technical or demanding, but isn't entirely superficial either' (Bryson 2004, 24). Medieval examples of the genre tend to be encyclopedias which cover a vast range of topics with great concision but often include surprising and pleasing details. Indebted to Pliny's *Historia Naturalis* (77 BC) and to Isidore of Seville's *Etymologiae* (560–636) and frequently citing their material, such works typically consist of a series of headings, sometimes phrased as questions, followed by brief explanatory paragraphs which are a happy mixture of what we would now term folk knowledge, scientific fact and religious interpretation – distinctions known if not overtly acknowledged at the time.

[8]   Clark refers to this as one of the instances of the 'passing interest in science' he attributes to the *Cloud*-author but for Clark this interest is worth noting only 'incidentally' (Clark 1995, 1: 18).

[9]   This phrase becomes 'simple language and without technical jargon' in the later edition, where the author's 'practicality' is also stressed (Hodgson 1982, li).

Crucially, all the information offered in all its various forms is regarded as valuable and somehow true, which allows these reference books (the *Wikipedia* of their day?) to reflect the eclectic mixture of knowledge available at the time, without being constrained to dismiss any of it. Some of these works have academically respectable pedigrees, such as Trevisa's translation of Bartholomaeus Anglicus's (fl. 1230–1250) *De Proprietatibus Rerum*, completed in 1398/9 and published several times thereafter. Others are less well regarded, particularly by modern scholars; *Sidrak and Bokkus* is one of these. The English version of a much-read late thirteenth-century French book of knowledge, *Sidrak* opens with a lively Prologue telling the story of Bokkus's conversion to Christianity, which concludes with a contest between Sidrak and Bokkus's other advisors. Sidrak wins in a series of events reminiscent of Elijah's defeat of the prophets of Baal (1 Kings 18:17–40). Following this, Bokkus asks Sidrak to answer a series of questions, and so the encyclopedic body of the text begins. It is an unusual opening to a book of science to say the least, which has led one critic to classify the work as both a romance and 'a catechism of medieval science', yet the very fact that it was possible to preface an encyclopedia with a romance indicates that the two modes share common ground and audience.[10] *Sidrak* thus testifies to the popularity of books of knowledge and offers a contrasting, but no less relevant context, to that of medieval mystical theology that has heretofore accompanied *The Cloud of Unknowing*. It is thus in their light that I read *Cloud*'s clouds here, but I do so without implying that the author gleaned his knowledge of clouds directly from either Trevisa or *Sidrak*. The author knew Latin and as a Carthusian he may well have acquired his knowledge directly from Latin sources, but he does not assume such Latinity in his audience. Indeed, as Cheryl Taylor points out, there is no Latin in the text at all, instead the author betrays an acute awareness of the flexibility and scope of English as a medium for theological and (I would argue) general intellectual discussion (Taylor 2006, 205).

There are three clouds in the treatise: two are rhetorical – the clouds of unknowing and forgetting, the third is actual – the one in which Moses dwelt for six days on Mount Sinai while waiting to receive the Ten Commandments (Exodus 24:15–18). This cloud is referred to simply as 'a cloud', without further exegesis, but that does not make it a

---

[10] H. L. D. Ward, *Catalogue of Romances in the Department of Manuscripts in the British Museum*, 1883. Quoted in Burton 1998, xxix–xx. Burton offers a full discussion of the standing of the work in his introduction, including a consideration of its place as a compendium of knowledge.

non-metaphorical cloud. Rather this is the most openly symbolic cloud in the text as the connection between the cloud which Moses entered as he ascended the mountain and in which he saw nothing, but heard God's voice, with the experience of mystic communion was well established within the mystical tradition, particularly that of the Dionysian *via negativa* and the Victorine school.[11] As such, despite its apparent actuality (mountain tops are often swathed in clouds) this real cloud is immediately highly metaphorical. It divides Moses from those waiting below, hiding them from him (so he is not distracted) and him from them (emphasizing his individual holiness) and veiling God. As a final touch it provides a sense of discombobulation appropriate for an encounter with Divinity. Since the treatise was probably written in the first instance as a guide for a particular disciple (see Hodgson 1982, l–li; Lees 1983, 455; Clark 1995, 1: 20; Whitehead 1998, 195) and only later opened out to a wider audience of unknown readers, it is likely that the text presumes on prior knowledge of the contemplative tradition, so the very word 'cloud' would immediately invoke the associations of purity, distance from earthly concerns and striving towards God that clustered around it in religious parlance.[12] That tradition meant that there was no need to make an explicit connection between Moses' cloud and the treatise's cloud of unknowing which defines the work of the contemplative

11 See Hodgson 1982, xli–lvi. Hodgson suggests that the author may well have drawn both the term 'cloud of unknowing' and the clouds of unknowing and forgetting from Richard of St Victor's *Benjamin Major* (Hodgson 1982, xliv n. 62). J. P. H. Clark elaborates on this (1980, 83–109). Christiania Whitehead further explains the author's adaptation of his Carthusian inheritance (1998: 105–212).

12 The *Middle English Dictionary* reveals that 'cloud' or 'clod' originally indicated a hill, cliff or mass of earth (modern 'clod'). This meaning persisted until the middle of the fourteenth century. 'Cloud' as atmospheric cloud, mist or fog made its appearance as late as 1300, when it is most often associated with overcast skies. Some examples given under this heading (2a and b) relate to purely meteorological clouds, or to the heavens in general, but many carry metaphorical meanings or indications of miracles; see the citations from the Legends of Saints Brendan and Becket (both c. 1300). Margery Kempe's (c. 1438) metaphorical statement 'þe sunne … sumtyme … is hyd vndyr a cloude, þat men may not se it' hints at her belief in her own unacknowledged virtue. Explicitly figurative uses are listed under the third heading where connotations of obscurity, shadow and darkness predominate. Despite the fascination and enjoyment inspired by cloud-gazing, claimed by Pretor-Pinney, and the strong associations of clouds with personal enlightenment in religious exegesis (Moses being a case in point) the citations listed in the *MED* and the *OED* emphasize less positive associations.

who likewise strives to attain a state of mental and spiritual preparedness for a direct apprehension of God.

It is thus remarkably easy to read *Cloud*'s clouds in purely figurative terms and this has been the usual reaction to the other two clouds in the text: those of unknowing and forgetting. The impulse to read them metaphorically is hard to resist, partly because of our common experience of clouds. Every reader knows what clouds are, how they can bemuse, disturb, envelop and disorientate; how some appear high and so, like the cloud of unknowing above us, hint at the brighter light beyond; others are heavy, low-lying, and so easily perceived as blankets (of forgetting). The use of clouds to describe the steps of contemplation thus seems perfect, and even allows for the inclusion of some Pretor-Pinney's cloudspotting pleasure. Such ease of comprehension may account for why so little has been said about the clouds themselves, as critics tend to accept entirely the 'strongly marked contrast between tenor and vehicle: on the one side a fully physical cloud "congealed out of the humors": on the other side, fully spiritual states of "unknowing" ' (Burrow 1977, 296). Burrow is keen to assert the need for latter-day readers to reject the post-Romantic use of 'symbols which seem to carry something of their physical reality over into the realm of the spirit' because 'this is precisely what the author of *The Cloud* does not want' (Burrow 1977, 296). This is true only up to a point. *Cloud* does indeed make a point of distinguishing between actual clouds that we can bring to our mind's eye by imagining them, and the cloud which is the metaphor for the contemplative state, but it also warns against anyone in this world seeking to separate the bodily and ghostly realms, since (as Burrow himself emphasizes) they are 'joined by God'. Burrow furthermore asserts that in *Cloud* 'the physical world has its own necessary and proper integrity as well as the spiritual world, and that to conceive either world in terms of the other imperils the integrity of both' (Burrow 1977, 289). It is surely right that the *Cloud*-author is keen to keep the physical, physical, but there is an alternative to the binary opposition underpinning Burrow's reading. The language of the text enacts 'joinedness', suggesting a fusion of the scientific and spiritual ways of comprehending the world which is more effective than a method that insists on the respective integrity of the physical and spiritual realms and so maintains a distinction between them. Far from employing the post-Romantic view as summarized by Burrow, which in effect removes the 'physical reality' into the spiritual, I wish here to invoke Onno Oerlemans' plea for a focus on 'the materiality of nature' (made, ironically, in a book devoted to Romantic poetry) which foregrounds the very physical and actual aspects of the natural world and imagery that are all too easily subsumed into the concept of 'metaphor' (Oerlemans 2002, 13–14).

The danger with metaphor is that it begs to be decoded and that decoding diverts attention away from the entity being employed as a symbol onto exclusive focus on the meaning behind the metaphor. As a result, that entity is denied intrinsic value; it is appraised only in respect of the concept it conveys or embodies. This is the danger attendant on Burrow's critique. The clarity of his reading is tempting, but the consequence is to make these clouds entirely figurative. What is particularly interesting about *Cloud*'s clouds is that while they are evidently effective as images, they also match well with the explanations of actual clouds found in books of popular science of the day. Moreover, the more one brings in the scientific information about clouds the more one becomes aware of exactly how much the attributes of real clouds underpin the apparently purely figural ones of the treatise. Thus although it could be argued that we are simply expected to recognize the figurative nature of clouds from the outset, and that the inclusion of Moses' cloud, the basis for that figural sense, at the end of the treatise in effect clinches the meaning and purpose of the clouds in the text as a whole, it still does not do to assume that there is therefore no trace of actual clouds at all. The *Cloud*-author does more than use just our immediate idea of a typical cloud; he draws on contemporary observations and understanding of how clouds work.

So let us return to those clouds. The cloud of unknowing seems to be always there, something the contemplative strives to enter and which is then both around and above him, between him and God.[13] The cloud of forgetting is one the contemplative must deliberately place, or even perhaps create, themselves. Apparently this becomes possible only when within the cloud of unknowing, at which point a further aspect of clouds is introduced – the fact that they inhabit different layers within the atmosphere:

> & ȝif euer þou schalt come to þis cloude, & wone & worche þerin as I bid þee, þee byhoueþ, as þis cloude of vnknowying is abouen þee, bitwix þee & þi God, riȝt so put a cloude of forȝetyng bineþ þee, bitwix þee & alle þe cretures þat euer ben maad. (Hodgson 1982, 13)

The separation used here (one cloud beneath and one around and

---

[13] I use 'him' here because it is a fair assumption that the disciple addressed in the text was a junior member of the male order to which the author belonged.

above) is maintained throughout the treatise. The contemplative is never within the cloud of forgetting and this second cloud is always beneath that of unknowing. This demarcation is exactly in keeping with the understanding of how clouds work. Trevisa cites Isidore of Seville:

> A cloude is impressioun imade in þe eyre of many vapoures gadred into one body in þe myddel regioun of þe eyr, iþickened togedres by cooldnesse of place ... And a cloude is gendred in þis manere: for hete of heuene by his owne vertue drawiþ to it wel sotile vapourable partyes of watir and of erþe, and wastiþ þe most sotile partyes þerof and makeþ þe oþirdel þicke and turneþ it into a clowde. Therof spekeþ Isidre and seiþ þat cloude is þickenes and gadred togedres by drawyng of vapoures and of fumositees of þerþe and of þe see.
>
> (Trevisa 1975, 577–78)

There are several points here which have a bearing on the clouds of *Cloud*. First is the sound meteorological fact that clouds inhabit the middle region of the air, the level which is cooler than that nearest the earth and so is a place where vapors will condense. They must be in this middle region because the highest region (there are only three) is heated by the sun, so any vapor rising that high is evaporated, while the lowest level's proximity to the earth makes it warmer than the middle level, but not as hot as the highest. This lower warmth means vapors rise from the earth, and it is these rising currents that condense in the middle (coolest) level to create clouds. This process is one of evaporation and condensation, in effect of distillation, which implies purification: an implication which is also found in *Cloud* as the things of this earth which will obstruct the contemplative must remain below the lower cloud. This indicates that they are not made of the subtle stuff ('sotile partyes') that can be sucked up into the ether and so purified: only the most pure elements are evaporated ('wastiþ') while the rest is turned into the vapor that creates the clouds. So the fumes themselves are not necessarily pure, they are simply whatever matter can be drawn up from the earth's surface by heat: that which is 'vapourable'. It is also worth noting that at this stage, predistillation, none of the matter is dark. The 'thickness' is a result of the pure elements being burnt off, leaving the other matter ('oþirdel') which is therefore denser and creates the clouds. This 'oþirdel' (surely the 'congelid humours' mentioned by Burrow which we meet in the fourth chapter of Cloud) is distinct from the 'sotile partyes' which continue to rise upward.

Also implicit within this explanation of cloud formation is the fact that it is a constant process involving constant movement. The subtlest matter continues to rise upwards becoming lighter and brighter as it does so, because the thinner it gets, the more the light of the sun shines through it:

> Also by lyȝtnesse of his owne substaunce a cloude meveþ vpward ... Also as þe vapoures of þe whiche a cloude is compowned beþ more sotile and pure, þe cloude fongiþ [þe] more schynynge and impressioun of sonne bemes (Trevisa 1975, 578)

Meanwhile the heavier matter continues to congeal, creating thicker and heavier clouds that are dark, obstructing the light of the sun:

> and for þe cloude is clere [liȝt] passiþ þereþurgh, but it be whanne þe substaunce þerof is ygadred in þe aire of fumositees þat ben grete and þicke. For þanne þe cloude is *dymme* and d[e]rke and bynemeþ vs þe liȝt of þe sonne and takeþ it out of oure siȝt ȝif he is set bitwene vs and þe sonne. (Trevisa 1975, 578)

Such clouds are lower and result in rain through which the matter within them is returned to the earth whence it came. Two of the terms that have begun to operate here are particularly resonant for a reader of *Cloud*: 'thick' and 'dark' are adjectives applied at various stages to both clouds within the text and these, with their opposite terms of 'thin' and 'light' or 'bright', are to be found in most popular explanations of clouds and how they work. Indeed for *Sidrak* the most pressing question concerning clouds is not how they are made, but why some of them are dark and some white.

> 'Why ben some clowdis of þe sky
> Whyte and some blak þerby?'
> > Clowdis sometime beeþ right þynne
> > For litel water þat is þerynne.
> Þanne cometh þe light of þe day
> And þe sunne þat shyneþ ay
> And ȝeueþ on þe clowde light,
> And þe clowde þat is of litel might
> Is þorghshyned þerwiþal;
> White þerfore he him shew shal,
> For þorgh waater may men se
> If þat it noght deep be.
> Þe clowde þat blak is to oure sight
> Is liche watir and of oon might
> And for þe þiknesse þat it has

May no light þerþorgh pas;
Þerfore holdeþ it not drie
For it is fer bynethe þe skye
And for it is þikke alowe
Blak byhoueþ him to to vs showe. (Burton 1998, 6621–40)[14]

It is worth noting that this highly popular and much derided text is well aware that clouds are entirely made up of water, there is no mention of the vaguer 'matter' that marks Trevisa's definition. It also makes clear that questions of darkness and lightness are dependent solely on density: the more water, the more opaque, so the darker the cloud appears. Added to this is the element of height, which also features in Trevisa. When it comes to clouds, darkness, thickness and lowness are often found together.

This gradual association is found in the treatise as well. Initially the cloud of unknowing seems to be analogous to darkness and is related to things forgotten as well as things unknown. We first encounter this cloud both as readers and contemplatives in chapter three, where it is explicitly figurative.[15] It accompanies the state of darkness the aspirant contemplative experiences when striving to focus entirely on God for the first time: 'bot a derknes, & as it were a cloude of vnknowyng, þou wost neuer what' (Hodgson 1982, 9). It is not entirely clear at this point if this cloud is solely a metaphor explaining the kind of darkness, or something independent, experienced alongside that darkness; regardless, that 'as it were' signals that here, at this first moment of use, the cloud is an image representing a state of uncertainty. By the next sentence, however, the cloud has become an established entity, just as the darkness, previously a trifle to be dismissed ('bot a derknes') has become a physical obstacle between the contemplative and God: 'Þis

---

[14] All references are to line numbers in Burton 1998. I have taken the Lansdowne manuscript as my text due to it being the fullest known English version (see Burton 1998, liv). Of the two versions in Burton's parallel-text edition, Lansdowne also happens to be the clearer on the matter of clouds.

[15] This is the first occurrence of a cloud in the body of the text. Although the treatise heralds the cloud of unknowing in its title, that cloud is not mentioned in the table of Contents. The only cloud mentioned in these Contents is the cloud of forgetting in chapter five. The chapter summaries which constitute the Contents are the only clues to where particular themes are discussed within the treatise, so we might reasonably expect the titular cloud to feature somewhere, but it does not. We are left to encounter the clouds as we read, without preparation beyond the title and this summary of chapter five, both of which present the clouds as substantives, not images or metaphors.

derknes & þis cloude is, howsoeuer þou dost, bitwix þee & þi God'
(Hodgson 1982, 9). So this cloud is between us and God, but at the same
time we are within it: 'it behoueþ alweis be in þis cloude & in þis
derknes' (Hodgson 1982, 9). This, then, is the kind of enveloping cloud
we might encounter on a mountain top, deliberately reminiscent of
Moses' cloud. Yet while this association may well come to mind (indeed
Gallacher's sole comment on these lines is a reference to the Biblical
passage) it is not a reference the treatise exploits. Instead we are led into
imagining or experiencing a more particular and perhaps more personal
cloud – 'þys cloude' – which is explicitly connected to darkness. The
darkness is important, not because it, too, is metaphorical, but because
it, too, is real.

However, although the darkness and cloud in which contemplatives
find themselves is an actual state, the treatise is at pains at this early
stage to ensure that neither is confused with common natural
phenomena. The few sentences that seek to ensure the reader avoids this
mistake again reveal the author's knowledge of the common definitions
of clouds:

> & wene not, for I clepe it a derknes or a cloude, þat it be any cloude
> congelid of þe humours þat fleen in þe ayre, ne ȝit any derknes soche
> as is in þin house on niȝtes, when þi candel is oute. For soche a
> derknes & soche a cloude maist þou ymagin wiþ coriouste of witte, …
> Lat be soche falsheed; I mene not þus. For when I sey derknes, I mene
> a lackying of knowyng; as alle þat þing þat þou knowest not, or elles
> þat þou hast forȝetyn, it is derk to þee, for þou seest it not wiþ þi
> goostly iȝe. & for þis skile it is not clepid a cloude of þe eire, bot a
> cloude of vnknowyng, þat is bitwix þee & þi God.
>
> (Hodgson 1982, 13)

We are able to imagine clouds which are made up of condensed vapor
('congelid of the humours') because they are part of everyday experience. What is interesting here is that to visualize such clouds demands a
'coriouste of witte' – a subtlety of the intellect, a term which implies
something rather different from a simple exercise of the imagination.
Such conceptual clouds evidently require some intellectual knowledge.
We need to know a bit about where clouds come from in order to visualize them, it seems. It may be, then, that it is not the picture of physical,
natural clouds that is the difficulty here, but the associations that such
envisaged clouds have with scientific knowledge, based on empirical
observation, human reason and deduction. This might seem tenuous
were it not for the emphasis on manmade darkness that accompanies

this warning against clouds understood as masses of congealed vapor drifting in the sky. The darkness we are told not to imagine is explicitly that created when a candle is put out. Why this? Why not the inevitable darkness of night, which would seem to have more direct association with clouds, as being also an inevitable part of the cycle of the natural world? I suggest that the answer lies in that phrase which is so difficult to translate: 'coriouste of witte'. Some connotation of the curiosity that killed the cat is surely present here, as is the association with something intricate, overintricate indeed, almost to the point of twisted. Here 'witte' is not the senses, but the intellect, the rational faculty which is often taken as the defining attribute that divides humans from the other beasts of creation. As such it has particular associations with knowledge based on deduction (*scientia*) whereas the mystical tradition tends to favor knowledge derived from revelation and apprehension (*sapientia*). So the exhortation, 'lat be soche falsheed', is a command to leave behind reliance on our human inventiveness and is a rhetorical device which recasts as falsehood the previously verifiable and observed phenomena of the darkness effected by the extinguishing of an artifact (the candle) and clouds as defined in books. In the course of this recasting, darkness shifts from lack of light to lack of knowledge and also, interestingly, all forgotten knowledge. And it is this lack of knowledge and knowledge once known but now gone that conglomerates to create the cloud of unknowing that gives the treatise its name.

Even when the second cloud, of forgetting, is introduced the associa-tion of darkness with the cloud of unknowing persists for some chapters. This is perhaps surprising, given what the books of knowledge say, but we must note that darkness, or thickness, is an attribute of all clouds; it is their opacity that makes them visible and proves their existence. As we have seen, that opacity is related to level, and this factor of height is also important in *Cloud*'s descriptions of clouds. Thus in chapter six while the cloud of forgetting must be trodden upon beneath the contempla-tive, it is the cloud of unknowing, above the contemplative, which is both dark and thick. Such darkness and thickness indicate that at this early stage the contemplative has not risen very high within the cloud of unknowing, and indeed is just at the start of the effort that must be made to break through the veil that separates him from God:

> & fonde for to peerse þat derknes abouen þee. & smyte apon þat þicke cloude of vnknowyng wiþ a scharp darte of longing loue, & go not þens for þing þat befalleþ. (Hodgson 1982, 14)

Despite the author's exhortation to resist visualizing a real cloud, we readily envisage here a kind of fog or low cloud enveloping the contemplative, who yet must strive to look *up*, battling the implied urge to find a way out of this thick, disorientating opacity to familiar ground below. At this point modern-day readers might like to consider later and more detailed categorization of clouds, which declare that Cumulonimbus can stretch across all levels of the atmosphere and can be dark or white, according to how much water they contain.[16] However there is more implied here than simply a probably involuntary reference to one of the commonest forms of cloud; that effort to pierce the cloud relies upon our shared knowledge that behind the clouds is light, the clear blue of the heavens and the sun. Density of matter, the vapor that makes up the cloud, prevents us from seeing this light above, but such matter is not permanent. The cloud can be dispersed in two ways, often operating together: through rain, which returns the implicitly heavy and impure matter to the earth, or through evaporation, as the purest particles are drawn ever higher, and made ever thinner until they finally disappear altogether. We find this process explained under the question about rain in *Sidrak*:

> And whan þe water is doun clenly,
> Þe clowde bileueþ white and faire
> Þat is þorgh colde of þe aire;
> And þat is wastid þorgh þe sunne clere,
> And so bycomeþ þe sky al clere. (Burton 1998, 5330–34)

All this concurs with Trevisa's description of clouds (quoted above) and shows that this distinction between clouds made up of 'more sotile and pure' vapors and those resulting from the gathering of 'fumositees' (to use Trevisa's terms) was firmly established in the popular imagination. It is this understanding of how clouds work through a process of purification by evaporation and simultaneous filtering (in effect) through gravity, which causes the heavier and less pure elements to thicken and eventually fall, which underpins the *Cloud*-author's use of clouds in his treatise. That use continues, and goes beyond simple analogy, when we look at how these clouds develop.

As I have shown, it was well known that the greater the density of matter, the darker the cloud. That density results from the conglomera-

---

[16] Pretor-Pinney (2006, 17) provides a clear and useful table showing which levels of the atmosphere different types of clouds inhabit.

tion of all sorts of less pure matter, and this finds an echo in the *Cloud*'s recommendation that the contemplative does not dwell on any individual thought, whether the recollection of sin done or of good deed or evidence of God's love, because such thoughts are necessarily connected to the earth and will thus distract from the endeavor of focusing solely on God above. All such thoughts are to be thrust beneath the cloud of forgetting, as contemplatives devote all their energy to piercing the opaque cloud above them.[17] However, although the contemplative must seek to penetrate this cloud, the author acknowledges that the effort must fail as the only light capable of getting through comes from above. In terms of religious apprehension this means that the only force that can pierce the cloud is God, but this will only be possible if the contemplative has succeeded in rising above all thoughts of the world. They must be 'hanging' (the term used in chapter twenty-one) in the dark cloud of unknowing, and have trodden all earthly notions below the thick cloud of forgetting: the adjectives have been split now and, when used at all, 'dark' is aligned with unknowing and 'thick' with forgetting. It is only when this is achieved that

> Þan wil he [God] sumtyme parauenture seend oute a beme of goostly liȝt, peersyng þis cloude of vnknowing þat is bitwix þee & hym, & schewe þee sum of his priuete, þe whiche man may not, ne kan not, speke. (Hodgson 1982, 34)

The beam comes from above, which is not at all remarkable given our conception of God dwelling above (and often depicted supported by a cloud), but it is a shift from the attempt to pierce the cloud from below. The contemplative must strive to reach upward, but only the implied sun above can actually get through the cloud. This fits with not only what is said in books of knowledge, but also our commonly perceived experience, as we have all seen shafts of light cut through clouds, often to dramatic effect. It is precisely such observations that give rise to the questions posed and answered by popular science, and, like them, the effect is not just to remind us of what is familiar, but to encourage us to look afresh with renewed understanding.

This returns us to the terms used in the further explanations of clouds and in particular to the way they disappear. The thin, white clouds that remain after rainfall are 'wastid' by the heat of the sun, while the lightest clouds are evaporated without the need for rain, as their purity means

---

[17] See in particular *Cloud* chapter seven (Hodgson 1982, 15).

they move ever upward. As Trevisa puts it, 'by lyȝtnesse of his owne substaunce a cloude meveþ vpward' (1975, 578). If we now focus on the sun's role in creating clouds we find another area in which understanding of cloud formation informs *Cloud*'s language. Again the process is most succinctly described by Sidrak when considering rain:

> Þe sunne, þat is hoot kindely,
> Draweþ the water faste him to
> …
> But whanne þe sunne his hete ȝildes,
> Þe dewe, þat is in towne and fildes,
> He takiþ vp and draweþ fast
> And comeþ to þe eir at þe last
> And is þere þikkinge liche a clowde
> (Burton 1998, 5313–14; 5319–23)

Lansdowne here is a little more circumspect than Laud, for whom the 'þykkynge' (thickening) is a cloud, not just like one. However, my focus here is on that word 'draw'. The sun draws up the water simply because, by very nature, the sun is hot and so draws cooler water to it. The process is both inevitable and irresistible. This is echoed in chapter nine of *Cloud* where God is described as drawing the contemplative up into the cloud of unknowing. Initially the contemplative is urged to lift their love up to the cloud, but the implication that the human has the initiative here is swiftly corrected: 'Bot ȝif I schal sey þe soþe, lat God drawe þi loue up to þat cloude' (Hodgson 1982, 19). Love is the pure affection and desire for God that inspires the contemplative and as such religious love or longing is the purest possible human emotion. It is thus in keeping with the idea of the sun drawing the purest elements up from the earth, ever higher until they disappear in the purity of evaporation. Once again the analogy is easy to see, as the contemplative desires to approach ever nearer to God and leave behind all associations with the world. However, the *Cloud*-author is careful to point out that full union with God is not possible in this world; the nearest one can hope for is to 'hang' within the cloud of unknowing, always striving towards the light that lies behind the cloud and sometimes blessed by a piercing shaft of light from above. This term 'hanging' is also found in Trevisa's aside on how clouds appear to border on heaven:

> Also a cloude þat hongiþ on hihe in þe hye regioun of þe eyr semeþ i-iunyed next to heuen, and is noþeles wiþouten comparisoun neer to þe erþe þan to heuene. (1975, 579)

Here again we find the mixture of simple observation, popular assumption and scientific knowledge. Those high, bright clouds *look* as if they must be in heaven, but in fact they are closer to earth than they are to heaven. Immediately we can see how this understanding of clouds is reflected in *Cloud*'s quietly made point that even Mary, the model for all contemplatives who achieve or seek to achieve this highest form of life, was within the cloud, which 'was þe best & þe holiest party of contemplacion þat may be in þis liif' (Hodgson 1982, 26). That last phrase is telling: the best possible on earth is yet a long way off from heaven. To those of us who are not in that cloud of unknowing, the contemplative seems to be all but joined to heaven, an aspirational model for us all, but true contemplatives know they are still far off; still within this cloud, rather than being part of that thinnest vapor which evaporates in the sunlight.

The persistence of this cloud for the contemplative leads it to be called 'combros' (cumbersome, obstructive) in chapter twenty-eight of the treatise, but it is also 'hiȝe' and 'wonderful' in chapter seventeen. Most importantly, though, it is always there, a point made strongly in chapter sixty-nine with the last mention of this cloud: 'for euermore he schal fynde it a cloude of vnknowyng þat is bitwix him & his God' (Hodgson 1982, 69). Perhaps surprisingly, given the information about how clouds evaporate, the medieval books of knowledge also contain the fact that clouds are always present, somewhere. *Sidrak*'s response to the question why we see fewer clouds in summer than in winter is

> As þicke ben clowdes ay
> In somer as in winter day
> And als greet and as derke
> ...
> Alþogh it be noght in þis cuntre,
> It is elleswhere so it be
> For þei ne faile neuermore
> Ouþer here or elleswhore.
> ...
> Clowdes on þe sky ful þicke clime
> Þere þat winter is þat time.
> (Burton 1998, 10489–91; 10495–98; 10503–04)

So clouds are always with us; an essential part of the seasonal cycle, as their formation and evaporation mark the process by which the fumes and water drawn up from the earth are purified and then some rained back down to fertilize the earth. Even this cyclical aspect is evident in

Cloud. Although it is a book devoted to contemplative life and how one might achieve it permanently, the earlier chapters admit that the novice will find it hard not only to achieve full contemplation, but also to sustain it. They will sometimes find themselves within the cloud of unknowing, only to fall out of it again due to some earthly concern, whether recollected sin, a good deed, or even an attempt to think in concrete terms about the goodness of God. It is only with practice and understanding that contemplatives will arrive at a state of sustained contemplation, always, presumably, within the cloud of unknowing. By this time that cloud is less the cumulonimbus of the early chapters that seemed to stretch down to the ground and envelop the contemplative, but more, perhaps, the pervasive cloud mentioned in Caxton's *Mirrour of the World* (1480) which 'hath not so moche obscurete that it taketh from vs the clernes of the day' (Caxton 1913, 117).[18]

Underlying this paper is the presumption that the *Cloud* author drew wittingly or otherwise on the way scientific understanding of clouds was expressed in the popular books of his day. There is nothing to say, however, that it might not have been the other way around. The writers of these books were making available to an interested, but not necessarily formally educated, audience the science known to schoolmen who were frequently also clerics. As such it is just as possible that the language used for religious discussion with those outside the universities has permeated the popular books of knowledge as that the process was the other way about.[19] Regardless of the flow of influence (and it may indeed have been a more circular current) the detailed yet also generalist knowledge found in such books as *Sidrak* and Trevisa's *On the Properties of Things* shows how popular it has always been to learn more about how the world works, particularly when the information on offer unites empirical science and straightforward observation. Popular science must establish a close and easy connection with its audience; it cannot rely on theories proved entirely through obscure experiments or measurable only with equipment not available to the majority of its readership.

---

[18] Caxton's text is an English version of the French *Image du Monde*, which Caxton translated in 1480.
[19] I am grateful to Sharon Ruston for pointing out the similarity between this comment and Gillian Beer's propositions in *Darwin's Plots: Evolutionary Narrative in Darwin, George Eliot and Nineteenth-Century Fiction* (2000). Space does not permit discussion of the exchange between Beer's arguments and those I offer here, but it is striking that Beer describes Darwin's famous term 'natural selection' as 'poised on the edge of metaphor because of the way it claimed an explanatory role before contemporaries had learnt what it meant' (xviii).

Where Hamblyn and Pretor-Pinney combine affability with research, others engage their readers by using as a guide figure a high-profile, non-specialist, for whom the subject matter is somehow relevant.[20] A latter-day example is the glossy and immensely appealing *Weather*, a book of photographs, particularly of clouds, accompanied by some explanatory text (Dunlop 2006).[21] The photographs and text are the work of Storm Dunlop, meteorologist and Fellow of the Royal Astronomical and Royal Meteorological Societies; a populist slant is lent by the Foreword by Chris Bonington, whose first phrase moves us into the world of literature: 'The earth's climate is a key protagonist in the story of humanity' (Dunlop 2006, 6). The combination of personal observation, traditional association, metaphor and empirical science found in popular science books of all ages, and, as I hope I have shown, also in *The Cloud of Unknowing* reveals a longstanding inclination for the kind of interconnectedness advocated by greens, be they environmentalists, ecologists, literary critics or political activists (and those terms need not be mutually exclusive). In addition it reveals how literature, religious treatises and books of knowledge use similar devices to engage readers and impart understanding. It is thus indicative of how we actually think about clouds, that they are chosen as vehicles for a text which seeks to expand the mind of its readers beyond the limits of the physical world, without denigrating that world. The fact that those same actual clouds have attracted so little academic discussion reveals how easily most readers overlook the presence of the material (rather than metaphorical) natural world within texts.

Works Cited

Beer, Gillian, 2000 (1983). *Darwin's Plots: Evolutionary Narrative in Darwin, George Eliot and Nineteenth-Century Fiction*. Port Chester, NY: Cambridge University Press.
Bryson, Bill, 2004. *A Short History of Nearly Everything*. London: Black Swan.

[20] It is possible, but I admit speculative, to regard the disciple addressed throughout *Cloud* as a fictional device designed to give readers someone to empathize with and to follow through the contemplative work involved. Readers would thus choose to align themselves with him, rather than with the rabble so explicitly excluded from the book.
[21] The cover of the book sports the subtitle 'Spectacular images of the world's extraordinary climate' and the information 'Foreword by Sir Chris Bonington'.

Burrow, John, 1977. 'Fantasy and Language in *The Cloud of Unknowing*', *Essays in Criticism* 27.4: 283–98.

Burton, T. L., ed., 1998. *Sidrak and Bokkus*. 2 vols. Early English Text Society. Oxford: Oxford University Press.

Caxton, William, 1913 (1480). *Mirrour of the World*, ed. Oliver Prior. Early English Text Society. London: Kegan Paul.

Clark, John P. H., 1980. 'Sources and Theology in *The Cloud of Unknowing*', *Downside Review* 98: 83–109.

———, 1995. '*The Cloud of Unknowing*': *An Introduction*. 3 vols. Analecta Cartusiana. Salzburg: Institut für Anglistik und Amerikanistik, Universität Salzburg.

Dawkins, Richard, 1986. *The Blind Watchmaker*. Harlow, Essex: Longman.

Dunlop, Storm. 2006. *Weather*. London: Octopus.

Frisinger, Howard H., 1977. *The History of Meteorology to 1800*. New York: Science History Publications.

Gallacher, Patrick, ed., 1977. *The Cloud of Unknowing*. Kalamazoo, MI: Medieval Institute Publications.

Garrard, Greg, 2004. *Ecocriticism*. London and New York: Routledge.

Gould, Stephen Jay, 2003. *The Hedgehog, the Fox and the Magister's Pox: Mending the Gap between Science and the Humanities*. London: Jonathan Cape.

Gribben, John, 2005. *Deep Simplicity: Chaos, Complexity and the Emergence of Life*. London: Penguin.

Hamblyn, Richard, 2001. *The Invention of Clouds*. New York: Farrar, Straus and Giraux.

Hodgson, Phyllis, ed., 1944. *The Cloud of Unknowing*. Early English Text Society original series 218. London: Oxford University Press.

———, ed., 1982. *The Cloud of Unknowing and Related Treatises*. Analecta Cartusiana. Salzburg: Institut für Anglistik und Amerikanistik, Universität Salzburg; Exeter: Catholic Records Press.

Lees, R. A., 1983. *The Negative Language of the Dionysian School of Mystical Theology: An Approach to 'The Cloud of Unknowing'*. Analecta Cartusiana. Salzburg: Institut für Anglistik und Amerikanistik, Universität Salzburg.

Minnis, A. J. M., 1982. 'The Sources of the *Cloud of Unknowing*: A Reconsideration', in *The Medieval Mystical Tradition, 2: Papers read at Dartington Hall, July 1982*, ed. M. Glasscoe. Exeter: Exeter University Press: 63–76.

Oerlemans, Onno, 2002. *Romanticism and the Materiality of Nature*. Toronto: Toronto University Press.

Pokorn, Nike Kocijanèiè, 1997. 'The Language and Discourse of *The Cloud of Unknowing*', *Literature and Theology* 11, 2 (December): 408–21.

Pretor-Pinney, Gavin, 2006. *The Cloudspotter's Guide*. London: Hodder & Stoughton.

Rudd, Gillian, 2007. *Greenery: Ecocritical Readings of Late Medieval English Literature*. Manchester: Manchester University Press.

Spearing, A. C., trans., 2001. *The Cloud of Unknowing and Other Works*. London: Penguin.

Taylor, Cheryl, 2005. 'Paradox upon Paradox: Using and Abusing Language in *The Cloud of Unknowing* and Related Treatises', *Parergon* 22, 2: 31–51.

———, 2006. 'The *Cloud*-Author's Remaking of the Pseudo-Dionysius' *Mystical Theology*', *Medium Aevum* 75, 2: 202–18.

Trevisa, John, 1975 (1398/9). *On the Properties of Things. John Trevisa's transla-tion of Bartholomaeus Anglicus' 'De Proprietatibus Rerum'*, general ed. M. C. Seymour. 3 vols. Oxford: Clarendon Press.

Whitehead, Christiania, 1998. 'Regarding the Ark: Revisions of Architectural Imagery in the Writings of the *Cloud* Author', *The Downside Review* 116: 195–212.

'dreams and plain dotage':
The Value of The Birth of Mankind
(1540–1654)

ELAINE HOBBY

WHEN *The Birth of Mankind* first appeared in print in 1540, it initiated a new kind of publication in Britain: this 'scientific' book was the first published text in English that sought to explain to the general reader where babies come from and how to look after them in their infancy. It was to become a phenomenal success, remaining in print in its revised and expanded version of 1545 for more than one hundred years, and passing through many more editions than have yet been counted.[1] This essay will sketch the book's history, before going on to use it as an example of the importance of reading scientific texts, and of reading them historically whilst applying literary critical techniques to analyse such features as metaphor and tone. Such a process both makes these writings a necessary part of the study of literature, and also shows how detailed engagement with materials of this kind necessitates a rejection of the assertions made in Thomas Laqueur's hugely influential *Making Sex* (1990) concerning the ways in which the differences between male and female bodies were understood in the early-modern period.

First, the book's history. Although when *The Birth of Mankind* appeared in 1540 it was the first of its kind, it was far from being a new book. The man acknowledged as its originator, Richard Jonas, who was probably the High Master of St Paul's School in London, had translated most of it from *De Partu Hominis* ('Of the Birth of Mankind').[2] To this he added materials gleaned from recent Latin editions of the ancient Greek

---

1 Good early studies of the book's history include Ballantyne (1906, 299–307 and 1907) and Power (1927). See also Raynalde (2008) for the large number of editions that either bear the erroneous date 1565, or are undated, and for other work on the book's history. Calculating on the basis that the book passed through many fewer editions than it actually did, Slack believes it to have been the sixth best-selling medical book of the sixteenth century (1979, 237–73).
2 A Richard Jones was Master of St Paul's Free School in London from 1532 to 1549. The evidence supporting the conjecture that he is the 'studious and

Hippocratic corpus. *De Partu Hominis* was not an original publication either, but itself was a translation of a work by a German physician, Eucharius Rösslin. That German book, *Der swangern Frauen und Hebammen Rosegarten* ('The Rose Garden for Pregnant Women and Midwives'), came out in 1513, designed as an instruction manual for midwives seeking state registration.[3] It was presumably well-suited to its task, because it remained in print for many decades, also being translated into Dutch in 1516 and staying in print in the Netherlands through at least twenty-eight editions into the eighteenth century. (The system of midwives' registration in the Netherlands resembled the German one, and sales to would-be midwives might well have been a factor in its popularity.[4]) *The Rose Garden* was also translated into Czech, Italian, French, Danish, and, possibly, Spanish (Ingerslev 1909).[5]

Identifying Rösslin as the author of *Der Rosegarten* does not, however, finish the task of tracing this 'new' book's origins. Research by Britta-Juliane Kruse (1994) and Monica H. Green (unpublished) has established that Rösslin drew extensively on a northern Italian Latin manuscript, and any close analysis of *The Birth of Mankind* can demonstrate that quotations from and summaries of the medieval Arabic physicians Avicenna (Ibn-Sinna) and Rhazes (ar-Rhazi), from Albertus Magnus's thirteenth-century *On Animals*, Paul of Aegina's seventh-century re-presentation of Soranus's first-century *Gynecology*, as well as the ubiquitous influence of Galen and Hippocrates make up most of this

learned clerk' who translated the book from Latin into English is outlined in Raynalde (2008, xxix–xxxiii).

[3] Some of the material in *Der Rosegarten* that is not taken from medieval and ancient sources relates closely to the skills that German midwives were legally required to demonstrate. As a whole, the book follows closely the stipulations of the German midwifery ordinances that are summarized by Merry Wiesner: 'What food, drink and baths will help a woman have an easy birth? … How does she know whether the foetus is healthy or sick, alive or dead? What is the normal position for birth, and how is this to be brought about in the case of abnormal presentations? What should be done with the umbilical cord and afterbirth, especially to make sure that the latter has emerged? How are the new mother and infant to be best taken care of, and what advice should she give the new mother?' (1993, 82).

[4] For midwifery regulation in the Netherlands, see Marland (1993), Green (1989, 450–51), Benedek (1977, 551–54).

[5] The possibility of a Spanish translation having appeared is raised both by Klein (Rösslin, 1910, xiv) and by Raynalde in 1545, but no such edition has yet been found.

book's content.[6] It was an extraordinarily wide-ranging compilation that the schoolmaster Richard Jonas (if schoolmaster he was) presented to his curious English reader in 1540.

Perhaps in part because the English-speaking world, where the state did not formally train midwives, did not provide the reading market for a midwifery manual that Germany and the Netherlands did, but also because of his own humanist educational goals, Richard Jonas addressed *The Birth of Mankind* not to medical practitioners but to a general Christian reader 'in this noble realm of England' (Raynalde 2008, 206).[7] This intended change in the readership is shown in various features of the book, including his introduction of 'An Admonition to the Reader', warning men not to use its sexual information in an 'ungodly' way, and his removal, on many occasions, of Rösslin's acknowledgment of the Arabic (read, Islamic) authority Avicenna as his source.[8] Perhaps though the most striking example of Jonas's change to his implied readership is shown in the five chapters of 'other fruitful things' that he advertises on the book's titlepage (Raynalde 2008, 203), and added to his source. Jonas's additional chapters deal not with the birthing process and the care of the new mother and baby (the sole concerns of *Der Rosegarten*), but with the mechanics of how to achieve pregnancy in the first place. No doubt it was the inclusion of this material, drawn from his own reading of Hippocrates, that prompted Jonas to warn his reader (or entice them?) to 'use it godly … utterly eschewing all ribald and unseemly communication of any things contained in the same, as they will answer before God' (Raynalde 2008, 204).

Whether Jonas's addition of these actually rather brief and perhaps disappointing 'fruitful things' to his book – they consist mostly of instructions on how to prepare medications to make a woman fertile – would have ensured the book's success in Britain is impossible to say, because at its next appearance, in 1545, *The Birth of Mankind* was again expanded, and spectacularly so. This expansion was the work of a physician, Thomas Raynalde, a man whose up-to-the-minute interest in

---

6   See the footnotes in the 2008 edition for indications of which parts of Rösslin's text are borrowed from what sources (Raynalde 2008).

7   In England and Wales, although midwives were supposed to hold a licence issued by their local bishop attesting to their good moral character and experience in assisting at births, there was no system of formal training. See Evenden (2000, 24–78), Guy (1982), Hitchcock (1967), Hess (1993), Sharp (1999).

8   See the footnotes in the 2008 edition for details of where references to Avicenna and other authorities were removed by Jonas or Raynalde (Raynalde 2008).

medical learning led him both to revise extensively the medical remedies that pepper it, and to add an extraordinary new first book. This new
first book is Raynalde's own synopsis and translation of the human
sexual anatomy of Andreas Vesalius, which had only just appeared – in
1543 – and only in Latin in a huge, very expensive folio edition
(Vesalius 1543). Raynalde extracted from Vesalius's text materials about
the female reproductive system, and published these in a cheap, small
quarto text that also includes copies of some of Vesalius's most startling
images, pictures of the womb (see Figures 1 and 2) and of the foetus in
utero.[9] The result of Thomas Raynalde's intervention in *The Birth of
Mankind* was that whilst in the rest of Europe only doctors and academics
could read Vesalius's work and engage with his new assertions about
human anatomy, a general reader of English could read these ideas, and
look at these images, almost as soon as the academic world itself could;
and could continue to do so for the next one hundred years, as the book
passed through its huge number of editions. Since for at least the first
fifty years of its life this book was the only one of its kind in English, it is
not unreasonable to assume that its 'general readers' included most
writers in the second half of the sixteenth century.

The potential interest of this book to those exploring the history of
medicine is clear enough; what of its significance to researchers in
literary and cultural matters? Its appeal is due in part to the book's
subject-matter, because early-modern readers of *The Birth of Mankind*
encountered between its pages an extraordinary range of topics. The
book engages not only with reproductive anatomy and the possible
complications of the birthing process, but with such concerns as the
importance of exercise and good diet in pregnancy, how to choose a
good wetnurse, and, in the final chapter added by Thomas Raynalde,
'beautifying receptes' that might be used by both women and men to
manage such 'tedious and loathsome' problems as 'the Rank Savour of

---

[9] Although most surviving copies of the 1545 and 1552 editions of *The Birth of
Mankind* lack most or all of the anatomical pictures, the text refers to them in
detail and repeatedly, indicating that Raynalde had planned for copies of them
to be included in his book. The Wellcome Library has a copy of the 1545 edition
that contains all of the illustrations (EPB 7358/B), which were redrawn in 1560
and made an integral part of the book. In later copies, the illustrations are usually
present. See Raynalde (2008, xxxv–xxxviii). The pictures that purported to
represent the fetus in utero were in fact based not on human but on dog anatomy,
as Vesalius later admitted. The resultant errors were corrected in subsequent
editions of *De Fabrica*, but continued to be reproduced in *The Birth of Mankind*
until 1654.

the Armhole' (Raynalde 2008, 202). The variety of the matters frankly discussed therefore provides today's reader with information on a surprising number of subjects, and the range of medieval and ancient sources relied on provides much material for research into the origins and contours of early-modern culture. For instance, although recent work on midwifery's history has sometimes asserted that early-modern people prevented any circulation of air in the birthing chamber (Wilson 1995, 26), *The Birth of Mankind*, in keeping with its German source, is explicit that in summer, fresh air is to be let into the room to prevent its becoming stiflingly hot (Raynalde 2008, 117). Similarly, any illusion that there was a lack of warmth in the way that people in the past viewed babies is brought into question by the tenderness of the book's Avicennan instructions to bathe an infant two or three times a day (Raynalde 2008, 155), to massage the baby before rewinding its swaddling bands (Raynalde 2008, 155), and to rock it gently in a cradle to settle it after feeding (Raynalde 2008, 160). If the child has a squint, there is the further suggestion that a baby's natural delight in bright colors can be used to encourage it to look in a particular direction and correct the impediment (Raynalde 2008, 183–84).

While many of these recommendations can be traced to medieval Arabic and earlier sources, some features of *The Birth of Mankind* are specifically attributable to its English 'authors', Richard Jonas and Thomas Raynalde, and these additions and adjustments have a particular interest for those working on early-modern British culture and its relationship with continental Europe. Jonas not only introduces 'fruitful' advice on fertility, but also makes other changes to his Latin original that could be indicative of his own experience as a London schoolmaster and father. (If the correct Richard Jonas has been identified as the translator, we know from his will that he was survived by several children, whom he commends to his wife's care.[10]) For instance, in discussing the possible need to stimulate menstrual (lochial) bleeding, Jonas assumes that 'few or no women be ignorant' of how to make remedies to achieve this (Raynalde 2008, 124), whereas *De Partu Hominis* indicates only that 'moderately skilful' women would have such knowledge (Rhodion 1535, 31v–32). In the light of modern speculation on how people in earlier times might have exercised control over their fertility, it is interesting to find such a casual assumption that women can make medicines of this

---

[10] Richard Jonas's will is in the Public Record Office, PRO PROB/11/32. There is a brief summary of its contents in Raynalde 2008, xxxiii.

kind.[11] Such abortifacients were not supposed to be used in a Christian country to end a pregnancy, of course, and in the next edition of *The Birth of Mankind* Thomas Raynalde was to add the reflection that the book might be attacked on the grounds that 'some wickedly disposed person' could

> abuse such medicines as be here declared for a good purpose, to some devilish and lewd use. What I mean by the lewd use of them, they that have understanding right soon will perceive. (Raynalde 2008, 19)

The key point of interest here, however, is Jonas's assumption that women would know how to stimulate their own bleeding.

Somewhat startlingly to a modern reader, Jonas also adds to his source a further possible way to stimulate lactation: a woman might take a warm bath and then 'cause some[one] to suck her breast' (Raynalde 2008, 159). This, combined with Jonas's adjustments to the Avicennan advice he inherited from *De Partu Hominis* on what should be borne in mind when feeding a baby, provides much material to explore both continuities and changes in ideas about these practices. A further systematic way in which Jonas amends his source text, giving his modern reader food for thought about divergences between English and German culture, is that he increases the number of references in the book to the likelihood that labor will be painful for the mother.[12] Unlike in the German *Rose Garden*, where such pain is linked in traditional Catholic fashion to Eve's punishment for sin in the Garden of Eden, Jonas treats this as a physical state that should cause men to have more sympathy and care for women. In 1513, Rösslin had explained to his patron that

> the almighty eternal God/ punished our first mother Eve/ for violating the commandment/ with the curse/ that she should bear her children in pain/ This curse is inherited from her by all women.
> (Arons 1994, 32)

This dedication of the book to Duchess Katherine of Brunswick and Lüneburg was omitted by the translator who produced *De Partu Hominis*, so Jonas's contrasting way of talking about a woman's pain in childbirth

---

[11] See McLaren (1984, 89–114), Pollock (1990, 55–59). Remedies to provoke the terms are also given in the works of two women almanac-makers: Sarah Jinner, *An Almanack* (1659, 1660, 1664), and Mary Holden, *The Womans Almanack* (1688, 1689); see Hobby (1988, 180–82).
[12] See the footnotes in the 2008 edition for details of where Jonas has increased the emphasis on a mother's pain (Raynalde 2008).

is not a direct response to Catholic tradition, but certainly comes from a very different theological perspective. He cautions his male reader to have sympathy for our 'even [fellow] Christians', women, 'which sustain and endure for the time so great dolour and pain for the birth of mankind and deliverance of the same into the world' (Raynalde 2008, 204).

Thomas Raynalde's re-editing of *The Birth of Mankind* in 1545 served to differentiate it further from the values and assumptions of its Latin and German predecessors, and also to introduce other new thinking. The first striking sign of his design in this book is his introduction of a new subtitle, 'The Woman's Book'. He has chosen this, he says, having read Jonas's translation and become convinced of 'the manifold utility and profit which thereby mought ensue to all women' (Raynalde 2008, 12). Such assertions of interest in attracting a woman reader at this time need to be treated with caution because, as Audrey Eccles (1974, 1977) and Suzanne Hull (1982) have shown, writers not uncommonly alluded to the likelihood of a female readership as an alibi for bringing out in the vernacular works that were traditionally available only in Latin, and so limited to an educated audience. An author might claim that he envisaged women as his readers as a way of masking his assumption that many male readers might not themselves be educated enough to attempt a book in Latin. In Raynalde's case, however, there is ample evidence both of an educational drive in this book, and of a particular interest in speaking to women. The address to women is explicit, for instance, when he remarks that his anatomical material will allow them 'the better to understand how everything cometh to pass within your bodies in time of conception, of bearing, and of birth' (Raynalde 2008, 12). The more general educational imperative is clear in many ways, including the fact that the Vesalian anatomy that Raynalde adds is actively presented 'as though ye were present at the cutting open, or anatomy, of a dead woman' (Raynalde 2008, 12), with descriptions, for instance, of the difficulty that can be experienced when trying to ease apart the layers of the skin (Raynalde 2008, 26), and of cutting through the skin, flesh, muscles and peritoneum to observe the appearance of the womb:

> the outside of it is very smooth, moist, glistering, and reddish, as it were a little red tempered with a great deal of white. The inside also of the matrix is smooth. (Raynalde 2008, 34)

He is also very much the teacher when he alludes to experiences in his reader's day-to-day life to explain how the body works. For instance, the 'skinny flaps' that serve to prevent urine running back up the ureters into the kidneys are likened to the mechanism in bellows that makes them blow air in only one direction (Raynalde 2008, 53–54), and a child's dried umbilical cord is compared to a harp-string (Raynalde 2008, 63). Raynalde also offers as a point of reference colloquial terms for some of the matters he discusses: of the terms (menses) he says, 'some name them their flowers' (2008, 57); in describing the membranes surrounding the fetus he offers the words 'coif' (cap), 'biggin' (hood), and 'shirt' as possible familiar expressions (Raynalde 2008, 60). He also proposes colloquial names for the cervix ('womb port', Raynalde 2008, 37) and vagina ('womb passage', Raynalde 2008, 32). It is worth pausing to reflect therefore that, despite Thomas Laqueur's assertion that there was no technical term for the vagina 'in the European vernaculars until around 1700' (1990, 5), this book's long life in print must have kept these terms current with readers from as early as 1545 until well into the seventeenth century. Raynalde's careful definitions and repeated use of these terms in this popular book indicates that it is not true to say that 'The language simply did not exist, or need to exist, for distinguishing male from female organs' (Laqueur 1990, 97).

I will return in a moment to the questions that this book's existence presents to Foucauldian theories of the body that were proposed first by Laqueur, and have been much elaborated since. First, though, it is neces-sary to say a little more about how Raynalde adapts and expands Jonas's version of *The Birth of Mankind* as he turned it into 'The Woman's Book'. Because part of the problem with Laqueur's thesis is that *Making Sex* confuses the conflicting theories concerning reproduction of Aristotle and Hippocrates/Galen, this also entails explaining briefly what those distinctions are, and how Raynalde responds to them.[13] Indeed, perhaps the clearest examples of Raynalde's educational goals appear in his engagement with what he calls the 'dreams and plain dotage' (Raynalde 2008, 66) of some of the scientific ideas he makes use of. The earliest hint of this appears in the first chapter that he added to his 1545 edition, where he explains the scope of what is to follow concerning 'the inward parts of a woman' (Raynalde 2008, 23). Making use of the conventional, implicitly passive metaphor of the womb as a 'field' where seed is sown, he comments:

---

[13] An excellent account of key shortcomings in Laqueur's thesis can be found in Park and Nye (1991). They also point out that early-modern accounts of the body do not use the 'one-sex' model that Laqueur believes he has found in them. What they used was a system of argument by analogy. This assessment of Laqueur's thesis is widely accepted amongst medical historians, but has largely been overlooked by literary critics.

And although that man be as principal mover and cause of the gener-ation, yet (no displeasure to men), the woman doth confer and contribute much more, what to the increasement of the child in her womb, and what to the nourishment thereof after the birth, than doth the man. And doubtless, if a man would demand to whom the child oweth most his generation, ye may worthily make answer that, to the mother; whether ye regard the pains in bearing, other else the confer-ence [contribution] of most matter in begetting. (Raynalde 2008, 23)

As the parenthetical 'no displeasure to men' indicates, Raynalde is taking a position here that would indeed be disapproved of by many of his male contemporaries, who vehemently supported Aristotle's asser-tions that women's contribution to human reproduction was much infe-rior to men's. According to Aristotle, women produced no 'seed' at all, but simply passive 'material', blood, that the active male seed worked on and added a soul to so as to make the child (1943, 1.19–21, 2.3). Raynalde's position, by contrast, is consistent with some parts of the Hippocratic corpus (*The Seed, Nature of the Child*), and with Galen's *On Semen*, in which both women and men are understood to contribute seed to conception.

Elsewhere in his book, Raynalde returns to this same argument. Implicitly rejecting the Aristotelian belief that a woman is 'an imperfect man' (Aristotle 1943, 2.3), when describing the seed that she contrib-utes to conception Raynalde concedes the medical 'fact' that by compar-ison with male seed, it is 'weak, fluey, cold and moist, and of no great firmity' (Raynalde 2008, 39). He is clear, however, that although some men might use this difference to argue for male superiority, they are making an error that misrecognises a divine plan: female seed is 'as convenient and proper for the purpose for the which it was ordained, as the seed of man for his purpose' (Raynalde 2008, 39); a woman is not, he says, 'unperfecter than man':

Neither is woman to be called (as some do) unperfecter than man (for because that man is more mightier and strong, the woman weaker and more feeble). For by this reason, the horse, the lion, the elephant, camel, and many other beasts, should be called more perfect than man, to the which man is not able to compare in natural might and strength. (Raynalde 2008, 47–48)

Whilst refusing Aristotle's one-sex argument that a woman is an 'imper-fect man', Raynalde does agree with 'Aristotle and other mo' (2008, 50) that the fluid that women produce during sexual activity is a result of their sexual pleasure. He rejects, however, any assumption (as was popular in the conduct book tradition) that there is something unpleasant or threatening about female sexual desire. Women who have undergone a painful delivery would never again agree to engage in sexual activity with men, he asserts, if it were not for the natural pleasure that God has designed for them in the activity:

> For ye shall hear some women, in time of their travail, moved through great pain and intolerable anguish, forswear and vow themself, never to company with a man again. Yet after that the pangs be passed, within short while, for entire love to their husbands, and singular natural delight between man and woman, they forget both the sorrow passed and that that is to come. Such be the privy works of God, and such be the pricks of nature, which never createth no special pleasure unaccompanied with some sorrow. (Raynalde 2008, 51)

Constantly in such reflections, Raynalde emphasizes the significance of the information he is providing, and demonstrates that he knows that some people use scientific facts to argue for social values that need not necessarily follow from those facts. If the way that he and his contemporaries understood human sexuality and the workings of the body is to be engaged with by the modern reader, it is also necessary to note that the body is not seen in purely physical terms. For Raynalde, as for most of his contemporaries, the body is a vessel for the spirit, and has to be read in religious terms: as this passage makes explicit, our physical characteristics are a direct result of 'the privy works of God'.

Raynalde's pausing on such occasions to reflect on the social and ethical significance of the scientific information he wishes to convey to his reader is also found at other moments when he writes about the beliefs that some people hold about the female body. The clearest examples here are in what he says about menstrual blood. According to Galenic tradition, menstruation is a result of the 'fact' that women, being naturally colder and wetter than men, cannot make use of all the blood that their bodies produce from the food they eat; every few weeks, therefore, this accumulated blood is shed as superfluous to requirements. In a much-cited alternative tradition, by contrast, menstrual blood is perceived as inherently dangerous or poisonous.[14] Ideas of this kind are

---

[14] These theories are clearly discussed in Crawford (1981), although her understanding of the distinctions between the different interpretations of these theories differs from that offered here. See also Delaney, Lupton, and Toth (1976). I

found for instance in the Bible in passages such as Leviticus 12, where Moses is instructed by God that a woman is 'unclean' after giving birth, just as she is during menstruation, and in the use of the phrase 'menstrual cloths' in Isaiah 30:22 to describe undesirable objects that must be 'cast away'. This biblical tradition underlies the practice of 'churching' women after delivery, a practice that was converted, as David Cressy (1993) has shown, from a ceremony of cleansing to one of celebration, as part of the redefinitions of female sexuality that English Protestantism promoted.

Meanwhile, the view of menstruating women as dirty or dangerous continued to be present in some key classical texts. Much alluded to, for instance, was Pliny's *Natural History*:

> Contact with it [menstrual blood] turns new wine sour, crops touched by it become barren, grafts die, seeds in gardens are dried up, the fruit of trees falls off, the bright surface of mirrors in which it is merely reflected is dimmed, the edge of steel and the gleam of ivory are dulled, hives of bees die, even bronze and iron are at once seized by rust, and a horrible smell fills the air; to taste it drives dogs mad and infects their bites with an incurable poison (1963, 7.15)

How commonly these views were asserted in early-modern times is indicated by their appearance in such texts as the phenomenally popular *Women's Secrets*, which circulated in Latin manuscripts throughout early-modern Europe, falsely ascribed to Albertus Magnus:

> women are so full of venom in the time of menstruation that they poison animals by their glance; they infect children in the cradle; they spot the cleanest mirror; and whenever men have sexual intercourse with them they are made leprous and sometimes cancerous.
>
> (1992, 60)

Raynalde's account of menstruation could not be more different from this. When he first introduces the topic of the blood in women's wombs, he explains that it is designed through the 'divine feats' of 'prudent Lady Nature' to be 'a very natural course, spring, fountain or well, evermore ready to arouse, water, and nourish the feature [foetus], so soon as it shall be conceived' (Raynalde 2008, 58). This blood is, then,

am grateful to Sara Read, whose doctoral research on early-modern menstruation has contributed to the analysis I am presenting.

even as pure and wholesome as all the rest of the blood in any part of the body else.

Is it to be thought, that Nature would feed the tender and delicate infant in the mother's womb, with the refuse of the blood, or not rather with the purest of it? (Raynalde 2008, 65)

In case his reader has not fully grasped the import of these descriptions, Raynalde closes this chapter with an explicit statement of his position in medical debates about menstruation:

Yet much more are to be detested and abhorred the shameful lies and slander that Pliny, Albertus Magnus, *De Secretes Mulierum*, and diverse other mo have written, of the venomous and dangerous infective nature of the woman's flowers or terms, the which all be but dreams and plain dotage. To rehearse their fond words here, were but loss of ink and paper; wherefore, let them pass with their authors.

(Raynalde 2008, 66)

As he set about fashioning his 'Woman's Book' from Jonas's translation and Vesalius's new anatomy, Raynalde had a clear sexual–political agenda within his educational aims.

Anyone familiar with Thomas Laqueur's arguments in *Making Sex* that early-modern thinking was characterized by a 'one-sex model', where differences between men and women were interpreted on the basis that a woman's body was an inside-out male one, will already have noticed that much of the argument to this point implicitly takes issue with that account. Although the Aristotelian model of *Generation of Animals* indeed read women as 'imperfect men', Hippocratic beliefs saw both similarities and differences between wetter and often colder women, and drier usually hotter men; and these differences were believed to be both physiological in origin and social in implication. Raynalde's comments in many places in *The Birth of Mankind* indicate the existence of active debate about what the differences between male and female bodies might be, and what, if anything, such differences might mean. No one reading *The Birth of Mankind* attentively would concur with Laqueur's assertion that before the seventeenth century,

sex, or the body, must be understood as the epiphenomenon, while *gender*, what we would take to be a cultural category, was primary or 'real.' Gender – man and woman – mattered a great deal and was part of the order of things; sex was conventional. (1990, 18)

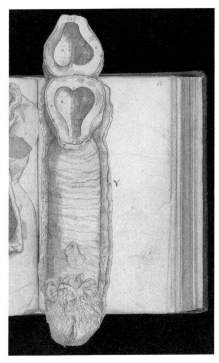

Figure 1. Image of the womb
and vagina from *The Byrth of
Mankind*. © The Wellcome
Library, London.

On every occasion that Raynalde names a body part or explains a function, he indicates his own familiarity with disagreements between his
contemporaries and their authorities about the social meaning of these
physical characteristics. For him, sex is a physical fact that has social
implications as a direct result of cultural values.

Given the centrality to Laqueur's argument of the perceived phallic
appearance of illustrations in Vesalius's *De Humani Corporis Fabrica* of
the female reproductive system, it is particularly interesting that these
very pictures are the ones taken up by Raynalde for his expanded version
of *The Birth of Mankind*. Laqueur states firmly that 'Women's organs are
represented as versions of man's in all three of Vesalius's immensely
influential and plagiarized works' (1990, 81), and it must be admitted
that anyone looking at the most famous of these images is likely to
perceive it as a penis before coming to see it as a vagina and womb (see
Figure 1). Raynalde, however, did not wish his reader to interpret this
picture in that way. His description of the figure focuses not on the
monstrous vagina, but on the womb itself (the 'found or bottom of the
matrix'):

Now ye shall understand that the found or bottom of the matrix is not perfectly round bowl-wise, but rather like the form of a man's heart, as it is painted, saving that the partition or cleft in the matrix between both corners, the right and the left, is not so profoundly dented inwards as the cleft in the heart. (Raynalde 2008, 35)

The female organs are presented in terms that relate them to an established symbol of love, 'the form of a man's heart as it is painted', not as an outside-in penis. Such a choice of words on Raynalde's part comes to seem all the more remarkable when his description is compared with the one that appears in Vesalius's own writing about the picture. This also draws attention to the shape of the womb, but imagines it in startlingly different terms. For Vesalius in his *Epitome*,

The shape of its fundus is not completely round but flattened in front and behind, obtuse above, and showing two blunt angles (one on each side) which resemble the immature horns on the foreheads of calves. (1969, 85)

What would cause Vesalius to look at a womb and think about 'the immature horns on the foreheads of calves' is a matter that might be thought about another time.

The re-imagining of the female body, and of the relationship between it and the male one, that Raynalde has undertaken in his reading of Vesalius's illustration of an excised womb is also found in his description of the cervix, or 'womb port'. In perhaps his most famous sentence concerning a woman's body, Vesalius explained in the *Epitome* of his new anatomical work that 'it [the cervix] projects like the glans penis into the cavity of the neck of the uterus' (1969, 85). Looking at this same (admittedly very strange) picture (see Figure 2),[15] Raynalde has a completely different way of having the image make sense to his reader:

The entrance of the matrix or womb is named the womb port, or mother port; the which in substance and fashion much doth resemble the form of an hawk's bell, or other little morris bells, saving that it is much bigger, having a clift overthwart the body thereof, as ye may more plainly perceive by the figure hereof. (Raynalde 2008, 37)

---

[15] This picture assumes that the vagina has mostly been removed, and that the viewer is looking at the cervix, beyond it seeing the rise of the womb with the ovaries on either side of that.

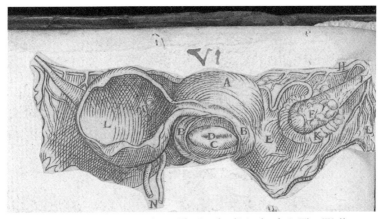

Figure 2. Image of the cervix from *The Byrth of Mankind*. © The Wellcome Library, London.

To liken the shape of the cervix to the bells used in the entertainments of morris dancers or in the sport of hunting is to associate female sexuality with festivity, play, and what would have been seen as the 'pleasurable' activity of hawking. In the case of Raynalde, at least, Laqueur's assertion that early-modern anatomists 'might have seen bodies differently – they might, for example, have regarded the vagina as other than a penis – but they did not do so for essentially cultural reasons' (1990, 16) is shown to be an oversimplification. Anatomists could, in fact, see women's bodies in terms that were not defined by male norms, and Raynalde did. This is not the place to engage in a reading of Vesalius's own similes and metaphors, but it is to be hoped that once the current massive project of translating *De Fabrica* into English is completed, someone interested in the history of the body will undertake this work.[16] As Laqueur has rightly argued, though not himself appreciating the full force of the observation, 'Ideology, not accuracy of observation, determined how they [sexual organs] were seen and which differences would matter' (1990, 88).

In 1545, Thomas Raynalde picked up the midwifery metaphors that

---

16 The only parts of *De Fabrica* that have so far appeared in English are Book 1, 'The Bones and Cartilages', Book 2, 'The Ligaments and Muscles', and Books 3 and 4, 'The Ligaments and Muscles' and 'The Nerves'. See Vesalius (1998, 1999, 2002), and Garrison and Hast (n.d.). A translation of some parts of Vesalius's description of the womb is given in Herrlinger and Finer (1964). These Vesalian drawings are discussed in Calbi (2005), Park (1997), Martindale (2001).

Richard Jonas had used when presenting the first version of *The Birth of Mankind* to his reader, observing that he 'thought my labour and pains should not be evil employed' (Raynalde 2008, 12) in revising Jonas's work, and hoping that the result would be 'pleasant and fruitful to all women' (Raynalde 2008, 15). Certainly many people must have found his work worth buying and reading through the one hundred years that it then stayed in print. If literary scholars were to read *The Birth of Mankind* today, they might be surprised by how complex, and self-aware, our fore-bears could be in the sense they made of the 'dreams and plain dotage' of writings on human reproduction.

Works Cited

Albertus Magnus (pseud.), 1992. *Women's Secrets: A Translation of Pseudo-Albertus Magnus's 'De Secretis Mulierum', with Commentaries*, ed. Helen Rodnite Lemay. Albany, NY: State University of New York Press.

Aristotle, 1943. *Generation of Animals*, trans. A. L. Peck. London: Heinemann; Cambridge, MA: Harvard University Press.

Arons, Wendy, 1994. *When Midwifery Became the Male Physician's Province: The Sixteenth Century Handbook 'The Rose Garden for Pregnant Women and Midwives', Newly Englished*. Jefferson, NC, and London: McFarland.

Ballantyne, J. W., 1906, 1907. 'The "Byrth of Mankynde" (Its Author and Editions)'; '(Its Contents)', *Journal of Obstetrics and Gynaecology of the British Empire* 10: 297–325; 12: 175–94, 255–74.

Benedek, Thomas G., 1977. 'The Changing Relationship between Midwives and Physicians during the Renaissance', *Bulletin of the History of Medicine* 51: 550–64.

Calbi, Maurizio, 2005. *Approximate Bodies: Gender and Power in Early Modern Drama and Anatomy*. London and New York: Routledge.

Crawford, Patricia, 1981. 'Attitudes to Menstruation in Seventeenth-Century England', *Past and Present* 91: 47–73.

Cressy, David, 1993. 'Purification, Thanksgiving and the Churching of Women in Post-Reformation England', *Past and Present* 141: 106–46.

Cushing, Harvey, 1943. *A Bio-Bibliography of Andreas Vesalius*. New York: Schuman's.

Delaney, Janice, Mary Jane Lupton and Emily Toth, 1976. *The Curse: A Cultural History of Menstruation*. New York: Dutton.

Eccles, Audrey, 1974. 'The Reading Public, the Medical Profession, and the Use of English for Medical Books in the 16th and 17th Centuries', *Neuphilologische Mitteilungen* 75, 1: 143–56.

———, 1977. 'The Use of English for Midwiferies 1500–1700', *Neuphilologische Mitteilungen* 78, 4: 377–85.

Evenden, Doreen, 2000. *The Midwives of Seventeenth-Century London*. Cambridge and New York: Cambridge University Press.

Galen of Pergamon, 1992. *On Semen*, trans. Phillip de Lacy. Berlin: Akademie-Verlag.

Garrison, Daniel and Malcolm Hast, [n.d.]. *On the Fabric of the Human Body: An Annotated Translation of the 1543 and 1555 Editions of Andreas Vesalius' De Humani Corporis Fabrica*. [electronic resource] http://vesalius.northwestern.edu

Green, Monica, (unpub. paper). 'The Sources of Eucharius Rösslin's *Rosegarden for Pregnant Women and Midwives*'.

———, 1989. 'Women's Medical Practice and Health Care in Medieval Europe', *Signs* 14: 434–73.

Guy, John, 1982. 'The Episcopal Licensing of Physicians, Surgeons and Midwives', *Bulletin of the History of Medicine* 56: 528–42.

Herrlinger, Robert and Edith Finer, 1964. 'Why Did Vesalius Not Discover the Fallopian Tubes?' *Medical History* 8: 335–41.

Hess, Ann Giardina, 1993. 'Midwifery Practice among the Quakers in Southern Rural England in the Late Seventeenth Century', in *The Art of Midwifery: Early Modern Midwives in Europe*, ed. Hilary Marland. London and New York: Routledge: 49–76.

Hippocrates, 1983 (1950). 'The Seed and the Nature of the Child', in *Hippocratic Writings*, ed. G. E. R. Lloyd, trans. I. M. Lonie. Harmondsworth: Penguin.

Hitchcock, James, 1967. 'A Sixteenth Century Midwife's License', *Bulletin of the History of Medicine* 41: 75–76.

Hobby, Elaine, 1988. *Virtue of Necessity: English Women's Writing 1649–1688*. London: Virago.

Hull, Suzanne W., 1982. *Chaste, Silent and Obedient: English Books for Women 1475–1640*. San Marino, CA: Huntington Library.

Ingerslev, E., 1909. 'Rösslin's "Rosegarten": Its Relation to the Past (the Muscio Manuscripts and Soranos), Particularly with Regard to Podalic Version', *Journal of Obstetrics and Gynaecology of the British Empire* 15, 1: 1–25; and 15, 2: 73–92.

King, Helen, 1998. *Hippocrates' Women: Reading the Female Body in Ancient Greece*. London and New York: Routledge.

Kruse, Britta-Juliane, 1994. 'Neufund einer handschriften Vorstufe von Eucharius Rösslins Hebammenlehrbuch *Der schwangeren Frauen und Hebammen Rosengarten* und des *Frauenbüchlein* Ps.-Ortolfs', *Sudhoffs Archiv* 78: 220–36.

Laqueur, Thomas, 1990. *Making Sex: Body and Gender from the Greeks to Freud*. Cambridge, MA, and London: Harvard University Press.

Marland, Hilary, 1993. 'The "*Burgerlÿke*" Midwife: The *Stadsvroedvrouw* of Eighteenth-Century Holland', in *The Art of Midwifery: Early Modern Midwives in Europe*, ed. Hilary Marland. London and New York: Routledge: 192–213.

Martindale, Kym, 2001. 'Author(iz)ing the Body: Monique Wittig, *The Lesbian Body* and the Anatomy Texts of Andreas Vesalius', *European Journal of Women's Studies* 8, 3: 343–56.

McLaren, Angus, 1984. *Reproductive Rituals: The Perception of Fertility in England from the Sixteenth Century to the Nineteenth Century*. London and New York: Methuen.

Park, Katharine, 1997. 'The Rediscovery of the Clitoris', in *The Body in Parts: Fantasies of Corporeality in Early Modern Europe*, ed. David Hillman and Carla Mazzio. New York and London: Routledge: 171–93.

Park, Katharine and Robert A. Nye, 1991. 'Destiny is Anatomy', *The New Republic* 18 (February): 53–57.

Pliny (the Elder), 1963. *Natural History*, trans. W. H. S. Jones. Vol. 8, libri 28–32. Cambridge MA: Harvard University Press.

Pollock, Linda, 1990. 'Embarking on a Rough Passage: The Experience of Pregnancy in Early-Modern Society', in *Women as Mothers in Pre-Industrial England: Essays in Memory of Dorothy McLaren*, ed. Valerie Fildes. London and New York: Routledge: 39–67.

Power, D'Arcy, 1927. '*The Birth of Mankind or the Woman's Book*: A Bibliographical Study', *The Library* 4th series 8, 1: 1–37.

Raynalde, Thomas *et al.*, 2008. *The Birth of Mankind: Or, the Woman's Book*, ed. Elaine Hobby. Aldershot: Ashgate.

Rhodion [Rösslin], Eucharius, 1535. *De Partu Hominis, et quae circa ipsum accidunt*. Florence: Ioannis Foucher.

Rösslin, 1910. *Eucharius Rösslin's 'Rosengarten'*, ed. Gustav Klein. Alte Meister in der Medizin und Naturkunde. Munich: Carl Kuhn.

Saunders, J. B. deC. M. and Charles D. O'Malley, 1982. *The Anatomical Drawings of Andreas Vesalius*. New York: Bonanza.

Sharp, Jane, 1999. *The Midwives Book: Or, the Whole Art of Midwifry Discovered*, ed. Elaine Hobby. New York and Oxford: Oxford University Press.

Slack, Paul, 1979. 'Mirrors of Health and Treasures of Poor Men: The Use of the Vernacular Medical Literature of Tudor England', in *Health, Medicine and Mortality in the Sixteenth Century*, ed. Charles Webster. Cambridge and New York: Cambridge University Press: 237–73.

Vesalius, Andreas. 1543. *De Humani Corporis Fabrica*. Basel.

———, 1969. *The Epitome of Andreas Vesalius*, trans. L. R. Lind. Cambridge, MA, and London: MIT Press.

———, 1998. *On the Fabric of the Human Body: A Translation of De Humani Corporis Fabrica Libri Septem. Book I, The Bones and Cartilages*, trans. William Frank Richardson and John Burd Carman. San Francisco: Norman.

———, 1999. *On the Fabric of the Human Body: A Translation of De Humani Corporis Fabrica Libri Septem. Book 2, The Ligaments and Muscles*, trans. William Frank Richardson and John Burd Carman. San Francisco: Norman.

———, 2002. *On the Fabric of the Human Body: A Translation of De Humani Corporis Fabrica Libri Septem. Book 3, The Ligaments and Muscles, Book 4, The Nerves*, trans. William Frank Richardson and John Burd Carman. San Francisco: Norman.

Wiesner, Merry, 1993. 'The Midwives of South Germany and the Public/Private Dichotomy', in *The Art of Midwifery: Early Modern Midwives in Europe*, ed. Hilary Marland. London and New York: Routledge: 77–94.

Wilson, Adrian, 1995. *The Making of Man-midwifery: Childbirth in England, 1660–1770*. Cambridge, MA: Harvard University Press.

Natural Rights and Natural History in Anna Barbauld and Mary Wollstonecraft

SHARON RUSTON

IN THIS ARTICLE I explore the ways that two writers, Anna Barbauld and Mary Wollstonecraft, used animals and natural history to push for natural rights. In the late eighteenth century cruelty to animals was a significant issue for those on all sides of the political spectrum, from radicals and dissenters to the socially and politically conservative Evangelical thinkers, such as William Wilberforce and Hannah More, who were against slavery and animal suffering but who did not argue for rights for all. Barbauld used animals to promote rights for dissenters, while Wollstonecraft explicitly used natural rights to argue for equality for women. The role of animals in these debates is often complex but also revealing of the political agenda of vulnerable or disenfranchised groups.

During the Romantic period a number of voices began talking insistently about 'natural rights', the rights that everyone had simply because they were alive. These rights became enshrined in the new republics emerging at this time: the American *Declaration of Independence* (signed on 4 July 1776) stated 'all men are created equal; they are endowed by their Creator with certain inalienable rights; that among these are life, liberty and the pursuit of happiness'. These rights are described as 'the laws of nature' (White 2006, 5). In 1789, the French *Declaration of the Rights of Man and of the Citizen* stated 'Men are born and remain free and equal in rights'; these natural, inalienable and even 'sacred' rights are defined as 'liberty, property, security, and resistance to oppression' (White 2006, 5). 1788 had been the centenary of the so-called 'Glorious Revolution' and English writers drew comparisons, both favorable and unfavorable, between the settlement reached between the monarch and people then and the events in France. Some radicals felt that the rights that had been given to Englishmen then had subsequently been lost, and that these rights needed to be restored; others felt that the changes of 1688 had not gone far enough. The understanding that there were rights which every person should expect and that should govern how people were treated is one that today we take for granted. As R. S. White has argued in *Natural Rights and the Birth of Romanticism*, a direct line can be drawn between the expression of these rights and such modern acts as the 1948 Universal Declaration of Human Rights and the Civil Rights movements in 60s America.

Of course the language of the twentieth century is quite different from that of the eighteenth, particularly in its attempt to be universal. The 1948 act is for Human Rights, rather than the rights of man. In Thomas Paine's book of that name, published in 1791, Paine argued that men were born free and equal and should therefore have equal rights. He was arguing against a system based on hierarchy and privilege, specifically, where power lay with the aristocracy and monarchy. Paine was not the only one to take up this call; Mary Wollstonecraft had published *A Vindication of the Rights of Men* in 1790, and reviews of the book, whether it was admired or condemned, all commented on the fact that a woman had written it. Many of them were sarcastic about the rights of man being asserted by a 'fair lady' (Wollstonecraft 1997, 11).[1] This seems to make the point clearly; the rights of man were not the rights of humans.

At this time, the rights of man were not even the rights of all men. The Society for Abolishing the Slave Trade was founded at this time too, in 1787. The Abolition of the Slave Trade Act was passed (in 1807) although it was not until 1833 that slavery was finally outlawed in British colonies. The antislavery movement was largely founded by Quakers and Anglican Evangelicals, and throughout the period religious toleration was contested for. Religious non-conformists, otherwise known as dissenters, particularly argued that they should have political rights: since the Test and Corporation Acts of the seventeenth century, dissenters had been unable to hold civil or military public office. During this period, dissenters, particularly Unitarians, often held important roles in literary, political, scientific and religious arenas. They tended to be from the educated middle classes, be politically liberal and to push for parliamentary reform and religious toleration. Again, it is testament to the changed mood at the end of the Romantic period that the Test and Corporations Acts were repealed in 1828. Similarly, Catholics were disenfranchised, denied the vote or any participation in politics, and the Catholic Relief Acts of 1778 and 1791 caused much turmoil and the worst riots on British soil during this period. Eventually bowing to the pressure of forces in Ireland, the Roman Catholic Relief Act was passed in 1829, which allowed Catholics to sit in Parliament.

---

[1] This is the edition I shall use when quoting from *Vindication of the Rights of Woman*, abbreviated here to *Vindication*.

Women were another disenfranchised group at this time. Mary Woll-stonecraft followed her book on the rights of men with *A Vindication of the Rights of Woman* published in 1792. In arguing for the rights of woman Wollstonecraft was reacting most immediately to the French minister Charles Maurice Talleyrand-Perigord's report on public educa-tion that had been presented to the National Assembly in France. The French Revolution offered an important opportunity: rather than be shackled by an unfair and inequitable government, as radical writers saw was the case in Britain, here was the chance to get things right. This was a new beginning. Unfortunately, Talleyrand's proposals did not live up to the promise of the revolutionary ideal that had asserted rights for all, and advocated that girls should only be educated in domestic duties. It seemed to Wollstonecraft that the *Declaration of the Rights of Man* precisely and specifically concerned men, not in a sense that included all human beings but in one that, in fact, actively excluded women. In her *Vindication*, Wollstonecraft set out to prove that women should be included in the general term 'man', that they were entitled to what she called the 'natural rights of mankind' (104). Wollstonecraft set out to prove that the mind has no sex, that men and women were all part of 'mankind', which was distinct from the rest of the animal kingdom by virtue of the ability to reason, that women were capable of reason, and that, therefore, women should be recognized as deserving of natural rights. I'll return to Wollstonecraft in the second half of this essay.

It is no accident that during this period when sensibility was a promi-nent literary movement people began to worry about animal cruelty. The RSPCA began life as the Society for the Prevention of Cruelty to Animals in 1809, and became the Royal Society in 1824. It is surely significant that among these societies' founding members was the Jew Lewis Gompertz, the Catholic Thomas Forster, and the MP who is now most famous for his efforts to abolish slavery, and who himself experi-enced an evangelical conversion, William Wilberforce. Amy Weldon makes the point that 'the degree to which humanity towards animals harmonized with Dissenting moral and political beliefs makes it likely that dissenters generally supported increased awareness of cruelty and measures to prevent it' and that 'Religiously based public opposition to cruelty against animals seems to have come mostly from outside the Anglican mainstream' (Weldon 2002).[2] Of course, it is also the case that

---

[2]   Weldon also notes that principal figures of the antislavery campaign 'were also founding members of the SPCA', citing Wilberforce and Fowell Buxton (2002, n. 2).

the orthodox and politically conservative showed great sympathy for animal suffering. At this time many people were becoming increasingly unhappy at the way that animals were being treated; on 22 July 1822 the Richard Martin's Act was passed in Parliament, to prevent cruelty to farm animals. Of course some people thought that such concerns showed that natural rights were being interpreted too broadly: Thomas Taylor's *Vindication of the Rights of Brutes* published in 1792 was a parody of the humanitarian calls for reform so prevalent at the time. Today, when many people demand products that have not been tested on animals and when vegetarianism is far more common than it was two hundred years ago, these ideas do not sound so ridiculous. The Great Ape Project is currently campaigning for a *Declaration on Great Apes*, asking that apes be given basic human rights, specifically the right to life, the protection of individual liberty and the prohibition from torture.

Elsewhere I have argued that a significant reason why these movements began and gathered momentum at this time is to be found in the scientific investigations of the Romantic period. I think there is a connection to be drawn between a new, extended and universalized perception of what it means to be worthy of rights and the study of life in plants, humans and animals.[3] Before the eighteenth century, people had been content with the classical idea of a Chain of Being, a hierarchical model showing the different species according to their lessening degree of perfection. God is at the top, followed by his angels, then humans, animals and finally rocks. The divisions between these gradations, however, began to blur as scientists found more similarities than differences between human, animal and plant life.[4] The term 'Biology' was coined in this period, otherwise known as 'the study of life'.[5] This was also the age of the museum, and the British Museum (founded in 1753) had collections of plants, fossils and other natural history specimens, while there were often shows of rare animals and the so-called 'monstrous' in London. One surgeon, John Hunter, amassed a huge collection of unusual skeletons, diseased body parts and deformities which now belongs to the Royal College of Surgeons; using these he developed the study of comparative anatomy. Scientists found that plants needed the same elements as humans in order to survive; Joseph Priestley isolated oxygen in 1774 (though he never called it that, leaving the French

---

[3]   For a fuller account of the science of life in this period, see Ruston 2005.
[4]   See Lovejoy 1936.
[5]   William Lawrence coined this word when he translated a word used by Gottfried Reinhold Treviranus (1819, 60).

chemist Lavoisier to name the gas after its acidity principle) and his work contributed to the eventual identification of it as the vital element in air that was needed to sustain all living things.[6] Without fully articulating the theory, he also discovered photosynthesis. There was a new, specifically Romantic recognition that man was not to be regarded as a separate species, set apart from and central to a divinely ordained hierarchy. Instead, the poet Samuel Taylor Coleridge would write of 'one Life within us and abroad', demonstrating a new awareness of a life that was shared by all living creatures.[7] Christine Kenyon-Jones argues that Coleridge 'articulates his thinking about what it means to be human through brilliant and extensive ruminations in prose about the status of animals vis à vis that of humankind' (2001, 66). His poem 'To A Young Ass' 'addresses animal treatment in language relating to the equality and rights of *human* groups, particularly slaves' (Kenyon-Jones 2001, 68).

There are two specific instances, one in a painting and another in a poem, when an animal's rights are brought to our attention. Priestley had discovered the importance of oxygen when he burned a candle in a jar turned upside down and the candle went out long before the wax was used up. He also tried this experiment on mice, and found that they too needed the re-introduction of air to survive. This experiment has been immortalized in Joseph Wright of Derby's *An Experiment on a Bird in an Air-Pump* (1768) (see Figure 3). Wright chose to paint subjects that showed the advances made in science, but this painting has long been recognized as rather ambiguous. In it, an itinerant lecturer is demonstrating to a well-to-do family how a vacuum can be created. The lecturer is rather wild looking, suggesting a figure like Mary Shelley's later character Victor Frankenstein; he stares out of the picture, looking directly at us in a rather challenging way, while his audience experience different reactions. The lecturer removes air from the pump and the white cockatoo droops, suffering from the deprivation of oxygen. If we look at the various reactions of those present, on the lecturer's right, a young man looks fascinated with the demonstration, perhaps by the angle of his head showing that he is looking for hidden tricks or simply that he is fully engrossed by the sight. Another man looks on, possibly at the experiment; hand on hip, he seems confident and assured of the knowledge being imparted. The two lovers have eyes for no one but each other. On the other side of the lecturer, an older man sits looking down at the floor, leaning on his walking stick, thinking deeply and perhaps

[6] My thanks to Simon Mills for clarifying this point.
[7] Coleridge, 'Aeolian Harp', line 26.

Figure 3. Joseph Wright 'of Derby', *An Experiment on a Bird in an Air-Pump*. Photograph © The National Gallery, London.

not positively about the march of science. The girls turn away in horror from the scene, revealing their feminine sensibility, while their father tries to get them to watch and learn. We do not know whether the lecturer will save the bird or not.

A similar fate awaits the mouse of Anna Barbauld's poem 'A Mouse's Petition', which is written as though from a mouse's perspective as he awaits Priestley's experiment on him. Barbauld and Priestley were both dissenters, and became good friends when Priestley worked as a tutor in the Warrington Dissenting Academy where Barbauld's father also taught. The dissenters had a close-knit community, bound by ties of faith and a recognition that they were disadvantaged by society, though they also felt that they were on the verge of gaining political rights. Many of Barbauld's poems in this first collection evoke scenes of domestic happiness, in which an ideal circle of family and friends join in the pursuit of intellect and liberty. The story goes that Barbauld wrote this poem as a joke for Priestley and when he came down in the morning to pursue his experiments on air, found it stuck in the bars of the mouse's cage.[8] The poem is partly an

8   See the headnote to the poem in Barbauld 2002, 69. Bellanca makes the point that this 'surreptitious deposit' of the poem into the bars of the mouse cage

in-joke, a mock petition, which is a form usually used to make demands of governments or monarchs. Barbauld certainly stated that she never intended to criticize her friend Priestley in this poem and yet, the fact that she is both a woman and dissenter is surely significant.[9] Barbauld is refused political rights (the right to vote, to hold government office, to go to university) on two counts: she holds, as Marlon Ross has put it, a position of 'double-dissent' (Ross 1994, 92).

A petition is a prayer or supplication to a higher power, asking in this case for mercy. It also possibly has a specific reference to 'The parliamentary declaration of the rights and liberties of the people, presented to Charles I in a petition in 1627 and assented to by the monarch in 1628' (OED). This meaning links the poem to a language of rights asked by a subject of its king. The poem is in ballad form with four-line stanzas of alternating iambic tetrameter and trimeter. The mouse appeals to his captor on the grounds of his sensibility initially: asking that Priestley 'never' allow his heart to be shut to a 'prisoner's cries' (line 3). In the third stanza he appeals to Priestley as a proud libertarian, someone who prizes his own freedom and having himself 'spurn'd' the 'tyrant's chain' should not then act the part of the tyrant (line 10). There is clearly a sense that Priestley having encountered such treatment himself should help others whom tyrants oppress.

The mouse appeals to his captor for his release on the grounds that he is 'a free-born mouse' and one of 'nature's commoners', pointing out that he breathes the same air as Priestley, drinks the same water, and that these are 'The common gifts of heaven' (lines 12, 23, 24). The word 'common' refers, as Mary Ellen Bellanca notes, to two meanings 'air both ordinary and shared by all' (2003, 56). To be a commoner also has multiple meanings that are all in play here: to be one of the common people, to 'share or take part' in something, 'one who has a joint right in common lands', and 'a member of the community who has civic rights' are all listed as definitions of this word (OED). Similarly, the *Oxford*

'epitomizes women's need to manoeuvre around cultural proscriptions when they wanted to speak about science' (2003, 53).
[9]   In a footnote to the third edition of her *Poems*, Barbauld wrote: 'The Author is concerned to find, that what was intended as the petition of mercy against justice, has been construed as the plea of humanity against cruelty. She is certain that cruelty could never be apprehended from the Gentleman to whom this is addressed; and the poor animal would have suffered more as the victim of domestic economy [ed. note 'i.e., in a mouse trap'], than of philosophical curiosity' (Barbauld 2002, 69).

English Dictionary defines 'free-born' as one who is 'born to the conditions and privileges of citizenship, inheriting liberty'. The mouse asks
Priestley what right he has to deny the rights that are natural to all, and
these are here defined as the right to life and liberty. The reference to
'the vital air' is surely a nod to Priestley's own discoveries in this field, his
recognition of oxygen as the vital principle, and the mouse's own part in
this discovery. In arguing for natural rights it was necessary to ask what
was natural to all, what was necessary for all living forms, and here
Barbauld uses an animal to make the point that we all share certain characteristics and needs, and thus should have the same rights. Of course,
this argument extends beyond mice to women, dissenters, slaves, and all
other peoples who are disenfranchised and oppressed. The medal cast by
Josiah Wedgwood, showing a slave petitioning on his knees, uses a
similar language of rights with the words: 'Am I not a man and a
brother?'

In the seventh stanza, the mouse appeals to Priestley as a scientist; if
he is 'well taught' he should treat all things equally, have 'compassion'
and feel 'for all' living beings (lines 25–28). There is some evidence that
Barbauld found Priestley wanting in these qualities. Deirdre Coleman
has argued that Barbauld set herself the task of trying to 'soften and
temper Priestley's masculine rigour', his 'philistinism' and 'rough and
unamiable rationality' (2002, 84, 88, 91). In the next stanzas, the mouse
also appeals to him on philosophical grounds, referring among those
'ancient sages', to Pythagoras's theory of metempsychosis (which had
originated in Ovid's *Metamorphoses*) in which souls are imagined as
transmigrating between creatures (line 29). This theory was used in
other animal rights writing.[10] The mouse issues a warning to Priestley; in
killing him he may in fact be dislodging the soul of a brother. Not
everyone believed that animals had souls (indeed there was also a question in some minds about whether women had souls as I will examine
later in this essay). The mouse in this poem leaves all possibilities open:
if, in fact, animals do not have souls, if they have no future existence to
look forward to in any form, then surely that is a reason to allow them to
enjoy the short life that they are given. The final stanza seems little short
of a threat: the mouse reminds Priestley that men can get into trouble
too and if he doesn't show compassion now will someone help him when
he needs help?

---

[10] See, for example, Ruston 2005, 113–32, and the note to line 32 in Barbauld
2002, 72.

Barbauld is using the perspective of a mouse, a vulnerable, disenfranchised creature to make a wider point. This political tactic is one that I shall continue to focus on for the remainder of the paper. Speaking about the children's writer Sarah Trimmer, G. J. Barker-Benfield has written that 'sentimental fiction's contribution to revolutionizing attitudes towards animals was a kind of surrogate feminism' (1992, 236). Barbauld's views on women's rights are difficult to fathom, and she seems not to have shared Wollstonecraft's more explicit feminism. Despite this, Wollstonecraft obviously found something of instruction to women in 'A Mouse's Petition' since she reprinted the poem in her book *The Female Reader*. The poem has also been seen as a 'likely source of inspiration' for Robert Burns' poem 'To a Mouse', which has itself been used by ecocritics to demonstrate that the rights of nature were being fought for; this poem has been seen as showing a 'green' sensibility toward non-human creatures (Hitt 2004, 127). Bellanca speculates that the particular association of mice and men (most famous today in John Steinbeck's novel of that name) represents their 'shared vulnerability to the vicissitudes of an uncertain world' (2003, 60). Mary Robinson, also influenced by Barbauld, published a poem called 'A Linnet's Petition' in 1775, in which a caged bird persuades his female owner to set him free and by doing so she learns the importance of compassion and freedom.[11] In my argument, I am, like others, culpable of what David Perkins has called 'displacing the animals' in reading these texts as anthropomorphic, as vehicles for arguing for the rights of specific groups of humans (2003, x).

The tactic of using a mouse to voice the political demands of dissenters was also used in *Evenings at Home*, a series of fables written for children, which Barbauld wrote with her brother, the trained physician John Aikin (1792–96, I, 98–99). Examining the book closely reveals what Aikin's daughter and biographer, Lucy Aikin, described as a 'hatred of every thing unfair and unequitable which was his leading principle and almost his ruling passion' (Brooks, 2004). Bellanca has noted that this text shares the 'passionate, if relentlessly empirical, fascination with nature that characterizes many educational texts of the 1790s' (2003, 49). Mice in particular figure largely in *Evenings at Home*, seeming to best represent those treated worst in society. In the story

---

[11] The particular association between women and caged birds has a long history in literature, culminating most famously in Maya Angelou's autobiographical novel, which is also commenting on slavery, *I Know Why the Caged Bird Sings*.

'Mouse, Lap-Dog and Monkey. A Fable', 'A poor little mouse, [...] half-starved', ventures into human society to eat 'a few crumbs which were scattered on the ground' only to experience people trying to kill her: 'and the poor terrified animal was driven round the room in an agony of terror' (Aikin and Barbauld, I, 98–99). The authors' sympathies are clearly with the mouse, and the fable teaches us that the world is a harsh place, where the 'fawning' of the lap-dog and the 'buffoonery' of the monkey are rewarded, while the mouse goes hungry (I, 100). At the end of the tale, the mouse says: 'Alas, how ignorant was I, to imagine that poverty and distress were sufficient recommendations to the charity of the opulent' (I, 100).

John Aikin had published *The Calendar of Nature: Or, Youth's Delightful Companion*, also written for young people, which he dedicated to his sister, Anna Barbauld (Aikin 1784). This book interspersed natural history with poetry by James Thompson and other authors. Here and elsewhere, Aikin made explicit the link between art and natural history. In his *Essay on the Application of Natural History to Poetry*, he finds in modern poets:

> descriptions faint, obscure, and ill characterized; the properties of things mistaken, and incongruous parts employed in the composition of the same picture. This is owing to a too cursory and general survey of objects, without exploring their minuter relations; and is only to be rectified by accurate and attentive observation, conducted on somewhat of a scientific plan. (Aikin 1777, 10)

This book was dedicated to Thomas Pennant, the foremost natural historian of the period. In the most general definition, natural history is the taxonomy or classification of species of animals, plants, and minerals; it presents the facts relating to and the properties of these species, and compares them to see how like or unlike each other they are. Since Pliny's natural history, such investigations had been exploited for political purpose; in the sixteenth century, for example, Thomas Elyot argued that the structure of a society of bees proved that it was natural for a single monarch to be head of state.[12] Not only did natural history in this

12 Thomas Elyot's, *The Booke of the Governor*, first published in 1531: 'One Sonne ruleth ouer the day, and one Moone ouer the nyghte; and to descende downe to the erthe, in a litell beest, whiche of all other is moste to be maruayled at, I meane the Bee, is lefte to man by nature, as it semeth, a perpetuall figure of a

period help pave the way for Darwin's ideas of the mutability of species, it also encouraged political and religious calls for equality, reform, toleration and enfranchisement. As I have shown, Aikin and Barbauld used natural history in their educational books for children, in a barely concealed attempt to promote civil and religious liberties. These writers tried to return to a concept of what was natural to argue that they should have equal rights with others. We find another example of this use of natural history in Thomas Percival's *A Father's Instructions to his Children*, which was published in 1775 by Wollstonecraft's, Aikin's and Barbauld's publisher, Joseph Johnson. Percival, another Unitarian, was the first student to attend the Warrington Academy, became a physician and the President of Manchester's Literary and Philosophical Society. Percival's book was 'designed to promote the love of virtue, a taste for knowledge, and an early acquaintance with the works of nature' (subtitle), and clearly used natural knowledge to instil morals into his child readers:

> Mark that parent hen! said a father to his beloved son. With what anxious care does she call together her offspring, and cover them with her expanded wings? … Does not this sight suggest to you the tenderness and affection of your mother? (1776, 34)

Barbauld's poem 'A Mouse's Petition' was included in *A Father's Instructions to his Children*, after an essay on the needlessness of animal cruelty in scientific experiments (Percival 1776, 62–65). Percival's book was extremely successful, going into at least eight editions, and it seems that his *Moral and Literary Dissertations*, published in 1784, and containing an essay 'On the Alliance of Natural History, and Philosophy, with Poetry' was intended as a sequel to this earlier work for children. In this essay, Percival refers to his 'friend' Aikin's earlier 'elegant and ingenious Essay, on the Application of Natural History to Poetry', again making explicit the coterie nature of such concerns and publications (1784, 223–74). While Barbauld did not agree with Wollstonecraft's later desire to reject sexual distinction, believing that 'Each is perfect in its kind. A woman as a woman: a tradesman as a tradesman', she did think that distinction should be ignored in the case of dissenters, who 'wish to bury every name of distinction in the common appellation of citizen'.[13] This similarity

iuste gouernaunce or rule: who hath amonge them one princpall Bee for gouernour' (Book One).
[13] Quoted in Taylor 2003, 184, 185.

has prompted Barbara Taylor to write that this 'serves as an important reminder of Wollstonecraft's own debt to Dissenting politics' (2003, 185). Like Aikin, Barbauld and Percival, Wollstonecraft used natural history to argue a political point; in *A Vindication of the Rights of Woman* she used natural knowledge to argue that women should share the natural rights that were being given to man.

For the remainder of this essay, I shall look at Mary Wollstonecraft's *Vindication*, to see, firstly, how she uses natural history to support her belief that women should be treated equally to men and, secondly, that much of the behavior used as evidence of woman's inferiority is learned rather than natural or instinctive; it is in fact a product of society and civilization.

During the period of the composition and publication of *Vindication*, Wollstonecraft reviewed a number of works of natural history for Joseph Johnson's *Analytical Review*: Thomas Bewick's and Ralph Beilby's *A General History of Quadrupeds* (in July 1790); William Smellie's *Philosophy of Natural History*; John Rotheram's answer to Smellie, *The Sexes of the Plants Vindicated* (both October 1790); *A New System of the Natural History of Quadrupeds*; and an abridged version of the Compte de Buffon's *Natural History* (both January 1792).[14] The effects of such reading can be found in *Vindication*, where Smellie's and Buffon's ideas are referred to specifically.

For women to be entitled to what Wollstonecraft calls, the 'natural rights of mankind', they had to prove that they were capable of reason; since, this, she argued, was what distinguished humans from other animals. She asked: 'In what does man's pre-eminence over the brute creation consist? The answer is as clear as that a half is less than the whole; in Reason' (1997, 104, 117). If women could be proved to be capable of reason, they would also be proved to be part of mankind in its most universal sense, and therefore entitled to the rights of man. Wollstonecraft had to prove that the intellectual, moral and even, partly, the physical inferiority of women to men was the corrupting and enervating effect of civilization. Through education Wollstonecraft believed that

---

[14] I am following the decision of editors Janet Todd and Marilyn Butler here in assigning these reviews to Wollstonecraft. See Wollstonecraft 1989, VII, 18. Wollstonecraft's reviews will be quoted from this edition hereafter. This is a vexed issue that has been much debated by critics, but given that Wollstonecraft refers to Smellie and Buffon in the *Vindication*, her authorship of these reviews seems even more likely (Wollstonecraft 1997, 204, 187).

woman could be restored to her natural state, be recognized as, in her words, 'a large portion of mankind', rather than a separate and lower species (1997, 158).

In *Vindication* Wollstonecraft had to face head on those who believed that woman was, in her words, 'the link which unites man with brutes' (1997, 146). In a 'chain of being' woman was considered by some to be *between* the most perfect or highest specimen of animal, 'man', and those beneath him in the hierarchy. A similar situation existed in contemporary accounts of race, where the European was placed above the African in the physical and intellectual scale. In the Chain of Being, was there a gradation between humans and animals? In different accounts women, Africans, or apes were cast as this link. Edward Long, writing in his *History of Jamaica* in 1774, did not think that 'an oran-outang husband would be any dishonour to a Hottentot female'.[15] The Manchester physician, Charles White, offered one of the best known theories of racial gradation; moving with apparent ease from an analysis of the material body to aesthetic and moral judgements on race, he argued that 'black people were a different, lesser, species, justifying their enslavement' (Fulford 2005, 97).[16]

At the beginning of *Vindication*, Wollstonecraft declares that she will 'pay particular attention to those in the middle class, because they appear to be in the most natural state' (1997, 111). This is a clear reference to Rousseau, who believed that man was born into his natural state but became corrupted by society and adults as he grew older: a child is born good but is corrupted by the company he keeps. In his educational treatise, *Emile*, Rousseau outlined the ideal education for a child, and argued that children had the right to be children but also should be educated in reason. Wollstonecraft was drawn to this idea, and others of Rousseau, but in his insistence that girls and boys should not be treated equally he seriously let her down. The child that Rousseau spoke about in *Emile* was explicitly a boy and not a girl. Wollstonecraft thought that the education women received from society caused them to be frivolous, to love pleasure, to be governed by feeling rather than sense. But, this did not 'prove that there is a sex in souls' (1997, 176). In other words, women did not behave in this way naturally; it was just the way that they had been educated.

Wollstonecraft concedes in her treatise that women tend to be infe-

[15] Quoted in Schiebinger 1993, 5.
[16] For an extended discussion of the issues of race in Romantic-period literature, see Kitson 2007, 18, 22, 51–66.

rior to men in terms of their physical strength, but even this difference is partly accounted for by the ways in which women are treated in society. She writes:

> In the government of the physical world it is observable that the female in point of strength is, in general, inferior to the male. This is the law of nature; and it does not appear to be suspended or abrogated in favour of woman. A degree of natural superiority cannot, therefore, be denied – and it is a noble prerogative! But not content with this natural pre-eminence, men endeavour to sink us still lower, merely to render us alluring objects for a moment. (1997, 110)

The use of the word 'endeavour' here makes clear her belief that men are actively and purposefully trying to push women further down the chain of being. Girls, she points out, are not allowed the physical exercise of boys, and throughout their lives they are taught that physical weakness is attractive to male suitors. Women are encouraged to starve themselves to achieve the appearance of a delicate constitution. Throughout the *Vindication* Wollstonecraft's efforts are to lessen the perceived gap between men and women, to show that many characteristics used to prove women's inferiority are not natural but learned.

Rousseau angered Wollstonecraft when he began to describe how a girl should be educated, in the fifth and final section of *Emile*: 'He advises them to cultivate a fondness for dress, because a fondness for dress, he asserts, is natural to them' (1997, 137). She bridled at 'The absurdity ... of supposing that a girl is naturally a coquette' and 'His ridiculous stories, which tend to prove that girls are *naturally* attentive to their persons, without laying stress on daily example are below contempt' (1997, 154, Wollstonecraft's emphasis). Finally, quoting *Emile* itself, she challenged his idea of women that 'a state of dependence being natural to the sex, they perceive themselves as formed for obedience' (1997, 204). It is Wollstonecraft's response to this last statement that I shall particularly examine here. Her efforts are to prove that such dependence and obedience are anything but natural. Indeed, she describes Rousseau's female ideal, Sophia in *Emile*, as 'grossly unnatural' (1997, 133). In order to ascertain which characteristics are truly natural to the sex, Wollstonecraft turns as Rousseau had done on occasion, to science, specifically invoking the natural historian William Smellie to refute Rousseau's claim that women are 'formed for obedience'. The entire concept of what is 'natural' to women or to humans generally, is in constant debate, and at these points in her argument Wollstonecraft has recourse to those writers who have observed such behaviour as is, in her words, 'common to the whole animal world', and relies on this knowledge to support her opinion (1997, 293).

In the *Vindication* Wollstonecraft uses evidence gained from Smellie's *Philosophy of Natural History* to compare woman in her civilized state to domesticated animals. Discussing Milton's portrayal of Eve, Wollstonecraft had written: 'How grossly do they insult us who thus advise us only to render ourselves gentle, domestic brutes!' (1997, 127). Domestic animals are defined by Smellie, and other natural history writers that Wollstonecraft had read, as animals who have been taught to act in a certain manner that is alien to their natural behaviour.

In *Philosophy of Natural History*, which Wollstonecraft reviewed on its publication in 1790, Smellie speaks of the 'empire of man' that has reduced animals to 'servitude'; he states that man's tyranny has 'degrade[d] and disfigure[d] Nature' (Smellie 1790, 460). Describing the 'mouflon', or, in Smellie's words 'the stock from which our domestic sheep have derived their origin' as 'comparatively a large animal', Smellie asks: 'How different is this from our domestic sheep, who are timid, weak, and unable to defend themselves? Without the protection of man, the whole race would soon be extirpated' (1790, 460). Compared to their wild or natural counterpart, sheep are physically weaker and reliant upon man for protection.

In her review of Thomas Bewick's and Ralph Beilby's *A General History of Quadrupeds*, Wollstonecraft quotes from only three sections of the text: specifically mentioning the mule, the shepherd's dog, and the wild cat, even though the book described many kinds of exotic animals (Wollstonecraft 1989, VII, 260–62). The mule and shepherd's dog, are linked by their domestication and utilitarian relationships with man, typified by either their submission to man and aid in his labor, or their ability to follow man's instructions. Indeed, the shepherd's dog is singled out for its 'faithfulness', 'discipline' and for being 'well-trained', its ability to receive commands and execute them promptly (Beilby 1790, 284).

In her review of Smellie's book, after quoting him on the 'docility and sagacity of animals', Wollstonecraft makes the point that such behaviour is not to be admired:

> The docility of animals is of the most ignoble kind – the *wonderful* instances which are here celebrated were produced by fear; a very strong passion. Animals soon forget their tricks when they are well fed, and are not reminded by signs of voice, of the cruel treatment they endured when they were learning them.
>
> (1989, VII, 299, Wollstonecraft's emphasis)

Wollstonecraft is at pains to point out that such behaviour is not natural to animals but learned; that they behave unnaturally in an attempt to please man, and only do this because they are scared and food is withheld from them otherwise.

To counter Rousseau's belief that 'dependence' and 'obedience' is natural to women in the *Vindication*, Wollstonecraft turns again to Smellie:

> This is begging the question; for servitude not only debases the individual, but its effects seem to be transmitted to posterity. Considering the length of time that women have been dependent, is it surprising that some of them hug their chains, and fawn like the spaniel? 'These dogs', observes a naturalist, 'at first kept their ears erect; but custom has superseded nature, and a token of fear is become a beauty.'
>
> (1997, 204)

Explicitly in the *Vindication* Wollstonecraft compares women to domestic animals whose strength has been tamed, and who know so little of their own nature that they 'hug their chains', oblivious to their servitude (1997, 204). Instead, she encourages women to 'endeavour to acquire strength, both of body and mind', in order, by inference, that they might break the bonds that hold them (1997, 111).

Allowing that women are naturally physically weaker than men, Wollstonecraft argues that the difference between them has been artificially widened by the fashions of society. She writes that: 'False notions of beauty and delicacy' encourage women to destroy their health and deliberately to forgo physical or mental exercise: they are, in her words, 'enervated by confinement and false notions of modesty' (1997, 246, 131). Wollstonecraft uses a physiological language to describe what happens to women's bodies:

> To preserve personal beauty, woman's glory! the limbs and faculties are cramped with worse than Chinese bands, and the sedentary life which they are condemned to live, while boys frolic in the open air, weakens the muscles and relaxes the nerves. (1997, 153)

The difference in the way that girls and boys are brought up, therefore, accounts for part of their comparative physical weakness later in life.

Wollstonecraft counters the advice given to women that they should not exercise too often. John Gregory, another of the writers Wollstonecraft engages with in *Vindication* and himself a medical man, advises in his *A Father's Legacy to his Daughters* that women should not 'dance with spirit' (1997, 137). Wollstonecraft asks: 'In the name of truth and common sense, why should not one woman acknowledge that she can take more exercise than another? or, in other words, that she has a sound constitution' (1997, 137). The idea that physical strength is something to be ashamed of is particularly frustrating to Wollstonecraft. In the society of her day she claims that even women who have retained their 'natural strength' by the exercise of their maternal, familial and marital duties are encouraged, she writes, 'to use art and feign a sickly delicacy in order to secure her husband's affection' (1997, 138). One only has to think of the delicacy of Lady Bertram in Austen's *Mansfield Park* and her use of physical weakness in getting what she wants. It is the case that the women Wollstonecraft points to as those who most use such arts are from the upper classes. In William Godwin's novel *Caleb Williams* Grimes' first sweetheart, Bet Butterfield, belonging to a lower social class, is described as a 'fine, strapping wench', 'as stout as a trooper' (Godwin 1970, 50–51). Her feats of strength include such masculine activities as romping and wrestling 'with the harvest men' (1970, 51). In contrast, Wollstonecraft recalls in the *Vindication*, 'a weak woman of fashion, who was more than commonly proud of her delicacy and sensibility' (1997, 155). According to this woman the lack of an appetite is proof of her 'exquisite sensibility' which, while raising her up the social scale, is, according to Wollstonecraft, simultaneously sinking her lower down the chain of being (1997, 155).

To conclude, Wollstonecraft believes that women should be included in the comprehensive term of 'mankind' and the gendering of virtues should, 'more properly speaking', be recognized as custom rather than indicating anything essentially female. This is her intention in the book: 'I shall first consider women in the grand light of human creatures, who, in common with men, are placed on this earth to unfold their faculties' (1997, 110). Women are to be regarded in the first instance as human and only in the second as specifically female, indicating her belief that gendered behaviour is learned rather than natural. Natural history is central to Wollstonecraft's text and argument. In her most famous statement, 'It is time to effect a revolution in female manners', she writes that women must take up the responsibility of being 'part of the human species' (1997, 158). Both Wollstonecraft and Barbauld were writers with sympathies for dissenters, and both used animals and natural history explicitly to promote natural rights. While some work has been done on Barbauld's links with Priestley and her access to scientific knowledge, little attention has been paid to the importance of science in

Wollstonecraft's writings. Her reviews of natural history books gave her additional evidence of the characteristics which were both natural and unnatural to women, and enabled her to argue that women should be given equal rights.

Works Cited

Aikin, John, 1777. An Essay on the Application of Natural History to Poetry. Warrington: J. Johnson.

———, 1784. The Calendar of Nature: or, Youth's Delightful Companion. Containing, details of natural history, the narrative variegated with poetical quotations from the most celebrated authors. Embellished with engravings, representing the four seasons. Warrington: J. Johnson.

[Aikin, John and Anna Letitia Barbauld], 1792–96. Evenings at Home; or, the Juvenile Budget Opened. 6 vols. London: J. Johnson.

Barbauld, Anna Letitia, 2002. Selected Poetry and Prose, ed. William McCarthy and Elizabeth Craft. Ontario: Broadview Press.

Barker-Benfield, G. J., 1992. The Culture of Sensibility: Sex and Society in Eighteenth-Century Britain. Chicago and London: University of Chicago Press.

Beilby, Ralph, 1790. A General History of Quadrupeds. The Figures Engraved on Wood by Thomas Berwick. Newcastle-upon-Tyne: Robinsons.

Bellanca, Mary Ellen, 2003. 'Science, Animal Sympathy, and Anna Barbauld's "The Mouse's Petition" ', Eighteenth-Century Studies 37.1: 47–67.

Brooks, Marilyn L., 2004. 'Aikin, John (1747–1822)', Oxford Dictionary of National Biography. Oxford: Oxford University Press.

Coleman, Deirdre, 2002. 'Firebrands, Letters and Flowers: Mrs Barbauld and the Priestleys', in Romantic Sociability, ed. G. Russell and C. Tuite. Cambridge: Cambridge University Press: 82–103.

Declaration on Great Apes. http://www.greatapeproject.org/declaration.php

Elyot, Thomas, 1531. The Booke of the Governor, in Renascence Texts. http://www.uoregon.edu/~rbear/gov/gov1.htm

Fulford, Tim, 2005. 'Science', in Romanticism: An Oxford Guide, ed. Nicholas Roe. Oxford: Oxford University Press.

Godwin, William, 1982. Caleb Williams, ed. David McCracken. Oxford: Oxford University Press.

Hitt, Christopher, 2004. 'Ecocriticism and the Long Eighteenth Century', College Literature 31.3 (Summer): 123–47.

Kenyon-Jones, Christine, 2001. Kindred Brutes: Animals in Romantic-Period Writing. Aldershot: Ashgate.

Kitson, Peter, 2007. Romantic Literature, Race and Colonial Encounter. New York: Palgrave Macmillan.

Lawrence, William, 1819. Lectures on Physiology, Zoology, and the Natural History of Man, delivered at the Royal College of Surgeons. London: J. Callow.

Lovejoy, Arthur O., 1936. *The Great Chain of Being: A Study of the History of an Idea*. Cambridge, MA: Harvard University Press.

Percival, Thomas, 1776. *A Father's Instructions to his Children: Consisting of tales, fables, and reflections; designed to promote the love of virtue, a taste for knowledge, and an early acquaintance with the works of nature*. London: J. Johnson.

———, 1784. *Moral and Literary Dissertations [...]*. Warrington: J. Johnson.

Perkins, David, 2003. *Romanticism and Animal Rights*. Cambridge: Cambridge University Press.

Ross, Marlon, 1994. 'Configurations of Feminine Reform: The Woman Writer and the Tradition of Dissent', in *Re-Visioning Romanticism: British Women Writers 1776–1837*, ed. C. Shiner Wilson and J. Haeffner. Philadelphia: University of Pennsylvania Press: 91–110.

Ruston, Sharon, 2005. 'Vegetarianism and Vitality in the Work of Thomas Forster, William Lawrence and P. B. Shelley', *Keats-Shelley Journal* 54 (2005): 113–32.

———, 2005. *Shelley and Vitality*. Basingstoke: Palgrave Macmillan.

Schiebinger, Londa, 1993. *Nature's Body: Sexual Politics and the Making of Modern Science*. London: Pandora.

Smellie, William, 1790. *A Philosophy of Natural History*. Edinburgh: C. Elliot, T. Kay and T. Cadell.

Taylor, Barbara, 2003. *Mary Wollstonecraft and the Feminist Imagination*. Cambridge: Cambridge University Press.

[Taylor, Thomas], 1792. *A Vindication of the Rights of Brutes*. London: Edward Jeffrey.

Weldon, Amy, 2002. ' "The Common Gifts of Heaven": Animal Rights and Moral Education in Anna Letitia Barbauld's "The Mouse's Petition" and "The Caterpillar" ', *Cardiff Corvey: Reading the Romantic Text* 8: 2 (June) http://www.cf.ac.uenca/corveyarticlescc08_n02.html

White, R. S., 2006. *Natural Rights and the Birth of Romanticism*. Basingstoke: Palgrave Macmillan.

Wollstonecraft, Mary, 1989. *The Works of Mary Wollstonecraft*, ed. Janet Todd and Marilyn Butler. 7 vols. London: William Pickering.

———, 1997. *The Vindications*, ed. D. L. Macdonald and Kathleen Scherf. Ontario: Broadview.

George Eliot, Geometry and Gender

ALICE JENKINS

SINCE THE PUBLICATION in the 1980s of Gillian Beer's *Darwin's Plots* and George Levine's *Darwin and the Novelists*, the map of Victorian literature has been almost wholly redrawn through critical interest in the relationships of literary and scientific writing. Very little attention indeed, however, has been given by literary scholars to the workings of *mathematics* in Victorian culture. This is a problematic absence from both Victorian studies and literature and science studies. It has resulted in a tendency to overemphasize the cultural impact of some scientific disciplines, and hence in a skewing of our understanding of the readership for and reception of scientific knowledge. To take one example, lack of attention to the variety and ubiquity of nineteenth-century engagements with Euclidean geometry makes us unresponsive to a wide range of metaphors, structures and key words which shape an extraordinary number of Victorian literary, political and polemical writings. Just as the Darwinian vocabulary of growth, development and inheritance can be traced in late Victorian literature whose thematic concerns are far removed from biology, the Euclidean vocabulary of proof, axiom and demonstration haunts even Victorian writing that has nothing explicitly to do with mathematics.

In this essay, however, I shall argue a more limited case, highlighting the ways in which Victorian culture ascribed contradictory, overdetermined and yet very powerful gender coding to Euclidean geometry. Because it was widely held to be a kind of knowledge that was perfect and timeless in its certainty, geometry was associated both with feminine purity and refinement and with masculine mental rigour. And because geometry was for many the epitome of a complete and fixed system of knowledge, it was often invoked to suggest the fixedness of other systems, including that of gender difference. At the same time, however, there are currents in Victorian writing about geometry which profoundly destabilize its use in the context of gender.

On 28 January 1851, a few weeks after moving to London to lodge in the publisher John Chapman's house, Marian Evans told her close friends Charles and Cara Bray that she had begun to study a new subject:

> I am attending Professor Newman's course of lectures on Geometry at the Ladies' College every Monday and Thursday. You will say that I can't afford this, which is 'dreadful true' – but the fact is that I happened to say I should like to do so and good-natured Mr. Chapman went straightway and bought me a ticket which he begged me to accept. I refused to accept it – and have paid for it – wherefore I must stint myself in some direction – clearly in white gloves and probably in clean collars. (Eliot 1954–56, I, 343)

The financial cost that the lecture ticket imposed on her was not very onerous; trickier was the ticket's role within the libidinal economy of the unconventional ménage 'good-natured' John Chapman had instituted in his house at 142 Strand, where he lived with his wife Susanna and his mistress, Elisabeth Tilley. Evans did not, of course, discuss *this* aspect of the 'cost' of the ticket with the Brays.

Evans was given the ticket in the course of what must have been a highly charged period of flirtation and seduction between herself and Chapman. The term at the Ladies' College began on Tuesday 14 January.[1] The first geometry lecture was probably given on Thursday 16 January, just two days before what Rosemary Ashton identifies as the start of Evans' sexual relationship with Chapman.[2] Evans' insistence on paying for the ticket can be read in this context as an attempted check to Chapman's sexual ambitions or perhaps as an assertion of her own independence, for the sake of her self-respect or her reputation.

Geometry lessons might seem a highly idiosyncratic seduction gift, of very limited suasiveness except to someone as intellectually hungry as Marian Evans. But in fact contemporary literature suggests that geometry had complex and fairly strongly marked sexual qualities for many Victorians and was surprisingly often used tropically to connote seduction, sexual availability or maturity.

Literary and cultural historical interest is growing in the British reception towards the end of the nineteenth century of the non-Euclidean

---

[1] *Times*, 14 January 1851, 4; issue 20698; col. A.
[2] Ashton 1996, 85, argues that 'it appears likely' that code marks in Chapman's diary for Saturday 18 and Sunday 19 January refer to sexual activities with Evans.

geometries developed by the European mathematicians Bolyai, Lobatchevski and Gauss. Steven Connor's Afterword to a recent book on the *Victorian Supernatural*, for instance, rightly emphasizes the connection between popularizations of the new geometry and late-Victorian spiritualism (Connor 2004). But long before these Fourth Dimensional geometries began to impinge on British culture, Euclidean geometry had been a seminal and ubiquitous part of the education of the British elite. And as well as having a central place in the education of the upper classes, geometry was also increasingly available to artisans and autodidacts from around the 1820s on, particularly through new textbooks and lectures at Mechanics' Institutes and other such fora. Though literary criticism and cultural history have as yet paid little attention to the fact, Euclid forms a major part of the shared cultural base of literate Victorian men.

For most of the Victorian period, mathematics and classics were the staple disciplines of English education for boys and men of the well-to-do classes. All through the nineteenth century, such students were taught Euclid's *Elements* in the same way as they were taught Latin: as the essential training of a gentleman and the indispensable gymnasium of the reasoning mind. This narrow curriculum dominated the traditional English universities until late in the nineteenth century. Although both Oxford and Cambridge began to diversify their curricula around mid-century, only very small numbers of Honours students opted for degrees other than the usual BAs which heavily emphasized classics (at Oxford) and mathematics (at Cambridge).[3] At Oxford mathematics was not greatly privileged in the curriculum, despite the efforts of Baden Powell, the Savilian Professor of Geometry from 1827 (and later the father of the founder of the Scouts and Guides), who led a movement to reform and modernize mathematics teaching there in the 1830s and 40s.[4] Cambridge, however, privileged mathematics to the extent that until 1854 even students reading classics were required to take mathematics until their final year. Thus, Cambridge-educated men, whatever their future profession, were all but certain to have been obliged to study mathematics at university to some extent. As the Cambridge mathematical Honours curriculum became increasingly advanced and specialist, Euclidean geometry was relegated to candidates for the 'poll' or non-Honours degree, until around mid-century it was minimized even

---

[3] Detailed accounts of curriculum change at Oxford and Cambridge can be found in Brock and Curthoys 1997 and Searby 1993.
[4] On Baden Powell's Oxford reforms, see Corsi 1988.

there. All students, however, would have had to show sufficient geometrical knowledge to pass the not very stiff entrance examination, which included two books of Euclid.

The heavy emphasis which this long-lasting system laid on mathematics and classics necessarily drove the curricular choices of public schools and tutors. Between the schools and the universities, a very broad spectrum of the male intelligentsia of Victorian Britain had an acquaintance, or more, with Euclidean geometry. Though, perhaps, few men actually remembered in later life much of what was often simply 'crammed' knowledge of those books of Euclid set for various examinations, they frequently retained a respect for the cultural and hence class prestige which surrounded Euclid. When reforms decreased the amount of Euclid taught at Cambridge in favour of more applied mathematics, for example, a review in *Blackwood's* reported that

> country clergymen, whose forgotten mathematics loomed grandly on their minds through the mist of years, were confounded with disappointment, in finding their sons, in whom they expected to find philosophers, return to them with an examination paper, apparently rather calculated to unfold the mysteries of engineering, well-sinking, and carpentering. (Prowett 1849, 238)

Two results of this combination of wide exposure to and belief in geometry are relevant for our purposes. The first is that until comparatively late in the century, men who were not professional mathematicians felt entitled and equipped to write on geometry, and many of their works were taken seriously enough to be reviewed and discussed in the press; and the second is that the widespread belief in geometry as the foundation of a patrician masculine education made it desirable and at the same time fearsome for many who were attracted to élite learning, including women like Marian Evans.[5]

Efforts to make geometry accessible to middle- and lower-class male

---

[5]   An interesting example of an amateur mathematician whose work on geometry was influential, being both highly praised and execrated for its reformism, was Thomas Perronet Thompson, who after graduating as seventh wrangler at Cambridge spent the first part of his career as an officer in the army and the second part as a radical politician, including seven years as MP for Bradford in the late 1840s and 50s. Shortly after retiring from active service in 1829 he published an anonymous reworking of the first book of Euclid's *Elements*, known as *Geometry Without Axioms*, which went through at least five editions up to 1834.

learners were not quite mirrored in girls' and women's education. Virtually no geometry textbooks were published in Britain aimed specifically
at female learners. Textbooks did not usually announce themselves as
intended for boys or men only, but they very rarely acknowledged that
girls or women might be among their readers. Where such acknowledge-
ments were made, the intention was often to emphasize that the book's
method was effective even for so ignorant and unorthodox an audience,
as, for example, when the clergyman Thomas Penyngton Kirkman
claimed in the preface to his horrifyingly rebarbative *First Mnemonical
Lessons in Geometry, Algebra and Trigonometry* (1852) that even 'school-
girls of fair capacity' could be taught basic mathematics by his method
(Kirkman 1852, vi).

Despite the absence of textbooks aimed at girls, however, opportunities for female geometrical education did exist, even if they were largely
informal.[6] Even though neither King's College nor University College
provided education for female students, a woman who, like Marian
Evans, wanted to study geometry in London in 1851 could choose from a
number of possibilities. First, of course, she could study at home, using
one of the plethora of new textbooks being published for autodidacts.
The letters and autobiographies of several mid-nineteenth-century
women indicate that they studied Euclid by themselves, usually of course
amongst many other tasks. Harriet Martineau, for instance, reported
herself in 1841 to be 'growing narcissus, tulips, hyacinths & crocuses in
my window, – studying Euclid, &, when sufficiently alone, drawing'
(Martineau 1990, 287). Alternatively, she could take private lessons. If
she preferred to attend lectures, there were other venues than the Ladies'
College. She was probably not much disadvantaged by being barred from
the all-male audience attending the lectures given by Robert Edkins at
Gresham College, since Gresham was in considerable decline at this
period.[7] But lectures on mathematics were provided for women at the
new Queen's College in Harley Street by T. G. Hall.

---

[6]   Though a number of very useful studies of prominent eighteenth- and nineteenth-century female mathematicians exist, much work remains to be done on
women and popular mathematics. Shelley Costa's study (2002) is highly infor-
mative about the *Ladies' Diary*, the most successful eighteenth-century popular
mathematical journal for both sexes, but nineteenth-century women's access to
mathematics remains little explored.
[7]   *Times*, 9 January 1851, 1; issue 20694; col. A. Gresham College had not
adapted much to the movement for expanding education from traditional elites.
Edkins' lectures, like most of those at the College, were advertised as given both
in Latin and in English, though in 1860 Dickens' enquiries after the Latin ones

The reason why Marian Evans attended Francis Newman's lectures at the Ladies' College was not, probably, because they were designed for a female audience (after all, at the same time she attended a lecture by Faraday at the Royal Institution, where audiences were mixed).[8] Instead, the reason is likely to have been the fact that Chapman knew Newman well, and Evans knew at least his work. Evans read his quasi-autobiographical theological book *The Soul: Its Sorrows and Aspirations* when it first appeared in 1849, calling Newman, with affectionate irony, 'our blessed St. Francis' (Eliot 1954–56, I, 282). Chapman had published several of Newman's books, including both *The Soul* and the lectures on political economy he had given the previous year at the Ladies' College; and when Chapman bought the *Westminster Review* in May 1851, Newman was one of the first people he invited to write for it (Newman 1851; Haight 1968, 89). But beyond these personal and professional connections, Newman was in some ways a surprising choice as a geometry lecturer – not just for Evans, indeed, but for his whole audience.

Newman was at the same time a central and a marginal figure of mid-century intellectual life. Not nearly so strongly identified with a single intellectual movement as his elder brother John Henry, Francis was famous as an upholder of unfashionable principles, including vegetarianism, the immorality of imperialism sustained by warfare and, most importantly and controversially, religious doubt. The Irish novelist Justin McCarthy describes him as disregarded by many of his contemporaries – 'nine out of ten men in London who took any interest in public affairs were apt to set down Francis Newman as hopelessly given over to crotchets' – but through his writings on Christianity, particularly *Phases of Faith* (1850), his influence on many advanced thinkers was strong (McCarthy 1903, 56). As Basil Willey puts it, 'his "fads" were the natural preoccupations of an ardent Victorian "progressive" ' (Willey 1980, 46). This may err a little on the side of generosity, but certainly Newman's reformism was a key factor in his interest in women's education and Dissenting and non-sectarian education.

Still, however various his interests and important his influence in Victorian intellectual life, Newman was not a professional mathematician. Evans rightly calls Newman 'Professor', but his chair at University

revealed that audiences were not large enough for any but the English to be given (Chartres and Vermont 1998, 48–49). As late as 1874 geometry lectures were still at least occasionally being given in Latin at Gresham (ibid., 49).

8   The ticket to the lecture at the Royal Institution (Marian wrongly calls it the Royal Society) was given her by Robert William Mackay. See Eliot 1954–56, I, 341–42.

College London was not in mathematics, nor indeed in political economy, but in Latin. The previous year he had lectured at the Ladies' College on ancient history and elocution, while the geometry lectures had been given by his colleague at University College, the far better qualified Augustus De Morgan, a very notable mathematician.[9] Newman's claim to appropriateness as a geometry lecturer was nowhere near so well founded as De Morgan's, being based largely on his outstanding achievements on the mathematical side of his 1822 Oxford undergraduate degree. Newman is a very good example of the role of amateur mathematicians in geometry education in this period. He was not only an occasional lecturer on the subject but also attempted to contribute to the progress of the discipline, publishing in 1841 a book on *The Difficulties of Elementary Geometry* which sought, like so many other works by amateur and professional mathematicians alike, to straighten out the pedagogical and logical flaws in Euclid's *Elements*.

It is difficult to be sure exactly what material Marian Evans studied with Newman, and how – or whether – he tailored his lessons particularly to female listeners, because (despite his association with Chapman) Newman did not publish his 1851 geometry lectures. Newman was, as one of his twentieth-century biographers notes, a 'whole-hearted' supporter of the rights of women, though his conception of those rights was sometimes quirky (Robbins 1966, 150). His work around the time when Eliot studied with him suggests a view of male and female which is conventional in being strongly bifurcated, but perhaps unconventional in the consequences it derives from that split. His 1849 book on *The Soul*, for instance, argues passionately for a highly gendered understanding of spirituality, culminating in an insistence that 'if thy Soul is to go on to higher spiritual blessedness, it must become *a Woman*; yes, however manly thou be among men' (Newman 1862, 82). By this Newman means that the soul must adopt towards God what he takes to be a feminine dependence and subservience, together with a complete abnegation of 'Rights *or* Liberty' (Newman 1862, 82). This account of gender as ideally saturated by inequalities of power does not reflect Newman's beliefs about women in the non-spiritual realm, however; he was active in promoting women's education and suffrage, and his most

[9]   *Times*, 12 January 1850, 4; issue 20384; col. B. The historian of mathematics Adrian Rice suggests that De Morgan's withdrawal from lecturing at the Ladies' College was not only to the lack of remuneration but also to the waste of time entailed in teaching 'girls who had only a very elementary knowledge of arithmetic' (Rice 1996, 395).

direct public statement on women's intellects, an 1874 review essay titled 'Capacities of Women', strongly praises the work of the best modern female writers, urging that 'it is surely high time that a man who dares to write insolently concerning the female intellect, should not only be regarded as rude, but should incur the imputation of deficiency in his own powers' ([Newman] 1865, 380). By 1891, when Newman was eighty-six, he listed among the signs supporting optimism about the future of society 'the power of women is about to signalize itself in most valuable directions – for the benefit of both sexes' (quoted in Robbins 1966, 162).

But Newman's support for female education and his goodwill towards female intellectuals does not give us much direct information about how he taught geometry to a female audience. Anna Swanwick, the writer and social reformer, also attended Newman's mathematics classes at the Ladies' College and reported him to be a highly effective teacher, sensitive to his students' progress (quoted in Sieveking 1909, 154–55). Along with this pedagogical talent, however, Newman brought his reformist views on religious, political and ethical matters to bear on his attitude to the subject matter and manner of teaching geometry. As he put it, he could 'see no reason why the beaten track should be held sacred, if a better offer itself' (Newman 1841b, 2).

Newman's association with the emergent non-Anglican education movement dated from as far back as his appointment to the chair of classics at the dissenting academy Manchester New College in 1840. In his inaugural lecture at Manchester, Newman outlined the enduring importance of classical literature in a modern curriculum. As part of his exposition he made the rhetorical move (common in early and mid-Victorian élite discussions of pedagogy) of comparing the effects of literary and mathematical education.[10] Newman explained that he valued geometry 'as an exercise of the mind', because it teaches logical thought and because it 'imparts the taste, and improves the faculty [for] lucid *arrangement*' (Newman 1841a, 10–11). Thus far, Newman's views typified the rationale for geometry as outlined by the early Victorian educational élite: ie., that geometry was an essential part of a liberal education not because of the special value of the subject matter itself, but because of the mental discipline it inculcated.[11]

[10] One of the most impassioned and influential contributions to this comparison was Whewell 1838.
[11] For an excellent discussion of the cultural importance of geometry in this period see Richards 1988.

But in *The Difficulties of Elementary Geometry*, published in the same year, Newman challenged the teaching methods that were often associated with this élite rationale. In particular, he attacked the traditional pre-eminence of Euclid's *Elements of Geometry* as a textbook, and the methods of demonstration the *Elements* adopted. Newman highlighted two problems that made Euclid a poor starting-place for learners: it was 'unbending', 'repulsive and unexplanatory'; and it was 'wholly unfit' to provide 'that large view which must be taken in the higher mathematics' (Newman 1841b, 8).[12] Euclid, he suggested, was downright out of date: 'in Geometry we have set up one of the ancients for our idol, and have cramped the science in its adult state by the trammels of its infancy' (Newman 1841b, 8). Marian Evans and her class at the Ladies' College, then, were studying with a professor who was something of a geometric iconoclast.

Evans' letters reveal nothing more about her progress in Newman's geometry class; but her later writing suggests that his impatience with geometric traditionalism was congenial to her. Nine years after she studied with him, she gave a highly critical account in *The Mill on the Floss* of the stuck-in-the-mud method by which the inadequate tutor Mr Stelling teaches Euclid to a resistant Tom Tulliver. In a passage that captures Mr Stelling's views but is a little too sarcastic to be quite in *style indirect libre*, George Eliot sums up his reasons for clinging to orthodoxy in the face of his student's obvious unreceptivity:

> a method of education sanctioned by the long practice of our venerable ancestors was not to give way before the exceptional dullness of a boy who was merely living at the time then present. (Eliot 1860, 169)

The idea that modernity required adjustments to educational methods was by no means obvious to all nineteenth-century teachers of geometry. Indeed it was a strong part of the claim of Euclid to a central place in the curriculum that the *Elements* had no need of moving with the times. Less than a generation before *Mill on the Floss* was published, the illustrious Master of Trinity College, Cambridge, William Whewell, the century's

---

[12] Newman's attack on Euclid seems to have gone further than his Manchester New College colleague, the professor of mathematics, R. Finlay, would have countenanced. Though Finlay agreed with Newman that the subject should be taught with attention to the work of modern geometers, in his own inaugural lecture he specifically praised the 'rigour', 'elegance' and 'beauty' of Euclid's geometry (Finlay 1841, 10–11). Newman, on the contrary, described the 'rigour' of Euclid as 'imaginary' (1841b, 8).

most vociferous and vehement defender of the traditional prestige of Euclidean geometry, summed up the patrician view of geometry's relationship with modernity by announcing that

> no new system of geometry can supersede the old. The old truths will always be true, and always essential. ... Euclid has never been superseded, and never will be so without great detriment to education. (Whewell 1838, 46)

This Canute-like view had by no means vanished even in 1860. But Eliot's implication that even geometry must be taught and understood differently in different periods is clearly consonant with Newman's view, which entirely contradicts Whewell's, that 'the works of a Greek geometer' alone cannot be appropriate for beginners 'in modern mathematics' (Newman 1841b, 8). And Eliot takes this reformist and skeptical position further, casting doubt on hallowed assumptions about the effects of geometry on the mind and character of youth.

The argument for the good effects of Euclid on the mind depended on the *Elements'* supposed tendency to teach students to reason in an abstract realm removed from sensory perception, a process, as it were, of anti-reification. Geometry could not and must not depend on the information of the senses: thus, in *Mill on the Floss*, Tom is condemned by Mr Stelling as 'a thoroughly stupid lad' because he entirely lacks a sense of the abstract and relies on his senses: though he can 'draw almost perfect squares on his slate without any measurement' and 'throw a stone right into the centre of a given ripple', he is 'in a state bordering on idiocy with regard to the demonstration that two given triangles must be equal' (Eliot 1860, 139). In particular, pedagogical approaches involving more than minimal use of visual aids were anathema to the upholders of traditional Euclidean teaching. Euclid had demonstrated geometrical truths using only a stick to scratch diagrams in sand: to interpose any more complicated technologies between the learner and these truths was widely considered a betrayal of Euclidean purity. Innovations giving technology a larger role in geometry risked devaluing the whole of Euclid by replacing its rational certainty with a mere matter of visual judgment. And this in turn might have dire consequences not only for mathematical ability, but for morality. As William Whewell put it,

> if [a student] be left to suppose that mathematical truths depend ultimately upon the evidence of the senses, he will look in other subjects for evidence equally palpable; and will not bring away from mathe-

matics that lesson which another mode of pursuing the study might impart to him, that there exist vast and solid edifices of truth, the foundations of which are not laid in the information which our external senses give us. (Whewell 1835, 9)

To hardline proponents of the élite rationale for geometry such as Whewell, innovations in favour of the real and the practical pulled geometry down from the sphere of ideal, perfect certainty and soiled it with the contingent, the everyday, and the human. Of course, these constitute exactly the milieu of the realist novel, and in the remainder of this essay I shall explore the cultural work of geometry in that genre – a task which has to begin with an acknowledgement of incommensurability.

Despite the efforts of geometrical reformers, geometry represented for many Victorians the epitome of certain knowledge: it signified a kind of certainty which it was barely possible to fit into the ethical and imaginative dimensions of the realist novel. The only comparable source of certainty, religious faith, came in too many varieties and shades to have the same effect on realist representation: geometry's certainties were, for many writers and readers, simply too universal and unarguable to be contained within the complicated, messy and mutable world of the novel. It is not surprising that there should be, therefore, on the face of it, an all but unbridgeable gulf between the procedures of geometry and those of realist fiction. Nonetheless, nineteenth-century literature generally is full of references and allusions to geometry, and even in realist fiction the subject is often invoked. Here, geometry is generally represented in heightened emotions, as an object of desire or of detestation, but rarely is it sufficiently congenial to the realist mode to be sustained long enough for its duration in the text to match the passion it provokes. In fact, the most important and frequently occurring scenes in which realist fiction tackles geometry are those in which characters are shown *giving it up*.

In autobiographical writing, as distinct from the novel, a number of nineteenth-century writers remark on the consolatory qualities of geometry's purity, abstractness and removal from the mundane. Wordsworth, most famously, found in Euclid an entrance to a ideal realm beyond the temporal and spatial, transcending the turmoil of human existence, 'an independent world,/ Created out of pure intelligence' as he wrote in *The Prelude* (Wordsworth 1979, 195).[13] De Quincey elaborated this: 'Words-

---

[13] Michael Simpson describes Wordsworth's adult interest in geometry as a regression but notes the profound importance of Euclidean geometry for Words-

worth was a profound admirer of the sublimer mathematics; at last of the higher geometry. The secret of this admiration for geometry lay in the antagonism between this world of bodiless abstraction and the world of passion' (De Quincey 1948, 149). Victorian writers, however, devoted a surprising amount of invention to exploring the connections between De Quincey's two worlds, and especially between the abstract objects and rigorous method of Euclid, and the physical objects and muddled methods of sexual identity and activity. Fictional representations of learning geometry are often used as counterpoints or contrasts with developing sexuality. The connections between geometry and sexuality partly reflect the fact that Euclid was for many pupils introduced later than Latin, for example, so that geometry was often apt to coincide with puberty. But perhaps more importantly, geometry is often used to signify the clarity and order of the presexual mind, which must be lost or renounced if maturity is to be reached.

Of course there are significant differences between the ways in which these losses and renunciations affect male and female characters. Let us take a first example from a not very distinguished novel which is nonetheless fairly typical in its representation of how geometrical certainty is destroyed by emerging male sexuality. On returning aged nineteen from adventures at sea, Robert, the narrator of Frederick Chamier's 1835 naval novel *The Unfortunate Man*, spends three years studying successfully, but on falling in love finds himself unable to concentrate on his work:

> in vain I pored over Euclid, or dived into Algebra; when I closed the volume ... I found my time and labour had been lost. I recollected not one word or figure of my occupation, and I wondered how, while I had been tracing a figure, I had only seen a face. (Chamier 1835, ch. 14)

The vestigial pun in Chamier's 'figure' connects diagrams with bodies, but the latter emphatically and disastrously displace the former. The episode is typical in that it uses geometry to indicate a kind of certainty which is simply incompatible with the complications of sexual adulthood. Robert's love affair results in serious consequences, including almost immediate dishonour and, interestingly, a loss of masculinity as he trembles 'like a frightened girl' at the thought of the deception he is

worth, suggesting that the 'overall scheme of "the thirteen-book Prelude" may even recall the standard thirteen books of Euclid's *Elements*' (Simpson 2003, 24).

practising on his beloved's father (Chamier 1835, ch. 14). Here Euclid
has to be abandoned for maturity to be achieved, but the achievement
turns out to be far less desirable than was expected.

When a female character of equivalent age studies geometry, the
outcome is also generally the abandonment of Euclid, but here the social
lesson tends to be even heavier than Robert's. Such scenes usually
involve strict reinforcement of gender difference, sometimes through
comedy, but more often involving renunciation or punishment. In the
former case, girls and young women characters are described as interested in Euclid in order to emphasize their virginity, highlighting a titil-
lating mismatch between their sexual charm and their ignorance of their
effect on men. When the elderly Sir Harcourt Courtley meets his
intended young bride in Dion Boucicault's 1841 smash-hit *London
Assurance*, for instance, he describes her as 'evidently not used to society.
Ha! – takes every word I say for infallible truth – requires the solution of
a compliment, as if it were a problem in Euclid' (Boucicault 2001, 100).
Here geometry is a marker of a naïve phase before sexuality initiates the
individual into the social realm. Rather paradoxically, Sir Harcourt
thinks that Grace will have to accommodate herself to the strenuously
enforced boundaries of gender-appropriate behaviour by giving up the
'infallible truths' of Euclid in favour of the murky and equivocal ambigu-
ities of adult life.

A more wholesale example of female characters being urged to give
up geometrical pursuits in favour of sexuality occurs in William
Courthope's 1869 'allegorical burlesque' poem *Ludibria Lunae, or the
Wars of the Women and the Gods*. Courthope was a highly respectable
literary scholar, producing among other works a well-regarded ten-
volume edition of Pope. This satire on women's education, though, was
written when he was in his mid-twenties and playfully describes sexuality of all kinds, lightly veiled by classical and pastoral trappings.
Despite its mildly risqué scenes, it was published by the highly respectable firm Smith and Elder and cannot have damaged Courthope's reputation irreparably, or perhaps even at all, since he was elected Professor
of Poetry at Oxford in 1895. In *Ludibria Lunae*, geometry signifies
anaphrodisia, a kind of knowledge so incompatible with female sexual
maturity that it can be used as both the alibi and the punishment for
sexual deviance. A group of women have set up an academy and dedicated themselves to study, but it is suspected that one of their number
has let her attention wander to love. All the women are put to trial by
ordeal. Each must kiss Amaryllis, the newest and most innocent student;
the one who shows signs of sexual excitement will be revealed as the

guilty party. A protracted scene of kissing follows, in which the girls 'with secret joy … comply'. Amid much imagery of bees and flowers, Celia is unable to control her physical reaction to kissing Amaryllis and is accused. She defends herself by referring to her devotion to geometry, but to no avail:

> 'Tis vain for Celia to protest;
> Still, so she swore, an honest Blue,
> Good Euclid's shrine was in her breast;
> Her eye proclaimed her oath untrue;
> Her convict cheek the crime confessed; (Courthope 1869, 76)

On conviction, Celia is punished by being fined her make-up and ordered to learn the first three books of Euclid by heart. The poem ends with full-scale war between the gods and women of advanced opinions, in which the gods triumph and women are urged not to aspire too high in future. The lesbian eroticism of the kissing scene is rehabilitated by the revelation that Amaryllis was all along Amadis, a man in disguise, and so the girls' sexual reaction to him was not only acceptable, but – within the gender ideology of the poem – praiseworthy.

Contrary to this strand of comic and satirical writing on women and geometry, realist fiction tends to focus on the earnestness and unhappiness of young female characters who study Euclid. Unlike boys, who are rarely shown as greatly interested in their mathematics, girl characters are often attracted to geometry for its intellectual rigour and its aura of masculine exclusiveness. Emmeline, in Charlotte M. Yonge's 1854 Keble-influenced novel *The Castle-Builders*, is just such a character. Rather like Ethel in Yonge's best-selling later novel *The Daisy Chain*, who studies classics with her brother until she sees that she must put intellectual ambition aside in favour of familial duty, Emmeline tries to teach herself geometry to keep her step-brother company. But not only is Emmeline forced to learn the conventional difference between feminine superficial quickness and masculine knowledge, the reader is shown that the latter is superior even when the present representative of masculinity is rather stupid. Emmeline and her sister Kate,

> being clever girls, could soon surpass a boy who was far from clever; and … all three launched into Euclid together, with great satisfaction, Emmeline rushing from proposition to proposition, fancying she understood all, but often 'brought up', as Frank called it, when obliged to make things clear to him. ([Yonge] 1854, 159)

For all he is not clever, Frank's insistence on solid understanding is far more in harmony with the spirit of Victorian geometrical education than Emmeline's enthusiasm. Yonge makes the episode serve as a miniature of her larger moral purpose. The central lesson of the novel – that it is unwise to delay one's first communion – enforces the same ideal of obedient progress by the steps laid down by authority as this lesson in geometry. For nineteenth-century defenders of Euclid's central place in education, studying geometry disciplined students to steady, linear effort, curbing the natural tendency of youth to skip from one half-digested idea to another. The remark which Euclid is (very likely apocryphally) said to have made to Ptolemy – 'there is no royal road to geometry' – was sometimes used to capture the beneficial lesson that geometry teaches: viz., that progress in learning of all kinds must be made step by step rather than by leaps and short cuts. The result was often to reinforce educational conservatism, as for example when Hannah More cited Euclid's remark in her very severe book on the education of girls, in order to clinch her determinedly reactionary argument that 'we cannot *cheat* children into learning, or *play* them into knowledge, according to the smoothness of the modern creed' (More 1799, I, 155).

Euclidean geometry thus represented for much of Victorian literature a prestigious and authoritative body of knowledge which had to be learned by submission rather than enthusiasm and steadiness rather than brilliance. It was layered with rich cultural meanings and emotional resonances. I want to close this essay as I began it, with Marian Evans/ George Eliot, probably the most interesting Victorian novelist writing on geometry, and to return briefly to Maggie and Tom Tulliver.

Like Emmeline, Maggie begins Euclid with great confidence and in order to help her brother. Where Yonge follows the conventional gender coding of geometrical education, however, contrasting a feminine tendency to superficiality with a masculine emphasis on solid progress, Eliot complicates the pattern. Maggie finds her first exposure to Euclid incomprehensible, explaining her difficulty as the result of starting in the middle of the book; Tom's response is that 'it's all the harder when you know what goes before: for then you've got to say what Definition 3. is and what Axiom V. is' (Eliot 1860, 147). Tom is in the unhappy position of being taught by the method of linear progress, but without the solid knowledge it is supposed to produce. He uses his knowledge of the cultural prestige of the method to support his rather bullying relationship with Maggie, slighting her capacity and causing his tutor to reinforce his strict and exclusive gender-coding of knowledge.

'Girls can't do Euclid: can they, sir?'

'They can pick up a little of everything, I daresay', said Mr Stelling. 'They've a great deal of superficial cleverness: but they couldn't go far into anything. They're quick and shallow.' (Eliot 1860, 150)

But Eliot complicates this absurdly conservative judgment by making Euclid part of a profound challenge to Tom's sexual identity. Though Mr Stelling's method of teaching is designed 'not to enfeeble and emasculate his pupil's mind', the first result of Tom's education is that through unhappiness he becomes 'more like a girl than he had ever been in his life before' (Eliot 1860, 140–41). The gender-coding with which Eliot replaces and reproves Stelling's is one based on a critique of unequal power: girls are not defined by their shallowness but by 'bruises and crushings'.

Much later, when Maggie is oppressed by the narrowness and meaninglessness of her life as a young woman at home, she returns to Tom's schoolbooks in search of 'masculine wisdom – ... that knowledge which made men contented and even glad to live' (Eliot 1860, 287). Despite her need, her attempt at autodidacticism does not appear to be successful. Eliot alludes obliquely to a version of the 'royal road to geometry' trope as Maggie goes on 'as if she had set out toward the Promised Land alone, and found it a thirsty, trackless, uncertain journey' (Eliot 1860, 287). Maggie, rather like Tom earlier, finds her inclinations wandering to the world of the real, physical and tangible rather than the abstract, and like Robert in *The Unfortunate Man*, she cannot concentrate on her studies: 'when she sat at the window with her book, her eyes *would* fix themselves blankly on the outdoor sunshine: then they would fill with tears' (Eliot 1860, 287).

Nonetheless, despite failure in the direct and formal knowledge she attempts to acquire, she does learn a more important and fundamental skill from her work. Both the exercise and the results of this skill are described in terms of geometry:

It flashed through her like the suddenly apprehended solution of a problem, that all the miseries of her young life had come from fixing her heart on her own pleasure, as if that were the central necessity of the universe; and for the first time she saw the possibility of shifting the position from which she looked at the gratification of her own desires, of taking her stand out of herself, and looking at her own life as an insignificant part of a divinely guided whole. (Eliot 1860, 290)

What has happened in Eliot's economy of metaphors here is a shift from theoretical to applied geometry, or an Eliotic application of geometry to the realm of morals. The perception of the 'solution of a problem' links Maggie's thought unambiguously to mathematics, and the flash of intuition with which it comes to her belongs to the Platonic school, to which William Whewell and the most traditionalist upholders of geometry belonged. But a little later, the adjective 'central' begins the change in the register of the metaphors which, by the end of the passage, has moved from strict textbook geometry to geometry as a relationship with the world. 'Central' recalls Tom's talent for throwing a stone 'right into the centre of a given ripple', which Mr Stelling failed to understand as a kind of geometric ability. Maggie's vision now of the possibility of 'shifting the position from which she looked' involves integrating geometrical authority with the contingencies of the world through the body, in a way that adopts and makes triumphant use of the overlooked practical geometry in which her unacademic brother excelled.

Maggie's epiphany rehabilitates geometry and its yearning towards abstraction and perfection, finding – however briefly – a way of making them serve a generous moral purpose, freeing them from aridity and using them to make the individual and the circumstantial world into a unity. It is unlikely that Eliot learnt this kind of geometry from Newman; but quite likely that he would have admired it.

Works Cited

Ashton, Rosemary, 1996. *George Eliot: A Life*. London: Hamish Hamilton.

Beer, Gillian, 1983. *Darwin's Plots: Evolutionary Narrative in Darwin, George Eliot, and Nineteenth-Century Fiction*. London: Routledge & Kegan Paul.

Boucicault, Dion, 2001 (1841). *London Assurance*. In *London Assurance and Other Victorian Comedies*, ed. Klaus Stierstorfer. Oxford: Oxford University Press.

Brock, M. G. and M. C. Curthoys, eds., 1997. *Nineteenth-Century Oxford*. Vol. 6, Part I. of *The History of the University of Oxford*. Oxford: Clarendon Press.

Chamier, Frederick, 1835. *The Unfortunate Man*. London: Bentley.

Chartres, Richard, and David Vermont, 1998. *A Brief History of Gresham College, 1597–1997*. London: Gresham College.

Connor, Steven, 2004. 'Afterword', in *The Victorian Supernatural*, ed. Nicola Bown, Carolyn Burdett and Pamela Thurschwell. Cambridge: Cambridge University Press: 262–75.

Corsi, Pietro, 1988. *Science and Religion: Baden Powell and the Anglican Debate, 1800–1860*. Cambridge: Cambridge University Press.

Costa, Shelley, 2002. '*The Ladies' Diary*: Gender, Mathematics and Civil Society in Early Eighteenth-Century England', *Osiris* 17 (2002): 49–73.

Courthope, William, 1869. *Ludibria Lunae, or the Wars of the Women and the Gods*. London: Smith & Elder.

De Quincey, Thomas, 1948 (1834–40). *Recollections of the Lake Poets*. London, Lehman.

Eliot, George, 1860. *The Mill on the Floss*. Edinburgh and London: Blackwood.

———, 1981. *The Mill on the Floss*, ed. Gordon S. Haight. Oxford: Oxford University Press.

———, 1954–56. *Letters*, ed. Gordon S. Haight. 7 vols. London: Oxford University Press.

Finlay, R., 1841. *Introductory Lecture [On Mathematics]*. London: Simpkin, Marshall.

Haight, Gordon S., 1968. *George Eliot: A Biography*. Oxford: Clarendon Press.

Kirkman, Thomas Penyngton, 1852. *First Mnemonical Lessons in Geometry, Algebra and Trigonometry*. London: Wheale.

Levine, George, 1988. *Darwin and the Novelists*. Cambridge, MA: Harvard University Press.

Martineau, Harriet, 1990. *Harriet Martineau: Selected Letters*, ed. Valerie Sanders. Oxford: Clarendon Press.

McCarthy, Justin, 1903. *Portraits of the Sixties*. London: Unwin.

More, Hannah, 1799. *Strictures on the Modern System of Female Education*. 2 vols. London: Cadell and Davies.

Newman, F. W., 1841a. *Introductory Lecture [On Classical Literature]*. London: Simpkin, Marshall.

———, 1841b. *The Difficulties of Elementary Geometry […]*. London: Ball.

———, 1851. *Lectures on Political Economy*. London, Chapman.

———, 1862 (1849). *The Soul: Its Sorrows and Aspirations*. 7th ed. London: Manwaring.

[———], 1865. 'Capacities of Women', *Westminster Review* 84, new series 28 (October 1865): 352–80.

[Prowett, Charles G.], 1849. 'The English Universities and their Reforms', *Blackwood's Edinburgh Magazine* 65 (February 1849): 235–44.

Rice, Adrian, 1996. 'Mathematics in the Metropolis: A Survey of Victorian London', *Historia Mathematica* 23 (1996): 376–417.

Richards, Joan L., 1988. *Mathematical Visions: The Pursuit of Geometry in Victorian England*. Boston: Academic Press.

Robbins, William, 1966. *The Newman Brothers: An Essay in Comparative Intellectual Biography*. London: Heinemann.

Searby, Peter, 1993. *A History of the University of Cambridge, 1750–1870*. Cambridge: Cambridge University Press.

Sieveking, I. Giberne, 1909. *Memoir and Letters of Francis W. Newman*. London: Kegan Paul.

Simpson, Michael, 2003. 'Strange Fits of Parallax: Wordsworth's Geometric Excursions', *The Wordsworth Circle* 34 (2003): 19–24.

Thompson, Thomas Perronet, 1833. *Geometry Without Axioms*. 4th ed. London: Heward.

Whewell, William, 1835. *Thoughts on the Study of Mathematics as Part of a Liberal Education*. Cambridge: Deighton; London: Whittaker.

———, 1838. *On the Principles of English University Education*. London: Parker; Cambridge: Deighton.

Willey, Basil, 1956. *More Nineteenth-Century Studies: A Group of Honest Doubters*. London: Chatto & Windus.

Wordsworth, William, 1979 (1850). *The Prelude* (1850). In *William Wordsworth: The Prelude: 1799, 1805, 1850*, ed. Jonathan J. Wordsworth, M. H. Abrams, and Stephen Gill. New York: Norton.

[Yonge, Charlotte M.], 1854. *The Castle-Builders*. London: Mozley.

On the Back of the Light Waves:
'Novel Possibilities in the "Fourth Dimension"

KATY PRICE

> 'The fourth dimension's out of joint. Oh spite
> That ever I was born to set it right!'
> (*Punch*, 1919a, 442)

IN 1934 Dorothy L. Sayers paid tribute to a popular science author whom she admired very much, when she had Lord Peter Wimsey travel '[o]n the back of the light waves' in solving a murder case (Sayers 1934b, 195). Her short story 'Absolutely Elsewhere' was published in *Strand Magazine* in February, having appeared across the Atlantic the previous month under the title 'Impossible Alibi' in *Mystery, the Illustrated Detective Magazine*. 'Absolutely Elsewhere' was subsequently broadcast by the BBC in 1940. By 1934 the trajectory of Wimsey's character development (commenced in 1920) was approaching completion and the aristocratic detective was well-known among readers of Sayers' novels; the best-seller *Five Red Herrings*, also published at the start of 1934, assured her celebrity status.[1] At the beginning of 'Absolutely Elsewhere' Chief Inspector Parker explains that 'all the obvious suspects were elsewhere at the time' (1934a, 185). Wimsey's response comes directly from Arthur Stanley Eddington's bestselling exposition of Einstein's relativity:

> 'What do you mean by "elsewhere"?' demanded Wimsey, peevishly. Parker had hauled him down to Wapley, on the Great North Road, without his breakfast, and his temper had suffered. 'Do you mean that they couldn't have reached the scene of the murder without travelling at over 186,000 miles a second? Because, if you don't mean that, they weren't absolutely elsewhere. They were only relatively and apparently elsewhere.'
> 'For heaven's sake, don't go all Eddington. Humanly speaking, they

---

[1] On the development of Wimsey's character see Plain (1996, 45–67); on Sayers' reputation see Reynolds (1993, 242).

were elsewhere, and if we're going to nail one of them we shall have to do it without going into their Fitzgerald contractions and coefficients of spherical curvature.'

Sayers' British readers would have empathized with Parker's plea for common sense to prevail over the technicalities of Einsteinian time and space. Those who had not looked at *The Nature of the Physical World* (1928) could scarcely have avoided all reference to this exposition, in magazines or on the radio.[2] By 1934 Eddington's name had been publicly associated with that of Einstein for fifteen years, following his appearance as Einstein's champion when relativity made headline news in November 1919. Wimsey fans could enjoy the detective's Eddington moment, as yet another instance of his tendency to blither in the face of brute reality; those who had read *The Nature of the Physical World* might well identify with Parker's riposte, recognizing the abstruse terms 'Fitzgerald contraction' and 'coefficients of spherical curvature' and knowing enough to dismiss them as irrelevant to the murder of William Grimbold, bachelor money-lender.

By incorporating the absurdity of mathematical science applied to human affairs into her characterization of Wimsey, Sayers appropriated a familiar source of entertainment from newspaper coverage of relativity, which in turn derived much of its energy from parodying the anthropomorphic conventions of popular science strategies. My aim here is to demonstrate how Sayers turned that energy to her own distinctive ends. To explore the full range of what it might mean for Wimsey to 'go all Eddington' I turn first to the early newspaper jokes about Einstein and then to Sayers' use of Einstein and Eddington in *The Documents in the Case* (1930); this is followed by a discussion of the specific passage from Eddington cited in 'Absolutely Elsewhere', before looking in more detail at the story itself. I argue that Sayers, along with a range of journalists, critics and other literary authors, found it useful to dramatize the disjunction between physical law and human affairs by tangling them up and exploring the consequences. Commentators at the time and more recently have tended to regret (or celebrate) the conflation of relativity with, for instance, relativism and subjectivism. I want to suggest that the mixing up of relativity with moral or political themes enabled writers to test at once the scope of physical law and the desirability of various

---

[2]   Whitworth discusses cheap editions of *The Nature of the Physical World* (1996, 65–68) and reviews of the book (1996, 68; 2001, 46); on Eddington's radio presence see Beer (1996).

social, cultural or political forms more extensively than if they had refrained from such imaginative (mis)appropriation of science in the first place.

The Fourth Dimensions

The Einstein story broke on 7 November 1919, just four days before the first anniversary of the Armistice. While Einstein and others had been working on relativity theory for over a decade, it was the announcement of star measurements taken during an eclipse that made headline news.[3] A key feature of this initial coverage was the trouble that even the President of the Royal Society (a privately sceptical J. J. Thomson) had to confess in trying to explain the new theory in accessible terms. The sheer difficulty of relativity opened it up to multiple appropriations, and columnists seized upon bent light rays and strange geometry to address a range of current topics from the failings of Lloyd George's administration and the specter of Bolshevism to the England cricket team's less than brilliant performance. Such jokes ran alongside serious coverage of the scientific debate over relativity.

'Light Caught Bending' announced the *Daily Mail*, on the same page as the King's call for two minutes of silence, a report on the Motor Show at Olympia and the news that a giant turtle had been found strolling across the sands at Cleethorpes.[4] The following day the government's heavily reduced estimate for running the railways was revealed, an 'Arithmetic Extraordinary' that was 'as hard to understand as Einstein's Theory of Relativity, which it puzzled all the wise men of the Royal Society to explain on Thursday night' (Anon. 1919b, 6). Later that month the *Times* went in for a more elaborate burlesque on familiar themes from popular astronomy and fiction:

> Does the past continue to exist? FLAMMARION, who had a genius for stating ultimate problems in simple language, asked us to imagine an intelligent observer receding from the earth with the velocity of light. Suppose him to have set out on his journey from the House of

---

3 Sponsel (2002) discusses the relationship between British astronomers and the press in promoting these results.
4 'Light Caught Bending' is one of the headlines to catch Arthur Gideon's eye in Rose Macaulay's *Potterism* (1920); this is probably the first reference to Einstein's relativity in an English novel (Crawford 1995, 64).

Commons at the moment when the PRIME MINISTER was listening
to the second (the optimistic) edition of the speech by the
CHANCELLOR of the EXCHEQUER on the national finances. He
would carry through all eternity, towards the limitless recesses of
space, the bland smile of MR. LLOYD GEORGE. It is an appalling
thought! But imagine the journey to be faster than light. The
observer, as he receded, would see the events precedent to the smile,
the colloquy which doubtless led to the revision of the speech, the
reading of the first edition, which led to the colloquy, and many other
episodes which would be illuminating to ordinary mortals who have
to guess at the past from the present. We need not pursue our illustration or make a reconstruction, in the fashion of a popular novelist, of
the evolution of a great statesman from the primordial slime.

([Mitchell] 1919, 13)

Connoting H. G. Wells, the Cheshire cat's smile from *Alice in Wonder-
land*, the reverse induction of detective fiction and the cinematograph,
this piece is as much concerned with readers and reading as it is with
politics or science. The prospect of reverse evolution into the primordial slime invokes concerns about the unraveling of British history and
empire, a prospect associated here with the coalition Prime Minister.
Alfred Harmsworth (Lord Northcliffe from 1905), who had founded the
Daily Mail in 1896 and acquired the *Times* in 1908, had little affection
for Lloyd George but there is more than a simple jibe at work here; the
concatenation of literary and political reference helps to consolidate a
relationship between journalistic writing and public life whereby
reading the *Times* can deflect such visions. The shift from third person
designation of the faster-than-light traveller to first person plural differentiation of the column itself from popular fiction helps to establish a
space between science and fiction where this relationship can continue
to develop. Readers of the *Times* might be well versed in mathematics
and read any amount of popular fiction but, the story implies, they
needed something else besides. Changes in the fabric of the universe or
society could be accommodated so long as people kept reading the
Times to find out how the past and the future, the old and the new, were
related to one another. Across its columns during November 1919
readers would find letters celebrating the vindication of relativist
philosophy alongside scepticism about Einstein from the older generation of British physicists defending the ether; the very act of reading
these columns helped to establish continuity between different
outlooks, giving 'ordinary mortals' a rounded view of every important
topic. The work of scientists might indicate that a 'new philosophy' was

dawning, but only the *Times* could properly delineate its scope and significance.

Northcliffe's determination that his papers should provide the greatest quantity and variety of news took a different form in the *Daily Mail*.[5] Here, readers were presented with a survey of extraordinary and extreme phenomena – from the deviant behaviour of light to the London hotels overflowing with unprecedented numbers of motor show visitors. These were exposed in the columns of the *Mail*, at once exhibited and uncovered, as readers were implicitly invited to participate in drawing the line between good showmanship and fraud. Science might contribute new spectacles but was itself subject to scrutiny; the commentary on Lloyd George's railway budget simultaneously hinted at question about the 'wise men' of the Royal Society and their work: would the puzzling arithmetic expose nature's workings, or merely the limitations of their own knowledge? Where the *Times* used the difficulty of relativity to offer 'ordinary mortals' a greater scope of vision and understanding than the Royal Society alone could provide, the *Mail* used elusive understanding to underline the promise of future exposures. Each paper drew the relativity story into the service of its own news values.

Popular enthusiasm for relativity was not simply a 'response' to publicity: it was an integral feature of that publicity right from the start. Pre-emptive jokes about the abstruse theory's ubiquity could be used to defuse undesirable possibilities, as in a series of formulaic gags produced by the *Daily Sketch*:

Novel Possibilities in the 'Fourth Dimension.'

The new theory of Einstein, which everybody is talking about and nobody understands, appears to hold some mighty possibilities.

One of them, which will be speedily seized upon by youth, is that the hated Euclid may have been talking through his hat all these years about the parallel lines that never meet.

We can imagine the joy of the young boy who gets up in school and on conscientious grounds refuses to work out a discredited problem.

The criminal in the dock is now provided with a novel defence:

'Your angle of vision is distorted, me lord', he might say. 'I appear to you a crooked man, but let me tell you my 'angle of divergence' is so great that I am as straight as you.'

5   On Northcliffe's philosophy of news see Chalaby (2000, 29–33).

The Up-to-Date Defence.

'But what made you steal the diamonds?'

'Ah, there, my lord, we have an error in the fourth dimension.'

This same 'fourth dimension' is also a tricky customer. We are told that in certain circumstances a three-foot rule is really the same as a six-foot rule.

Imagine the plight of a man with £200 a year applying for a rise of salary to an employer who believes in Einstein.

'Have you considered your salary in the light of the fourth dimension?'

'No, sir.'

'Well do so, and you will find that £200 is really £400.'

And the happy father of twins who sees instead a fourth-dimensional quartette will probably set out to look for Einstein with a hammer. ('H. V. M.' 1919, 2)

Potential Bolshevist sympathies are deflected by making Einstein the target of violent action and mathematical wizardry the means of oppression, while conscientious objection is placed on a footing with classroom frustration and criminals are supplied with new puns rather than liberty. But whose side is Einstein really on? The fourth dimension is over-mobile, enlisted on the part of schoolboys, criminals and employers. This set of simple jokes shares a form with an argument subsequently put forward by Bertrand Russell in his *ABC of Relativity*: that because Einstein's theory may be enlisted in support of virtually any philosophy, it amounts to a support for none (Russell 1925, 220). Russell's view emerges in the context of his structuralist philosophy of science, but for *Sketch* readers the levelling of relativity's extrascientific possibilities serves to re-affirm the normal constraints of education, justice and employment. By toying with Einstein's 'new philosophy' each publication translated the dislocations of postwar society into a dislocation between cosmic and human affairs. Such encounters affirmed the service of newspapers to their readers while raising questions about what interests could or should be served by scientific theory.

Just as relativity's popularity was pre-empted, so was its resonance in literary culture. *Punch* exploited the fourth dimension's diverse possibilities, offering a revised couplet from *Hamlet* (quoted at the head of this essay) which was said to benefit from 'omission of the harsh and unseemly epithet "cursèd"' (Anon. 1919a, 442). Conceding that 'I know a bank where the wild fourth dimension grows' might seem 'at the first blush somewhat disconcerting', *Punch* urged appreciation of its 'more impressive and sonorous' qualities, suggesting that 'the new form of the phrase ... can be defended as a legitimate application of the principle of *vers libre*'. Adaptation of Watts' hymn to incorporate 'The fourth dimension, like an ever-rolling stream' might be 'difficult to reconcile with popular predilections ... but the task ... ought not to be beyond the powers of a great prosodist such as the present Poet Laureate'. There were limits to the extent of revision, however; readers were advised that 'for the present there is no intention on the part of Lord Northcliffe to change the title of his chief paper to *The Fourth Dimensions*'. The 'Einstein Upheaval' enabled *Punch* to affirm its satirical scope, levelling the cultural aspirations of Robert Bridges, Alfred Harmsworth and the exponents of free verse. Einstein's own contribution to the *Times* was followed by a full treatment of the 'Einsteinized' syndrome:

> I had been reading Dr. Einstein's article in the morning paper, and the train (as I deduced by an analytical mental process), apparently in disproof of the theory of perpetual motion, was retarding relatively to the platform. The station was teeming with moving mass points and my mind was alive with science as I propelled the door outwards.
>
> Grasping my bag I flew into space.
>
> Arriving at a fixed point and accelerating my speed through a system of co-ordinates in a high state of motion, I followed the deviation of light rays to the end of the spectrum, and deposited my bag in the place for inert and heavy masses. Satisfied with my calculations I placed myself in a stable rotation, when unfortunately, while theorising, I collided with an immovable object.
>
> He opened up a whole string of new theories.
>
> I gave a warp into space and landed on my basal principle. I've given up science. (Anon. 1919c, 498)

A double burlesque operates here, as this piece sends up in turn the newspaper trend for parodies of scientific exposition. Where the newspapers dramatized the absurd effect of Einsteinian thinking on ordinary life, thereby questioning its relevance, *Punch* exaggerates those effects while making them a direct result of reading the paper, hinting that it would be similarly absurd to live one's life according to what the papers say. Aspiration to higher forms of knowledge might not ultimately make much difference to the average train passenger but Punch will always be there to lampoon every scientific or literary pretension, in a satirical obverse of the continuities established through Northcliffe's 'chief paper'.

The effects of reading about Einstein in the papers were of pressing concern to literary authors whose relationship with the reading public was often uncertain. Relativity entered literature as a newspaper phenomenon first and a scientific theory second, as the example of Rose Macaulay's *Potterism* testifies.[6] Steinman (1987) and Whitworth (2001) have explored the engagement with relativity by American and British literary modernists respectively, focusing on the publications and communities through which ideas about science and technology circulated and the significance of those ideas in terms of metaphor, audience and literary form. In her epistolary novel *The Documents in the Case* (1930), Sayers made a direct address to Einstein as a newspaper phenomenon, problematizing his theory not for its popular manifestations, aesthetic qualities or commodity status but for the ways in which the circulation of popular and specialist knowledge about the new theory was related to sexual identity. The combined ubiquity and incomprehensibility of Einstein's theory is drawn into the service of the murder plot's underlying debate about marriage.

'A copulation of politic tape-worms'

The Documents in the Case exploits the full range of responses to relativity that would have been available to non-mathematical readers through newspapers and magazines from 1919 onwards. While Sayers' collaborator 'Robert Eustace' (Eustace Barton) furnished her with medical, chemical and psychiatric details, the novel's preoccupation with cosmology stems from her own reading of Eddington.[7] Margaret Harrison has been reading about Einstein in the Sunday paper, and her failed attempt to engage her husband in conversation on the topic is presented by Aggie Milsom, her paid companion, as yet another example of 'the calm assumption of superiority that a man puts on when he is talking to a woman' (Sayers and Eustace 1973, 12). George Harrison's insistence that Einstein is 'a charlatan who was pulling people's legs with his theories' places him firmly in the nineteenth century, an outlook that is confirmed by his verdict on 'the virtues of the old-fashioned domestic woman and the perpetual chatter of the modern woman about things which were outside her province', as Aggie relates to her sister (13). Another Einstein conversation ensues when the upstairs tenants, artist Harwood Lathom and writer Jack Munting, are invited to tea. Writing to his fiancée, Munting reports his initial 'social charm' in

6   See note 4 above.
7   On Eustace Barton and Sayers see Reynolds (1993, 213–24).

voicing the schoolboy's delight in finding that 'straight lines were really curly … because it would have annoyed the geometry master so much'; but on realizing that his hostess has chosen the topic for some purpose of her own he more 'guardedly' ventures that 'the theory was now generally accepted by mathematicians, though with very many reserves' (26). Margaret Harrison's gushing enthusiasm against 'deadening … materialism' is mischievously countered by Munting's observation that 'you are *really* only made up of large lumps of space, loosely tied together with electricity', and her protest elicits a retort from her husband in the name of 'common sense', which she sweeps aside in an appeal to 'poetry and imagination and the beautiful things of the mind … the only true realities after all'.

This shift from curly straight lines to lumps of space helps to locate the Einstein conversation in the late 1920s, connoting the debates around materialism in which Eddington's *Nature of the Physical World* became a familiar reference point. In congenial opposition to materialism is the parson, Perry, who believes that relativity has made his job 'much easier' (27), a view subsequently elaborated when Munting learns that he is 'thankful to find that the scientists would at last allow him to believe what the Church taught' (35). Inclined at first to class this as 'the usual shifty ecclesiastical clap-trap', Munting is impressed enough by Perry's Cambridge mathematics degree and his reading of 'Eddington … Jeans and Japp and one or two other fantastic scientists whose names I had never heard of' to enlist the parson's help in working out the sections on Victorian materialism for a biography he is writing. The authenticity of Perry's outlook is affirmed by T. S. Eliot's verdict, broadcast two years after the publication of *Documents*, on 'the popular attitude of hailing modern physical science as a *support* of religion', an attitude he found 'very misguided' (Eliot 1932, 429). Maintaining that 'no scientific discovery influences people either for or against revealed religion', Eliot regretted the 'uncritical attitude of the public' towards writers such as Eddington and Jeans, 'an attitude shared, I am sorry to say, sometimes by theological writers who ought to know better'. Materialistic science had not destroyed religion in the first place, he argued; it was only 'our preference of unbelief' that had made 'illegitimate use of science'. Eliot was not alone in adopting a 'separationist position' with regard to the relations between science and religion; Whitworth has shown that the 'separation of all science from cultural, philosophical and theological questions' became an increasingly prominent theme throughout the 1930s, often in direct response to the writings of Eddington and James Jeans (2001, 54–57). But the example of Sayers points to a contrasting strategy of differentiation, where scientific themes are brought into closer proximity with belief and conduct only to have their bearing on these issues subjected to deeper questioning. In the work of writers as divergent as Dorothy Sayers and William Empson, who were prepared to entertain 'misguided' relationships between mathematical science and human affairs, the separation of relativity from moral, spiritual or social questions was harder won and more nuanced for their having seriously entertained a connection between them.[8]

In *Documents* Sayers flirts with relativity as relativism under the name of Einstein, as a way to open up questions about how men and women can be on equal terms with one another. The type of support each character obtains for their opinion on the significance of Einstein is directly related to their sexual identity. Margaret Harrison is dismissed by her husband and teased by Munting (she 'frowned attractively' at the 'lumps of space' remark) but ultimately finds solidarity with Lathom through sexual attraction masquerading as aesthetic debate; Munting and Perry find terms through the younger man's recognition of his elder's learning; George Harrison invokes '[m]y friend Professor Alcock' in support of his own dismissive opinion (Sayers and Eustace 1973, 26). Narratorless, the bundle of correspondence exposes each character's assumptions and blindnesses, while giving the reader grounds for sympathy with each of them. The parson's outlook, with which Sayers undoubtedly concurred, is subjected along with every other argument to the relativizing effect of the novel's form. Yet *Documents* only adopts the form of relativism to disavow it. There is a valid answer to the murder case, just as there will be preferred answers to questions about marriage and materialism, and the dramatization of multiple perspectives helps to engage the reader in the search for satisfactory solutions. As the plot develops, the characteristically 'modern' ability to see every side to a question is itself put under pressure. The relationship between John Munting and Elizabeth Drake is represented as a bold attempt at a frank and free partnership, in contrast to the cramping misery of the Harrisons' marriage. But the artist Harwood Lathom casts doubt upon the ability of human creatures to truly see beyond their own selfish concerns. Writing to Munting, he suggests that the pair may be

> Gods, probably – with that dreadful temperateness of the knowledge of good and evil, seeing two sides to every question. You will analyse

---

[8] I have discussed two of Empson's relativity poems in Price 2005 and 2007.

your bridal raptures, if you have any, and find the whole subject very interesting. You will have, Heaven help you! a sense of humour about the business, and your friends will say how beautiful it is to see such a fine sense of partnership between a man and a woman. A copulation of politic tape-worms! But where is the use of my being offensive to a man who will allow for my point of view? I hate being allowed for, as if I were an incalculable quantity in an astronomical equation.

(Sayers and Eustace 1973, 56)

Munting proposes to take refuge from the disarray caused by Lathom's suburban affair with Margaret Harrison by reading 'astronomy or physics or something' (60), but finds that thinking about the finite universe, time's arrow and the disintegrating atom do not ultimately help resolve the question of how to conduct his own personal or professional life; as he writes to his fiancée, 'Our own immediate affairs are as important as the loves of the electrons in this universe of infinitesimal immensities' (67). Lines that sound as though they have come from popular science books are drawn into the novel's debate about marriage, helping to establish a tension between messy human passions and cold abstraction.

The names 'Einstein' and 'Eddington' serve slightly different functions in relation to this tension. While 'the Einstein topic' stimulates and signals divergence of outlook across the novel's *personae*, references to Eddington accompany moments of more measured individual reflection, as when Munting wonders to his fiancée whether 'Eddington and those people are right in supposing that we are rather a freak sort of planet, with quite unusual facilities for being inhabited, and that space is a sort of cosy little thing which God could fold up and put in his pocket' (25). Sayers begins her novel by appropriating the social satire of journalistic misapplication of cosmology to society, using the Einstein coverage to provoke dissent between outlooks and underline the need for an adjustment to traditional sex relations; she then invokes the vulnerability of Eddington's 'freak sort of planet' to signal the possibility of a return from the cosmological to the human scale, on renewed terms.

Sayers' own letters indicate the respect she held for Eddington's worldview and his writing style. She urged her son to read *The Nature of the Physical World* when he was fourteen years old (Sayers 1997, 87), and enjoyed the way that reading Eddington 'enlarges and disorientates the mind' (Sayers 1998, 338). In her Royal Institution lecture on Dante she sent a posthumous Eddington back in time for a meeting with the poet, producing an engaging pastiche of the expository dialogue form that was designed to illuminate affinities between the medieval and the twen-

tieth century world view (Sayers 1957, 78–85). But in her fiction Sayers
set Eddington's anti-materialist outlook to work on the sex question,
voicing flippant comments drawn from his writings through male characters as part of her concerted attempt to find a workable form of modern
marriage. Wimsey's Eddington moment is shaped by this search, in ways
that become evident when we look more closely at its source in the
'Time' chapter of *The Nature of the Physical World*.

'She will have to think of you continuously for eight hours on end'

Throughout *The Nature of the Physical World*, which began as a series of
Gifford Lectures at Edinburgh in 1927, Eddington was concerned to
dispel the apparent contradiction between relativity theory and
common sense. 'Your protest in the name of commonsense against a
mixing of time and space is a feeling which I desire to encourage', he
asserted early in his third chapter, agreeing wholeheartedly that '[t]ime
and space ought to be separated' (Eddington 1928, 37). Explaining that
what happens 'Now' will vary according to the reckoning of different
observers (the relativity of simultaneity), he stressed that the 'Absolute
Future' and 'Absolute Past' were very much a part of the Einsteinian
picture. 'The common impression that relativity turns past and future
altogether topsy turvy is quite false', he insisted (48). Eddington's aim in
this discussion was to show that the familiar conception (with three
dimensions of space enduring through time) actually relied on an
unhelpful jumbling of time and space, and that Einstein's theory had
shown how to separate them more deeply. 'Come back with me into the
virginal four-dimensional world' he invited his reader, 'and we will carve
it anew on a plan which keeps them entirely distinct' (37–38). Wimsey's
'absolutely elsewhere' is discovered during this voyage into the virginal.

What follows is a series of diagrams populated by lines and circles,
leading step by step away from the familiar location of events in time and
space, with its false absolutes, and towards the more reliable four-
dimensional picture. Noting that different observers with different
velocities relative to one another will disagree about what is happening
Now, Eddington explains that two observers passing close to one
another will at least agree on what is 'Seen-Now' (47). They will also
agree on which events lie in the Absolute Future; such events may be
reached by any observer from Here-Now, 'since the required velocity is
less than that of light' (50). Events that could only be reached by
observers from Here-Now by travelling faster than light are considered

to be 'absolutely Elsewhere'; these events inhabit a 'neutral zone' in Eddington's diagram, a 'wedge' that is Elsewhere to all observers from Here-Now.

To illustrate, Eddington invites his reader to imagine that they have fallen 'in love with a Lady on Neptune and that she returns the sentiment' (49). It will, he suggests,

> be some consolation for the melancholy separation if you can say to yourself at some – possibly prearranged moment, 'She is thinking of me now.' Unfortunately a difficulty has arisen because we have had to abolish Now. There is no absolute Now, but only the various relative Nows differing according to the reckoning of different observers and covering the whole neutral wedge which at the distance of Neptune is about eight hours thick. She will have to think of you continuously for eight hours on end in order to circumvent the ambiguity of 'Now'. … From this point of view the 'nowness' of an event is like a shadow cast by it into space, and the longer the event the farther will the umbra of the shadow extend.

The shadow of Now cast into space by the Lady on Neptune's eight hour vigil turns romance into a hard day's work with no prospect of physical intimacy, giving it a funereal quality and hinting that it may be safer to remain out of the shadow's reach. When Eddington reaches for organic metaphors to help transcend divergent outlooks and affirm the common sense of the new absolutes, the same sense of vulnerability attends the newly reconstituted self and world in four dimensions. He represents the world as a pig and the (male) human self as 'a kind of four-dimensional worm', with 'considerable extension towards the Past and presumably towards the Future, and only a moderate extension towards Elsewhere' (42). Insisting that 'to think of a man without his duration is just as abstract as to think of a man without his inside', he argues that our familiar acquaintance with 'the section of the worm (the man Now)' is an arbitrary construct, an abstraction that 'is made differently by different observers'. It is in forming these arbitrary abstractions that the FitzGerald contraction, invoked by the exasperated Parker in 'Absolutely Elsewhere', plays a part. Eddington looks beyond the effects of this contraction to emphasize the 'non-abstract man enduring through time', the 'common source from which the different abstractions are made' (53).

The clinical abstraction implied by a 'section of the worm' carries a violent undertone thanks to a preceding analogy between the four-dimensional world and a butchered pig:

We have been accustomed to regard the world – the enduring world – as *stratified* into a succession of instantaneous states. But an observer on another star would make the strata run in a different direction from ours. We shall see more clearly the real mechanism of the physical world if we can rid our minds of this illusion of stratification. The world that then stands revealed, through strangely unfamiliar, is actually much simpler. There is a difference between simplicity and familiarity. A pig may be most familiar to us in the form of rashers, but the unstratified pig is a simpler object to the biologist who wishes to understand how the animal functions. (47)

Two competing visions of science are offered through these analogies: the slicing of a living creature into sections is a familiar habit that we are asked to discard in favor of a 'simpler' view that reaches beyond individual perspective to view the living, enduring being. In moving from the former to the latter, Eddington's exposition is carefully balanced between fostering relativity (between individual reference frames or ways of slicing) while minimizing relativism (with regard to the choice between rashers and wholeness). Through his analogies of slicing, shadows, and separated lovers, the 'Time' chapter resonates with mutilation and estrangement in postwar Europe, as does the argument about competing schemes for carving up the world (Eddington is tellingly silent on the Absolute Past, leaving readers to infer it for themselves from his definition of the Absolute Future). The old scheme seemed natural and universal, but it relied on arbitrary distinctions; the new scheme may be unfamiliar and difficult to inhabit but it offers a restored and more reliable, far-reaching sense of unity. A committed Quaker and conscientious objector, Eddington minimized relativism in order to promote a science that needed to be in contact with other modes of experience to be meaningful.[9]

In later chapters of *The Nature of the Physical World* Eddington argued for severe limits to the scope of physical law and sought to establish spiritual experience as an equally valid approach to 'the hard facts of experience' (289). Sayers' allusion to Eddington in 'Absolutely Elsewhere' is unusual among literary appropriations of Eddington (including *The Documents in the Case*) in that it ignores the ultimate message of his best-selling exposition, a message that Sayers herself found convincing and important. Wimsey (unlike Parker) has no religious commitments, giving Sayers occasion to produce a rare example of literary engagement

---

[9] On the relationship between Eddington's faith and his science, see Beer (1995), Stanley (2003) and Stanley (2007).

with *The Nature of the Physical World* through its more technical language. In this vacuum of belief the analogies and anecdotes surrounding Eddington's discussion of 'absolutely Elsewhere' carry an implicit sense of painful disjunction between mathematical physics and human interaction. Such disjunction was used by the newspapers to consolidate readership, and by Eddington to promote the need for spiritual experience to be recognized; but Sayers' characters are made to dwell in this discomfiting state. In *Documents* the problems of intimacy and communication are established though textual means: newspapers, popular science books, letters and book manuscripts. In 'Absolutely Elsewhere' isolation and disorientation are more subtly diffused through the domestic details essential to the murder plot of a short fiction.

'An expensive little item'

What does it mean for Wimsey to 'go all Eddington'? Towards the end of 'Absolutely Elsewhere' the household and police await Wimsey's promised telephone call from London, over forty miles away. Parker goes into the hall to take the call and, following an exchange about car licence plates, is instructed to return to the dining room:

> As he entered the room, he got an instantaneous impression of six people, sitting as he had left them, in an expectant semi-circle, their eyes strained towards the french windows. Then the library door opened noiselessly and Lord Peter Wimsey walked in. 'Good God!' exclaimed Parker, involuntarily. 'How did you get here?' The six heads jerked round suddenly.
> 'On the back of the light waves', said Wimsey, smoothing back his hair. 'I have travelled eighty miles to be with you, at 186,000 miles a second.' (Sayers 1934a, 195)

It is essential to the story's genre that Wimsey has not physically travelled at the speed of light: this is detective fiction, not supernatural or science fiction. It is in his mind – and, until the denouement, the minds of his audience – that Wimsey is able to reach the limits of physical law: a marker of his class and education, and of his unconventional methods of deduction. In asking him not to 'go all Eddington', Parker cajoles Wimsey into focusing on material facts rather than highbrow theoretical science.[10]

10 On Eddington and the BBC's 1930 'highbrowism' debate see Beer (1996, 163–64).

The investigation in 'Absolutely Elsewhere' centres on the service of
Grimbold's last meal and its interruption by a telephone call from his
nephews in London. Wimsey and Parker begin with Hamworthy the
butler, 'whose spherical curvature', the reader learns directly from the
narrator, 'was certainly worthy of consideration' (185). In addressing
this point directly to the reader Sayers tacitly places Hamworthy in the
category of those who have not tried to read Eddington. From Parker's
comments we gather that he has himself looked at *The Nature of the
Physical World*, but his recollection of the text may be less detailed than
that of Wimsey, whose remarks follow Eddington's attempt to convey
the relativity of time quite closely. In his exasperation Parker mixes up a
term used in that section ('Fitzgerald contraction') with the 'coefficient
of spherical curvature', used later when Eddington turns to Einstein's law
of gravitation (Eddington 1928, 120). These distinctions between
different levels of familiarity with Eddington's text connote the amount
of leisure time available to each character and the ways they may choose
to fill it. As with Wimsey's Piccadilly flat his reading habits function as a
status symbol that the reader is likely to appreciate rather than feel alien-
ated by. The rotund butler inhabits a social 'elsewhere' enabling Sayers
to create an understanding between her readers and her protagonist,
mediated by Parker.

Hamworthy gives an elaborate account of his master's last, unfinished
meal, which is interrupted first by the telephone and then by the door-
bell, during which interval the killer strikes. First Neville Grimbold, the
nephew calling from London, tells the butler that his brother Harcourt
wants to speak with him; then Harcourt comes on to say that he is
coming to visit his uncle that night. During the call, the grandfather
clock in the nephews' Jermyn Street flat is heard striking eight; then
Neville comes back on to ask for various items of country clothing to be
cleaned and sent to him as he prepares to travel to Scotland. During this
conversation a visitor rings twice at the front door of 'The Lilacs', but
Hamworthy is saved from interrupting Neville's instructions when he
hears Cook going to answer the door. The telephone call is also interrupted at three minute intervals by the Exchange and is renewed twice,
making it 'an expensive little item' (192).

These multiple layers of interruption to the dinner show traditional
service roles compounded and stretched by the rushed and simultaneous
demands of modern life, with its expensive telephone calls and
long-distance travel on a whim. Through the telephone system, urban
places and voices are simultaneously present at Grimbold's country
home, and each is associated with measuring time: the Exchange with its

three-minute intervals and the London flat with its grandfather clock. It is significant that the clock at The Lilacs is heard striking immediately afterwards, so that the two are not perfectly synchronized: a familiar theme from relativity exposition is used to signal that we are in a world of human interaction and not the idealized realm of geometry. At the end of the story, mimicking the murderer's trick with the aid of his manservant Bunter, Wimsey demonstrates just how easy it is to sound as though one is forty miles away in London while simply joining the London line by lifting the receiver of a another telephone in the house. During the call, a clock at the London residence must strike the hour as 'proof' of one's bodily location. Wimsey, following the example of Harcourt Grimbold, has been speaking into the telephone set in the library at 'The Lilacs'. Early in the story it is established that the library telephone does not need to go through the set in the hall to get an outside line; Wimsey explains at the end that Harcourt's voice in the library really 'was coming from London, because, as the 'phones are connected in parallel, it could only come by way of the Exchange' (196). Special relativity, with its emphasis on simultaneity, was developed in the context of Einstein's work assessing patents for the synchronization of clocks; thanks to Sayers' faithful recording of apparently mundane material details, the story tacitly acknowledges the communication technologies on which the formulation and exposition of modern physics depended.[11] By exposing our faith in what our senses absorb from these technologies, Wimsey is able to expose the murderer and uphold the law; he needed to 'go all Eddington' in order to work out precisely how the murderer's movements were not at all 'Eddington', but were instead confined to everyday time and space. He ventures into the world of geometrical abstraction, mixing human affairs up with mathematical physics, in order to reestablish order in the everyday world of money lenders, cooks and butlers.

The Eddington reference can best fulfil this function when it is separated from the debates around materialism; in contrast to his role in *Documents*, Eddington is used here more for his language and the sheer technicality of his exposition than for the ideas that his name had come to stand for. The function of the allusion is closer to that served by the earlier relativity jokes in newspapers; like the criminal's answer in the *Daily Sketch*, Wimsey's explanation to the amazed audience invokes the abstruse theory only to reaffirm its distance from the ordinary order of

11 On Einstein and clock synchronization see Galison (2003).

things. But in contrast to the news values serviced by Einstein and relativity in the newspapers, the social values explored in Sayers' fiction are questioned rather than affirmed by the references to 'Fitzgerald contraction' and 'spherical curvature', for the stability of life at 'The Lilacs' cannot be regained following the revelation of the telephone trick. In the story's American publication as 'Impossible Alibi', instead of saying 'don't go all Eddington' Parker simply retorted 'be reasonable' (Sayers 1934b, 19). Without Eddington's name, the technical terminology tends to connote highbrow reading habits in a fairly straightforward way. But for British readers of *Strand Magazine* who shared at least Parker's level of familiarity with *The Nature of the Physical World*, the inclusion of Eddington's name had the potential to locate the murder of William Grimbold in a postwar society where intimacy between men and women is impossible and bodies are only just held together. The end of the story leaves us with bachelor loves poised on the verge of separation from society: the nephews will go to prison or be hanged; Hamworthy no longer has a job or a place to live; Wimsey will, presumably go back to his flat and take refuge in Eddington as a diversion from the pain of bringing another man to the gallows; Parker's romance with Wimsey's sister may or may not be underway, for the story's date in relation to Wimsey's timeline is uncertain. The only female character apart from the cook is Mrs Winter, Grimbold's mistress living in Paris whose vicious alcoholic husband has recently died. Harcourt confirms that she and his uncle were probably about to marry and Wimsey deduces that the murder has been precipitated by the prospect of a change in Grimbold's will. The lady returning from Paris/Neptune, liberated at last from the vigil of an abusive marriage, ironically triggers an end to the only prospect of intimacy contained within the story.

Given the coded form of terms such as 'Fitzgerald contraction' and 'coefficients of spherical curvature' – a language that is understood between selected bachelor characters – the tendency for a man to 'go all Eddington' signals a homosocial existence in which ladies are kept at a distance and wartime experience undermines coherence of the self.[12] Wimsey's indulgence in Eddington enables him to inhabit this lonely and painful condition with characteristic humour; in the process Wimsey does a service to Eddington, for through him Sayers teases the science writer's highbrow status while using Parker to establish a knowing bond between technical terminology and her readership. In

[12] On male hysteria and 'homosexual economy' in the Wimsey stories, see Plain (1996, 45–67).

'Absolutely Elsewhere' mathematical physics may not apply directly to human affairs, but the prospect of inhabiting a four-dimensional world helps to clarify what is needed to get along in everyday circumstances. Even without the mysticism of his later chapters, Eddington represents the hope of a return from abstract theory to warm bodies, and the need for readers and lovers to find ways of living in the shadow of nowness.

Works Cited

Anon. 1919a, 'The Einstein Upheaval', *Punch*, 26 November: 442.

Anon. 1919b, 'Arithmetic Extraordinary', *Daily Mail*, 8 November: 6.

Anon. 1919c, 'Einsteinized', *Punch*, 10 December: 498.

Beer, G., 1995. 'Eddington and the Idiom of Modernism', in *Science, Reason, and Rhetoric*, ed. Henry Krips, J. E. McGuire and Trevor Melia. Pittsburgh: University of Pittsburgh Press: 295–315.

———, 1996. ' "Wireless": Popular Physics, Radio and Modernism', in *Cultural Babbage: Technology, Time and Invention*, ed. Francis Spufford and Jenny Uglow. London: Faber: 149–166.

Chalaby, J., 2000. 'Northcliffe: Proprietor as Journalist', in *Northcliffe's Legacy: Aspects of the British Popular Press, 1896–1996*, ed. Peter Catterall, Colin Seymour-Ure and Adrian Smith. Basingstoke: Macmillan: 27–44.

Crawford, A. 1995. *Paradise Pursued: The Novels of Rose Macaulay*. Madison: Fairleigh Dickinson University Press.

Eddington, A. S., 1928. *The Nature of the Physical World*. Cambridge: Cambridge University Press.

———, 1939. *The Philosophy of Physical Science*. Cambridge: Cambridge University Press.

Eliot, T. S., 1932. 'Religion and Science: A Phantom Dilemma', *The Listener*, 23 March: 428–29.

Galison, P., 2003. *Einstein's Clocks, Poincaré's Maps*. London: Hodder and Stoughton.

' H. V. M.', 1919. 'Euclid Up-to-Date', *Daily Sketch*, 10 November: 2.

Macaulay, R., 1920. *Potterism: A Tragi-farcical Tract*. London: Collins.

[Mitchell, Peter Chalmers], 1919. 'The Past and the Future', *The Times*, 22 November: 13.

Plain, G., 1996. *Women's Fiction of the Second World War: Gender, Power and Resistance*. Edinburgh: Edinburgh University Press.

Price, K., 2005. 'Flame far too hot: William Empson's non-Euclidean Predicament', *Interdisciplinary Science Reviews* 30: 312–22.

———, 2007. 'Monogamy and the Next Step? Empson and the Future of Love in Einstein's Universe', in *Some Versions of Empson*, ed. Matthew Bevis. Oxford: Oxford University Press: 242–63.

Reynolds, B., 1993. *Dorothy L. Sayers: Her Life and Soul*. London: Hodder & Stoughton.

Russell, B., 1925. *The ABC of Relativity*. London: Kegan Paul.

Sayers, D. L., 1934a. 'Absolutely Elsewhere', *The Strand Magazine*, February: 185–96.

———, 1934b. 'Impossible Alibi', *Mystery: The Illustrated Detective Magazine*, January: 19–21, 104, 106, 108.

———, 1957. *Further Papers on Dante*. London: Methuen.

——— and R. Eustace 1973 (1930). *The Documents in the Case*. London: New English Library.

———, 1997. *The Letters of Dorothy L. Sayers*, ed. Barbara Reynolds. Vol. 2, *From Novelist to Playwright: 1937–1943*. Cambridge: Dorothy L. Sayers Society.

———, 1998. *The Letters of Dorothy L. Sayers*, ed. Barbara Reynolds. Vol. 3, *A Noble Daring: 1944–1950*. Cambridge: Dorothy L. Sayers Society.

Sponsel, A., 2002. 'Constructing a 'revolution in science': The Campaign to Promote a Favourable Reception for the 1919 Solar Eclipse Experiments', *British Journal for the History of Science* 35: 439–67.

Stanley, M., 2003. ' "An Expedition to Heal the Wounds of War": The 1919 Eclipse and Eddington as Quaker Adventurer', *Isis* 94: 57–89.

———, 2007. *Practical Mystic: Religion, Science, and A. S. Eddington*. Chicago: Chicago University Press.

Stebbing, L. S., 1937. *Philosophy and the Physicists*. London: Methuen.

Steinman, L. M., 1987. *Made in America: Science, Technology and American Modernist Poetics*. New Haven: Yale University Press.

Whitworth, M. H., 1996. 'The Clothbound Universe: Popular Physics Books, 1919–39', *Publishing History* 40: 53–82.

———, 2001. *Einstein's Wake: Relativity, Metaphor, and Modernist Literature*. Oxford: Oxford University Press.

Le Fanu's 'Carmilla', Ireland, and Diseased Vision

MARTIN WILLIS

JOSEPH SHERIDAN LE FANU's vampire narrative 'Carmilla' (1872) has come to prominence through two seemingly very different scholarly endeavors in the last twenty-five years. The first is Irish studies, given impetus by W. J. McCormack's (1980) political and literary biography of Le Fanu, which has sought to revisit Irish and Anglo-Irish literary history utilizing a historicist political methodology. The second is gothic studies, which has given 'Carmilla' a position of some esteem as a short story that can very profitably be examined by recourse to emerging theories of gender and sexuality. Recently, these two fields of study have moved closer together, generating a series of books and articles on the subject of Irish gothic, again led by McCormack (1998), and followed by Declan Kiberd (2000) and Richard Haslam (2007).

The role of science remains undeveloped, however, in both Irish and gothic studies and there has been no substantial analysis of its importance in Le Fanu's 'Carmilla'. It would be commonplace to state that 'Carmilla' is a narrative of infection – a good deal of the criticism of vampire fictions would point to the metaphors of disease that Le Fanu employs – and uncontentious to point out that Irishness was often equated with disease and contagion. Yet there has been no critical assessment of Le Fanu's 'Carmilla' as an Anglo-Irish fiction that particularly examines theories of disease and their relationship to the cultural politics of Ireland.

It is the purpose of the present article to revisit 'Carmilla' in light of this absence, to consider the story as an important articulation of the intersection of Victorian disease theories with Anglo-Irish ethnicity that reveals how entwined were science and politics in the Victorian cultural imagination. The article therefore has two aims: first, to offer a new way of considering 'Carmilla' that interrogates its status as a gothic and Irish fiction; second, to argue that in the study of literature and science, science never remains unadulterated when it enters the public sphere, and that public understandings of science, as well as misunderstandings, are just as much a part of *science* as the theoretical and experimental work of the scientist. To these ends, the article will interweave its discussion of the fictional narrative, disease, and Irish political and cultural history, offering, it is to be hoped, suggestive cross-correspondences that illuminate Le Fanu's contribution to Victorian gothic and the Irish question.

How, then, in the broadest terms, does 'Carmilla' represent disease and Ireland? Certainly the narrative's vocabulary invites a medical reading: the evolution of the story's vampirism is littered with both medical terminology and specific medical images. The narrator and central protagonist, Laura, situates her victimization by the vampiric Carmilla within prevailing discourses on infection. She describes her declining health as similar to the 'mysterious complaint' (Le Fanu 1993, 279) suffered by the local working classes, and imagines that Carmilla has 'been stricken with the strange epidemic that ... had invaded the country' (Le Fanu 1993, 274). Laura's father, dismissive of the existence of vampires, regards local superstition as an 'infect[ion]' (Le Fanu 1993, 269) and employs medical expertise – two doctors – to restore Laura's health. By the conclusion of the story Carmilla's death is likened to ridding the land of a plague (Le Fanu 1993, 315–16). Further, the importance placed on sight – most importantly on how one can or cannot *see* the vampire and its effects – parallel common mid-Victorian medical discourses on the discoveries of infection by microscopic observation and methods of social surveillance and control.

The narrative's Irishness is less well developed through specifically prescribed discourses. Indeed there is nothing explicitly Irish about the story at all. Yet the placing of the events in Styria is suggestive of an implicit Irish context. As Matthew Gibson (2006) has shown, Styria might well be read as a transposed Ireland; its own politics of Protestant and Catholic conflict and colonial intervention similar to Ireland's political and religious history. Added to that is the more circumstantial evidence of various critical commentators that Le Fanu's English publisher demanded non-Irish settings for his work, and that almost all of Le Fanu's fiction can be seen as Irish-inflected even when superficially unconnected to Ireland. Equally important is that 'Carmilla' includes many tropes regarded as particular to the genre of Irish gothic: the employment of traditions of folklore and superstition (the vampire and responses to it), the central symbol of the grand house (Laura's father's 'feudal residence' [Le Fanu 1993, 244]), and the sexualized Irish female figure (Carmilla). It is possible, perhaps even probable, that alert contemporary readers of 'Carmilla' performed a simple geographical substitution of Styria for Ireland and read the story as an examination of the

Anglo-Irish, albeit with the added gothic frisson of Eastern European exoticism.

Disease and Ethnicity

'Carmilla' draws on two existing theories of disease in its imaginative composition of vampiric infection. By 1870, the date of the story's conception, theories of disease were evolving slowly towards what would become germ theory, heralding the beginning of the bacteriological era. The dominant paradigms of disease and infection in 1870, however, were characterized by two opposing positions: contagionist and anticontagionist (or miasmatist).

Contagionists believed that infectious diseases were passed from one person to another through close contact or touch. Diseases, they argued, produced similar effects on the human body as the processes of fermentation did on liquids – where there began an agitation of fluid that could escape its immediate surroundings and come into contact with another body. Contagionism could claim to be closer to a scientific orthodoxy in the first half of the nineteenth century, due largely to its status as a venerable scientific belief. As Erwin Ackerknecht has shown, 'contagion and the contagium animatum were rather old theories around 1800' (Ackerknecht 1984, 564). Certainly a writer on disease like Edward Bancroft, member of the Royal College of Surgeons, physician to the British Army and at St George's Hospital, could discuss contagion in an 1811 work on Yellow Fever as though it were a long established theory: 'are all fevers naturally contagious', he speculates, or might it be possible that they are 'generated, by an accumulation of filth' (Bancroft 1811, 87–88). It is clear from Bancroft's prose, especially his rather incredulous 'might it be' when speaking of filth, that contagion is the more acceptable proposition within medical science.

Contagionist strategies of disease management tended to focus on the individual: 'physicians tended to assume that most medical diseases had internal and often spontaneous origins, hence they only thought of external factors as predisposing rather than exciting causes' (Worboys 2000, 193). Any attempts at containment therefore began with the containment of the individual believed to be contagious. Quarantine was the most widely used state practice designed to contain the spread of contagious diseases (Maglen, 2001). Yet quarantine caused great disruption both for the individual and for communities and their socioeconomic progress. Indeed as most points of quarantine existed at natural borders, say between land and sea, trading ports and other places of economic importance were far more likely to suffer the economic conse-quences of contagionist theory. There was also a price to pay for any individual whose social identity fell within contagionism's range of suspicion. Foreign sailors and travellers, British seamen who had returned from abroad, and port prostitutes, all fell within that range. The body of the other therefore becomes the prime site of disease: be that the visible foreignness of the sailor or the invisible, but presumed, pollution of the prostitute.

Such sanctions against the individual or the small community ran against the grain of a liberal Victorian Britain that valued 'the concerns of affected individuals' more highly than 'the public weal' (Baldwin 1999, 563). This led to serious and sustained opposition to contagionist practices, of which the opposition to the Contagious Diseases Act is the most prominent. There was another reason for opposition to contagionism. The apparently random nature of contagious disease – which disconnected it from other causes such as poverty and urban deprivation – meant that little was done to effect change in those places where disease commonly struck. As Charles Rosenberg has argued, 'con-tagion seemed morally random and thus a denial of the traditional assumptions that both health and disease arose from particular states of moral and social order' (Rosenberg 1979, 117). Contagion, therefore, promoted a democracy of disease that denied the relevance of any form of social inequity.

Anticontagionists, or miasmatists, found this an anathema to their project of social regeneration. The anticontagionist position on disease was that infection was the product of environmental factors such as contaminated water, foul air and poor hygienic conditions. Denying that diseases were contagious in any way, they believed that exposure to an environment predisposed to disease because of its putrid air or water supply, its inappropriate drainage and bad smells, its lack of light or ventilation, gave rise to vapours that penetrated the human body and caused infection. Such infection was not passed between individuals but would affect individuals who resided within the particular locale that gave rise to such vapours. Those holding to this position were known as miasmatists because the root of many of their beliefs arose from early scientific analyses of diseases seemingly caused by marsh miasmatas such as malaria.

By far the most persuasive and authoritive voice in defence of anticontagionism was that of sanitary science. From the 1830s sanitary science became increasingly influential in opposing contagionist arguments and promoting practical anticontagionism. Contagionism, as far as the sanitarians were concerned, did a great deal of harm to the health of Victorian Britain by continually refusing to accept that the predis-posing character of the environment led to an increase in infectious disease. Early sanitarians such as Edwin Chadwick were supported by disease experts like Southwood Smith and hospital managers such as Florence Nightingale, both of whom were leading figures of the sani-tarian movement. In 1830 Smith published *A Treatise on Fever*, his manifesto for anticontagionism. In this work he argued that 'the imme-diate, or the exciting cause of fever is a poison formed by the corruption or the decomposition of organic matter' (Smith 1830, 349). Such decomposition leads to 'a new compound' which 'produces the phenomena constituting fever' (Smith 1830, 349). This new compound is most infective when it is 'formed by exhalations given off from the living bodies of those who are affected with fever, especially when such exhalations are pent up in a close and confined apartment' (Smith 1830, 364). Here was a theory of disease to challenge contagionism. Indeed Smith even offered a reason for the contagionists' mistaken belief in the contagious, diseased individual. What they believed was a contagious disease, Smith argued was actually a particularly potent compound arising from environmental conditions and carried by individuals suffering from the fever it excited.

Put into context, these two disease theories gave rise to different presumed causes for outbreaks of infection. The European cholera epidemic of 1832 – which hit Ireland particularly badly and is one of the touchstones for future stereotypes of the Irish as disease-ridden – could be understood either as a contagion spreading from a foreign source or as a disease whose geographical distribution correlated with places of already existing squalor. Yet public understanding of contagion and anticontagion rarely allowed for such a clearly articulated difference. Instead, contagionism and miasmatism were routinely bound together, and often misapplied. During the 1832 epidemic, the port city of Glasgow returned all Irish beggars to Derry, fearing that they might spread cholera to Scotland, despite the fact that cholera struck in Ireland while the beggars were in Glasgow. Alternatively, the Irish establish-ment, reflecting both contagionist and miasmatist rhetoric, blamed, variously, 'manure heaps', 'the poorer quarters of Dublin', 'prostitutes' and working men 'of irregular habits' (Robins 1995, 66–68).

'Carmilla' is similarly imprecise in its application of theories of disease, yet it is clear that Le Fanu infuses his narrative with imaginative reconfigurations of both contagionist and miasmatist discourse.

Carmilla's unexpected arrival at the home of Laura and her father is prefigured by a change in the surrounding environmental conditions, where 'over the sward and grounds a thin film of mist was stealing, like smoke' (Le Fanu 1993, 250–51). Carmilla arrives from out of this mist, a portentous symbol of miasma from which the disease of vampirism emerges. Yet neither Laura, her father nor their servants recognize the danger of the mist and of Carmilla, preferring instead to reserve their concern for the 'hideous black woman' (Le Fanu 1993, 257) whose obvious ethnicity makes her a far more suitable candidate for suspicion.

After Carmilla's arrival disease spreads rapidly throughout the local area, killing the wife of a pig farmer and the daughter of a forest ranger, both members of the Styrian working class. Laura fears that their deaths signify the beginning of a 'plague or fever' (Le Fanu 1993, 266) but even when this disease closes in on her home, reaching 'the sister of a young peasant on [her father's] estate, only a mile away' (Le Fanu 1993, 269) Laura is convinced that disease will not reach her. When Carmilla asks Laura if she is afraid of infection Laura replies, 'I should be very much if I fancied there was any real danger of my being attacked as those poor people were' (Le Fanu 1993, 270). This is the language and etiology of contagion: constructing disease as the spreading plague that attacks individuals randomly. Yet it is also implicitly the discourse of miasmatism; Laura's confident assertion of her safety is largely premised on the difference between a presumed cleanliness of her own home and the polluted environment of the local population. While class difference undoubtedly contributes to Laura's opinion, her perceived separation from the infected locals is also based on ethnicity. Just as Carmilla's black companion is visibly different to Laura (and to Carmilla) so too are the local peasant class recognizably Styrian (Irish), even if, for Laura, this comes through local knowledge rather than any visible sign of ethnic difference.

With these patterns of ethnic difference and disease in place it is possible to begin to discern the schema of Le Fanu's narrative. Disease, whether contagious or miasmatic, is an attribute of ethnicity, of the visibly othered black woman or the known (but ethnically invisible) Styrian. As the progenitor of disease, the vampire is therefore inevitably ethnically different to Laura. Of course, this is exactly the case; Carmilla, we discover, is Styrian, or Irish, while Laura is Anglo-Styrian (Anglo-Irish). Taking a step further, Le Fanu therefore locates disease as Irishness, with the vampiric Carmilla acting as a synecdoche of the infecting potential of the Irish on the clean, unpolluted Anglo-Irish Laura. The importance of drawing on both miasmatic and contagionist understandings of disease transmission becomes more apparent in this schema. Miasmatism, after all, focuses on place as the exciting cause of disease, while contagionism privileges the centrality of the body. In Le Fanu's organization of disease both the bodies of the Irish and Ireland itself become sites of infection, and it is the vampire Carmilla who holds these two together; she is both the dangerously contagious Irish individual and the locus for a miasmatic Ireland.

Seeing Disease, Seeing the Irish

The evidence and suppositions of both contagionism and miasmatism would certainly support Laura's confident belief in her own immunity from disease. After all, contagionist practice suggested ethnicity, as well as low social and class positions, were at the root of infection, while sanitary science's social agenda focused on the most socially deprived areas of urban Britain and Ireland. With the evidence of these opinions and statistics in the Irish national consciousness it would have been remarkably easy for Laura, a member of the Anglo-Irish aristocracy, to believe herself to be exempt from infection. Yet the sustained invisibility of Carmilla's vampirism cannot wholly be attributed to self-satisfied superiority on the part of Laura and her father. Rather, what are illuminated in the consistent failure to *see* that Carmilla is the exciting cause of disease are the complex structures of vision involved in detecting both infectious potential and the qualities of Irishness that may lead to dangerous pollution.

The role of two guardians – Laura's father and General Spielsdorf – are important in this respect. Both appear to suffer from the same inability to recognize the signs of vampiric infection, or indeed to believe in the reality of such a mythological creature. Laura's father scorns the local doctor for suggesting that a vampire has caused the fatal illnesses in the neighbourhood:

> He and papa emerged from the room together, and I heard papa laugh, and say as they came out: 'well, I do wonder at a wise man like you. What do you say to hippogriffs and dragons?' (Le Fanu 1993, 271)

Likewise, General Spielsdorf admits that his was as disbelieving an attitude when he talked with his physician: 'being myself wholly sceptical as to the existence of any such portent as the vampire, the supernatural theory of the good doctor furnished, in my opinion, but another instance of learning and intelligence oddly associated with some one hallucination' (Le Fanu 1993, 310). Both men regard the vampire as a creature of superstition, believed not only by the gullible but also, crucially, by those of scholarship and knowledge who become hoodwinked by an illusion they take to be real. Their scepticism of expert opinion is fuelled by their inability to accept what seems to them to be fantastical. Within the textual economy of 'Carmilla' vampirism is a reality, but for Laura's father and General Spielsdorf a lack of visible evidence turns it into myth.

The same epistemological stranglehold is characteristic of Victorian debates on disease. With technological advancement in one of the most important visual tools available to science, the microscope, medicine made rapid progress in understanding disease. However, the public were still caught between scientific opinion and phenomenological evidence. Contagionists passionately described the animalculae they found during microscopical examinations of diseased tissue, and sanitary scientists beseeched the public to rid their homes of the infinitesimally small particles of organic dust (illuminated by the microscope) that posed such a danger to health. Yet the public could not see the parasite or the dust mote: and their incredulity was not reduced by the scientific community's own disagreements over microscopical evidence that threw into doubt the reality of the visions it offered.

The power of the microscope to reveal new and ever smaller worlds gave rise to a sense of awe amongst observers. In the many popular accounts of microscopy it is the sense of wonder at what can be viewed that dominates. William Carpenter, for example, stresses that the size of objects viewed through the microscope does not detract from their ability to inspire the observer:

> We cannot long scrutinize 'the world of the small' to which we thus find access, without having the conviction forced upon us, that all size is but relative, and that mass has nothing to do with real grandeur. There is something in the extreme of minuteness, which is no less wonderful, – might it not almost be said, no less majestic? – than the extremes of vastness. (Carpenter 1856, 37)

For Carpenter and other users of the microscope, the new worlds that it revealed existed both in reality and in imagination. For one microscopic enthusiast it was a complex interaction of the two:

> The microscope displays to us, in each object, a thousand others which escaped our knowledge. Yet, in every object discovered by this

instrument, others yet remain unseen, which the microscope itself can never bring to notice. What wonders should we see, if we could continually improve those glasses, which are invented for the assistance of our sight. Imagination may, in some measure, supply the defect of our eyes, and make it seem as a mental microscope to represent in each atom thousands of new and invisible worlds.

(Anon. 1806, 12–13)

There is a process of myth-making here, the construction of a microscopic world that does not exist except in the imagination. Such visual slight of hand – shifting from actual vision to mental vision – was a product of the wonderment which, as Carpenter suggests, was a common experience of looking through the microscope. Jabez Hogg describes that experience as 'astounding [in] its revelations' and leading to a point where 'our facts become stranger than fiction, and far beyond the imaginings of the most poetic brain' (Hogg 1856, 450). Similarly Gideon Mantell compares the discoveries of 'that noblest instrument of natural philosophy, the Microscope' to 'the realisation of the imaginings of Shakespear [sic] and of Milton, or of the speculations of Locke and of Bacon' (Mantell 1846, 7).

For many microscope observers there is a belief in the microscope as a 'phantasmagoric' (Crary, 1990, 132) instrument, providing visions that, while tentatively accepted as real, are much more in line with the mental images conjured by the imagination. How have these visions occurred? The answer is two-fold: either the microscope is an object of mythic power far in excess of the sum of its mechanical parts, or, the eye and the mind of the observer are being tricked, again by some opaque system within the microscope itself. Although microscopic commentators would not have been able to articulate this historical sense of their own vision it is the case that their belief in the microscope's own power does reveal itself throughout their writing. Jabez Hogg, for example, talks of discovering things *with* the microscope rather than using the microscope (Hogg 1856), and an anonymous writer of a book of popular microscopy discusses not what the *observer* discovers but what the *microscope* discovers (Anon. 1806). These accounts implicitly acknowledge the active involvement of visual technology in the visions which reach the eye of the observer. The microscope becomes a participant in the creation of a vision that is no longer simply real but now also a product of a phantasmagoric imagining.

For scientists intent on pursuing further evidence of contagionism or miasmatism, discoveries made with the aid of the microscope were therefore problematic. Images of microscopic life might easily be the false vision of one overcome by imagination or, worse, prone to accept myth as reality. Edward Bancroft had argued this case early in the century, when the images produced by the microscope were limited: 'our belief frequently depends upon supposed causes and effects, whose existence and relations are not capable of being either seen, heard or felt; and yet men will frequently imagine they have seen, heard or felt all that is necessary to warrant their belief' (Bancroft 1811, 95). In 1870, with far more powerful microscopes available, John Tyndall had also been tentative: 'it is difficult for an outsider like myself to read without sympathetic emotion such papers as those of Dr. Budd, of Bristol, on cholera, scarlet-fever and small-pox. He is a man of strong imagination, and may occasionally take a flight beyond his facts; but without this dynamic heat of heart, the stolid inertia of the free-born Briton cannot be overcome' (Tyndall 1870, 340–41). The greatest strength of feeling is to be found in the writing of sanitarian Florence Nightingale. The 'most important practical lesson' that her 'Notes on Nursing' offers, is 'what to observe – how to observe' (Nightingale 2004a, 122). As Nightingale tells her reader, it is a lack of skilled observation that most often leads to medical error: 'almost all superstitions are owing to bad observation, to the post hoc, ergo propter hoc, and bad observers are almost all superstitious' (Nightingale 2004a, 130).

Microscopic vision showed the Victorians that a world invisible to the eye did exist, but it also challenged them to be able to differentiate between reality and superstition. In view of this, medical use of the microscope to aid research into disease highlighted the importance of skilled observation. John Hughes Bennett, Professor of Medicine at the University of Edinburgh, argued this point in his opening lecture to histology students in the 1840s. 'It is not enough to have good instruments', he said, 'we must know how to use them' (Bennett 1841, 11). Many of the misinterpretations and errors of microscopists, he argued, 'arose more from their want of knowledge, than from any fault in the instrument' (Bennett 1841, 11). John Quekett, also in a lecture on histology, agreed with Bennett when he hinted at the importance of appropriate and skilled observation. He believed 'the utmost benefit both to science and their fellow-creatures' to come from 'those who have employed the microscope … with the greatest assiduity' (Quekett 1852, 3). Samuel La'mert remained the most outspoken supporter of the observer's skill over the microscope's revelations: 'It must be especially observed', he warned his reader at the end of his treatise on disease, 'in connexion [sic] with the efficacy of the microscopic examination, that *competency to use that instrument with advantage can only be acquired by a long course of study and practice*' (La'mert 1859, 150). Without this education, he continues, 'some gentlemen, who have attempted microscopic inquiries without acquiring a sufficient amount of experience, have from time to time *fallen into such serious blunders*' (La'mert 1859, 150–51). Truth, then, comes only to the scientist who is the 'positive ideal of the observer', as characterized by Lorraine Daston and Peter Galison, 'patient, indefatigable, ever alert, probing the limits of the human senses' (Daston and Galison 1992, 119).

Le Fanu is fascinated by vision in 'Carmilla'. The narrative is permeated with references to observation, visibility (and invisibility), hallucination and superstition. Laura's encounters with Carmilla are described as dream-like hallucinations; evidence of Carmilla's heredity is hidden behind the accumulated dust on the family portraits; and, most interestingly, the traveling beggar with the 'piercing black eye' (Le Fanu 1993, 268) notices in Carmilla's 'sharpest tooth' (Le Fanu 1993, 269) the partly visible signs of her vampirism, offering Laura a charm that is 'an antidote against the malaria' (Le Fanu 1993, 281). The common denominator in these examples is Carmilla: vision is tied explicitly to disease. Progress towards the discovery of Carmilla's vampirism follows a pattern similar to the microscopic investigations of the medical establishment. Although vampirism is *seen* very early in the narrative, by Laura herself, it is initially disregarded as hallucination. Medical opinion is sought and vampirism is seen once again, but this time ruled out as superstition. The beggar then makes it visible for the third time, but is ruled out as a less than ideal observer. Only when General Spielsdorf, whose long investigation makes him the ideal observer, advocates vampirism as the source of disease is Carmilla's true identity accepted and, in the concluding moments of the plot, made visible.

It is Le Fanu's symbolic scheme for the narrative – that imagines disease as the vampire – that so astutely binds together the discourses of science, vision, and Irish identity. By employing the mythological monster of the vampire as representative of disease, Le Fanu interrogates ideas of evidence and belief as they occur in both cultural myth and experimental microscopy. Both myth and the microscope give rise to questions over the ontological status of perceived phenomena and the relationship between these phenomena and the human observer. Just as disease occurs primarily at the subepidermal level and is therefore invisible without the aid of visual technologies, and even then might only reflect the fallibility of the irrational observer, so too is the vampire an object of cultural invisibility reliant on the transformation of superstition into truth, or else disempowered by rational thought as no more than a product of the overwrought human imagination. While this attenuation of science with myth is a complex enough over-determination of the symbol of the vampire, the narrative's gothic coda overlays them with the discourse of Anglo-Irish ascendancy. Carmilla's hidden identity, her association with superstition and myth, and her representation as infectious disease all conform to, and in some respects exceed, what Le Fanu would clearly have recognized as a common pattern (especially in gothic fictions) denotative of Irishness.

Carmilla's ethnicity is as invisible as her infection, and for the same reasons. While disease was, at this period, understood as existing invisibly inside the body (whether it had begun in the surrounding environment or in the body itself), it was therefore often imagined as hidden from view below the visible layers of the skin. Similarly, Carmilla's Irishness cannot be seen: she does not wear her identity on the skin as did so many of the colonial subjects of Victorian Britain. This was always a problem for the Anglo-Irish ascendancy class in their imperialist rule over Ireland: there was no 'epidermal schema', in Frantz Fanon's phrase, from which to see ethnic difference (Fanon 1967, 111). Like disease, Carmilla's Irishness is subepidermal, invisible to the naked eye. Le Fanu pushes this point at several moments in the text. One of Carmilla's first appearances in the narrative is at a masked ball where the identity of all participants is hidden from view, and at which she stubbornly refuses to reveal her identity. This refusal is continued in Carmilla's discussions with Laura, and made manifest in the dust-covered and therefore opaque portraits of the Karnstein family that are only made visible by thorough cleaning.

While Carmilla's Irishness cannot be detected by visual surveillance, her characterization as the gothic vampire provides another avenue for recognition. It was one of the central generic tropes of Anglo-Irish gothic to associate the native Irish population with ancient folklore and mythic traditions. As Jarlath Killeen argues, Anglo-Irish writers were fascinated by 'antiquarianism, folkloric studies and Irish "superstitions"' (Killeen 2006, np) and often employed these in their gothic fictions. R. F. Foster goes further, indicating that it was common in Protestant ascendancy gothic to figure the Irish as 'occult' figures, whose 'Catholic magic' engenders both 'repulsion and envy' (Foster 1993, 220). Carmilla is entirely in line with this gothic tradition: as the vampire she both represents Irish myth and instigates the superstitious fears of the local population. Vampirism is also her own brand of Catholic occult magic, imagined in the narrative as a variety of supernatural characteristics from shape-shifting through dream appearance to vampiric attack. Seeing native Irishness, then, is vitally important for the Anglo-Irish, because to be Irish was to have the hidden potential for violent opposition to the Protestant ascendancy.

To be able successfully to see disease and Irish ethnicity is to become empowered by vision. Clear sight is masterful surveillance, knowledge and power. It is also a disruption of all efforts to hoodwink the observer and is therefore an adumbration of the power of the other. For disease theorists, confidence in the visual veracity of the microscope would lead scientists, as Samuel La'mert believed, 'to detect the latent causes of human suffering with a view to their removal' (La'mert 1859, 145–46). For the Anglo-Irish, recognizing the Catholic Irish's propensity for violent intervention in the colonial supremacy of the Protestant ascendancy was a first step towards maintaining that supremacy intact. 'Carmilla' suggests that, for Le Fanu, these two things are inextricable. Read through contemporary disease theory and the politics of Irish gothic the underlying narrative emerges as a rather overbearing conservative political allegory: where the native Irish are imagined as diseased and violent insurrectionists preying on an unsuspecting and innocent Anglo-Irish ruling class, who, awakened to the danger of their position, mercilessly put down the Irish and free Ireland from its contagion.

Disease and the Irish Question

There are fault-lines in such a reading. For example, what significance is there in Laura's familial relationship to Carmilla? Or, why does the native Irish population also suffer from Carmilla's vampirism? Finally, would Le Fanu, often sympathetic to Irish self-determination, construct a narrative that so avowedly opposed Irish nationalism? There are, then, legitimate reasons to believe that there is a broader range of meanings in 'Carmilla' and that this range can be illuminated if we accept that Le Fanu's consideration of science is at the same time a consideration of politics. That is, in constructing a gothic vampire narrative that evokes and interrogates the varied public conceptions (and misconceptions) of infectious disease Le Fanu is also drawing on the political impact of such scientific knowledge to articulate his position on the Irish Question.

Le Fanu's politics are complex. As Michael Begnal has revealed, after the Tithe War in 1831, Le Fanu realized 'he was of the Anglo-Irish, Protestant ascendancy' and that 'the constant tension and opposition between two kinds of Irishmen and two visions of Ireland … [was] a problem and a paradox with which he was to struggle' (Begnal 1971, 15). In the 1840s Le Fanu was sympathetic to certain Irish nationalist causes, such as the Young Ireland movement of Charles Gavan Duffy. Yet in the 1850s, and in part because of the foundation and agitation of the more aggressive Irish Tenant League, Le Fanu returned to a traditional Tory position. He was involved in the periodical *The Warder*, which W. J. McCormack calls 'a robust champion of Irish Toryism', (McCormack 1980, 92) and retained a partnership in the newspaper of the Tory aristocracy, the *Dublin Evening Mail*. In the 1860s, the *Mail* withheld all support for Disraeli's Irish parliamentary candidates and although, as the decade proceeded, Le Fanu himself became more moderate on the Irish Question, he still opposed Gladstone's attempted reconciliations with Catholic Ireland after 1868. Despite publicly supporting the creation of a middle party rather than those in favour of, or against, Irish home rule, Le Fanu greatly feared the increasing agitation for disestablishment and the rise of violent Fenianism. Fenianism, in particular, was frighteningly alien to the Anglo-Irish; it had arisen as though from nowhere and was associated with a Continental Catholicism that was foreign and unknowable. Although McCormack argues that Le Fanu's opposition to Fenianism was 'the background to [his] renewed activity as a novelist' (McCormack 1980, 211) in the 1860s and 1870s, the work he produced 'embodies that awareness of history's multiple levels which preoccupied the Protestant elite in its more attentive moments' and was 'dominated by transitional stasis, a state of consciousness in which the inevitability of change is both acknowledged and resisted' (McCormack 1980, 253, 260). McCormack's historical analysis of Le Fanu's work is reinforced by Jarlath Killeen's literary critical view of Anglo-Irish gothic as a genre working in a 'mode of hesitation, [a] psychological ambivalence' (Killeen 2006, n.p.) towards politics and history.

In 'Carmilla' Le Fanu does not attempt to work his way out of such ambivalence. Rather he encapsulates that in-betweenness by working the Irish Question into existing and contradictory scientific ideas of disease transmission, themselves already employed politically in discussions of land and identity. Theories of disease were perfectly placed for political treatment. Miasmatism was politicized by sanitary scientists to promote social reform in areas of deprivation: making issues of land pollution a question of political as well as scientific action. Contagionism had an even longer history of political influence: it played a key role in the continuation of state-sanctioned quarantine and made the diseased body the responsibility of the government as well as the medical profession. It is, therefore, important to trace miasmatism and

contagionism in the narrative, for it is by recognizing their role in politi-
cizing the vampire as a mode of infection that Le Fanu's political project
might be better understood.

The most telling instance of hesitancy in decrying the Irish as an
infectious disease attacking the Anglo-Irish ascendancy class is the
complex familial relation between Carmilla and Laura, which is in turn
imagined within a paradigm of miasmatic disease etiology. Laura's
mother was descended from the Karnstein family, as was General
Spielsdorf's wife, meaning that Laura, and potentially General
Spielsdorf's ward (his niece), were also descendants of that same
ancient Styrian family. The vampire, Carmilla, is not only a Karnstein
but the original Countess from whom these mothers and their daughters are descended. We have, therefore, a direct lineage from the
vampire through the dead mothers to their infected daughters. To draw
such a clear line of descent from Carmilla to Laura is to make much
more liminal the position of the Anglo-Irish. More than this, it suggests
that Laura's aristocratic ancestry – the historical roots of her social and
political power in Ireland, further reinforced by her English father – is
actually the source of the narrative's present infection. It is not, then,
the disenfranchised Irish to which the source of vampirism might be
traced but an ancient Irish aristocracy from which the present political
aristocracy is descended. Nevertheless, it is the Irish Carmilla and not
the Anglo-Irish Laura who spreads disease. However complex the
historical ties between the ancient Irish aristocracy and the present
ruling class it remains the case that it is the Irish who are characterized
as violent, dangerous and unclean. There is, therefore, a vacillation
between one source of infection and another, between the Anglo-Irish
and the Irish.

If the source of infection is the Anglo-Irish then it is also miasmatic
in origin. This makes sense, as miasmatism was always associated with
specific sites of disease, and this association between place and disease
was commonly known outside scientific circles, not least because of the
work of sanitary scientists. While we recall that Carmilla appears to
Laura from a mist that can be read as symbolizing a miasma, it is more
pertinent to note that the infections from which Laura and General
Spielsdorf's ward suffer only have an effect when the vampire resides in
their homes. Likewise the local population falls ill when Carmilla's
infective potential reaches out to them from her base within Laura's and
her father's household. While disease can be traced to Laura's family
seat, it can also be traced to another locale: the Karnstein family grave-
yard within the nearby 'ruined village' (Le Fanu 1993, 244). There, the

'mouldering tombs' (Le Fanu, 245) of the Karnsteins include the one
from which Carmilla has arisen as a vampire.

These twin miasmatic sites further illuminate the ancestral connection between Laura and Carmilla, and indeed play on the different
meanings of ancestral within general public discourse and the specific
scientific discourse of miasmatism. While ancestral has a common
linguistic meaning that signifies linked intergenerational biological
inheritance, in miasmatic conceptions of disease it signifies instead a
long-existing and specifically sited infectious potential. Miasmatists
used the phrase ancestral disease as a particular recognition of the
phenomenon of an infection that lay dormant over a long period of time
within a specific place and, when agitated by unique environmental
conditions, again give rise to disease in the human population. Whether
Le Fanu understood the different meanings of the term ancestral, or
simply mistook ancestral disease as infection connected through fami-
lies, the collapsing together of the two meanings very neatly evokes the
political complexity at which he was straining. Miasmatism, in its political context, implicates both the present Anglo-Irish ascendancy class
and their aristocratic predecessors in the current problems of Irish insurrection. In this reading, the present infection of Ireland is not an alien
and violent Fenianism but rather the historically miscegenated
Anglo-Irish ascendancy class who continue to spread infection across
Irish land.

If Le Fanu's politics of miasmatism highlights the historical valences
of the Irish Question and, as a result, appears to favour a nationalist position, then the narrative's politicized contagionism refocuses attention
on the native Irish and on Fenianism. Although miasmatism appears to
be the dominant disease theory for the majority of the narrative, it does
not account for every movement of disease nor every process undertaken
to deal with infection. The story of Carmilla's own transformation into
the vampire is one example where contagion appears to be the mode of
transmission. The legend of Carmilla with which Laura closes her own
narrative describes how disease in the form of vampirism arises initially
from the suicide of Carmilla's lover. Unable to cope with her early death,
he took his own life and became a vampire, subsequently infecting
Carmilla. This direct transmission from individual to individual is
clearly based on the principles of contagion, as is the obvious attribution
of disease to personal immorality. It is implicit in the legend that the
moral debasement of the suicide was the exciting cause of vampirism.
Such causal connection from an individual's lack of morality to their
diseased state was a commonly held popular belief that had been encour-

aged by contagionist principles of infection. While miasmatism did propose a link between disease and immoral activity this link began with infection and led to vice: Florence Nightingale, for example, argued that 'sick streets produce sick people and bad people' (Nightingale 2004b, 533). Contagionism usually reversed this process; linking, say, prostitution to infection in such a way as to suggest that the moral laxity of the activity would excite disease.

This narrative of the emergence of vampirism is entirely concentrated on the native Styrian population: characterizing them as immoral and diseased in exactly the way the native Irish had been regarded in popular colonial narratives. The legend, then, is a myth of a diseased Ireland with the infectious Carmilla as the dangerous native Irish woman at its centre. This association of Carmilla with a native Irish culture is further developed by the story's geography. The site of Carmilla's tomb, the particular place of the disease of Irishness is to the west of Laura and her father's home. This cannot be without political resonance in a narrative that symbolizes its geographical locations so carefully. For the Anglo-Irish of the 1870s it was in the west of Ireland that the roots of the present disturbances could be found. Fenianism was traditionally believed to have its strongest roots in the west and the stereotypical spread of 'Fenian fever' (McCormack 1980, 211) was from the rural west to the urban east (centred on Dublin). Carmilla's own emergence from the west to infect the Anglo-Irish in their eastern manor-house is certainly a strong indication that one representation of the vampire is as the Fenian agitator.

Laura's father and General Spielsdorf certainly regard the vampire as a dangerous contagion. Their involvement in the appropriately named Imperial Commission, created to eradicate Carmilla, finds them following the procedures of disease containment favoured by contagionists; focusing on the diseased individual rather than the environment. After the opening of the tomb, Carmilla's body:

> was raised, and a sharp stake driven through the heart of the vampire, who uttered a piercing shriek at the moment, in all respects such as might escape from a living person in the last agony. Then the head was struck off, and a torrent of blood flowed from the severed neck. The body and head were next placed on a pile of wood, and reduced to ashes, which were thrown upon the river and borne away, and that territory has never since been plagued by the visits of a vampire.
>
> (Le Fanu 1993, 315–16)

Rather than considering it important to undertake a cleaning and disin-
fecting of the polluted site, as would have been commonly advocated by
sanitary science, the Imperial Commission decapitates and burns the
individual associated with the spread of infection. Clearly the two
Anglo-Irish patriarchs regard the vampire as having arisen from native
Irish insurrection rather than their own colonial oppression of Irish land
and communities.

Having constructed a contemporary political narrative from disease
theories framed within the traditions of Irish gothic, Le Fanu appears, at
the conclusion of that narrative, to have retreated into a Tory
mythology of the Irish vampire vanquished by Anglo-Irish heroism. If
there is, as W. J. McCormack argues, 'a pervasive symbolism' in Le
Fanu's work 'from which it is impossible to amputate political implications' (McCormack 1980, 256) the resonances in 'Carmilla' suggest that
Le Fanu's position on the Irish Question is of ultimate opposition to
Fenianism and a re-entrenchment of Tory resistance to change. Yet, at
the very end of Laura's narration, hesitancy and doubt resurface. Despite
Carmilla's destruction Laura, for years afterwards, still 'heard the light
step of Carmilla at the drawing-room door' (Le Fanu 1993, 319). The
Tory solution to the Irish Question is overshadowed here by the spectre
of Fenianism's return – a visible contagion eradicated, perhaps, but an
invisible ancestral miasma awaiting the coalescence of social and environmental conditions that will excite it into violent action once again.

Works Cited

Ackerknecht, Erwin H., 1948. 'Anticontagionism between 1821 and 1867',
    Bulletin of the History of Medicine 22 (1948): 562–93.
Anon., 1806. *The Wonders of the Microscope; Or, An Explanation of the Wisdom of
    the Creator in Objects Comparatively Minute, adapted to the understanding of
    Young Persons.* London: Tabarat & Co.
Baldwin, Peter, 1999. *Contagion and the State in Britain, 1830–1930.* Cambridge:
    Cambridge University Press.
Bancroft, Edward Nathaniel, 1811. *An Essay on the Disease called Yellow Fever,
    with Observations Concerning Febrile Contagion, Typhus Fever, Dysentry, and
    the Plague, partly delivered as the Gulstonian Lectures, before the College of Physi-
    cians, in the years 1806 and 1807.* London: T. Cadell & W. Davies.
Begnal, Michael H., 1971. *Joseph Sheridan Le Fanu.* Lewisburg: Bucknell Univer-
    sity Press.
Bennett, John Hughes, 1841. *On the Employment of the Microscope in Medical
    Studies. A Lecture Introductory to a Course in Histology.* Edinburgh:
    Maclachlan, Stuart & Co.

Carpenter, William B., 1856. *The Microscope: and its Revelations*. London: John Churchill.

Crary, Jonathan, 1990. *Techniques of the Observer: On Vision and Modernity in the Nineteenth-Century*. Cambridge, MA: MIT Press.

Daston, Lorraine and Peter Galison, 1992. 'The Image of Objectivity', *Representations* 40 (Autumn 1992): 81–128.

Fanon, Frantz, 1967. *Black Skin, White Masks*. New York: Grove Press.

Foster, R. F., 1993. *Paddy and Mr Punch: Connections in Irish and English History*. London: Allen Lane.

Gibson, Matthew, 2006. *Dracula and the Eastern Question: British and French Vampire Narratives of the Nineteenth-Century Near East*. Basingstoke: Palgrave Macmillan.

Haslam, Richard, 2007. 'Irish Gothic: A Rhetorical Hermeneutics Approach', *The Irish Journal of Gothic and Horror Studies* 2 (2007): n.p.

Hogg, Jabez, 1856. *The Microscope: Its History, Construction, and Application. Being a Familiar Introduction to the Use of the Instrument and the Study of Microscopical Science*. London: Herbert Ingram.

Kiberd, Declan, 2000. *Irish Classics*. London: Granta.

Killeen, Jarlath, 2006. 'Irish Gothic: A Theoretical Introduction', *The Irish Journal of Gothic and Horror Studies* 1 (2006): n.p.

La'mert, Samuel, 1859. *Self-Preservation: A Medical Treatise on Nervous and Physical Debility, Spermatorrhea, Impotence, and Sterility with Practical Observations on the use of the Microscope in the Treatment of the Diseases of the Generative System*. London: Samuel La'mert.

Le Fanu, Sheridan, 1993 (1872). 'Carmilla', in *In a Glass Darkly*, ed. Robert Tracy. Oxford: Oxford University Press.

Maglen, Krista, 2001. 'Interpreting Infection: Quarantine, the Port Sanitary Authority and Immigration in Late Nineteenth and Early Twentieth Century Britain'. Unpublished Ph.D. thesis, University of Glasgow.

Mantell, Gideon, 1846. *Thoughts on Animalcules; Or, A Glimpse of the Invisible World revealed by the Microscope*. London: John Murray.

McCormack, W. J., 1980. *Sheridan Le Fanu and Victorian Ireland*. Oxford: Clarendon Press.

———, 1998. 'Irish Gothic', in *The Handbook to Gothic Literature*, ed. Marie Mulvey-Roberts. London: Macmillan.

Nightingale, Florence, 2004a (1860). 'Notes on Nursing for the Labouring Classes (1860)', in *Florence Nightingale on Public Health*, ed. Lynn McDonald. Ontario: Wilfrid Laurier University Press.

———, 2004b (1867). 'Letter to Henry Parker, 1 May 1867', in *Florence Nightingale on Public Health*, ed. Lynn McDonald. Ontario: Wilfrid Laurier University Press.

Quekett, John, 1852. *Lectures on Histology, delivered at the Royal College of Surgeons of England, in the session 1850–51*. London: Hippolyte Bailliere.

Robins, Joseph, 1995. *Miasma: Epidemic and Panic in Nineteenth Century Ireland*. Dublin: Institute of Public Administration.

Rosenberg, Charles E., 1979. 'Florence Nightingale on Contagion: The Hospital as Moral Universe', in *Healing and History: Essays for George Rosen*, ed. Charles E. Rosenberg. New York: Science History Publications.

Smith, Southwood, 1830. *A Treatise on Fever*. London: Longman, Rees, Orme, Brown and Green.

Tyndall, John, 1870. 'On Haze and Dust', *Nature* (27 January 1870): 339–42.

Worboys, Michael, 2000. *Spreading Germs: Disease Theories and Medical Practice in Britain, 1865–1900*. Cambridge: Cambridge University Press.

Evolution, Literary History and Science Fiction

BRIAN BAKER

THE FIRST LINE OF the Preface of George Levine's study of Darwinian discourse and its connection to the nineteenth-century novel, *Darwin Among The Novelists* (1988) quotes G. H. Lewes's remark 'that "science is penetrating everywhere" ' (Levine 1988, vii). Twenty years later, this volume of *Essays and Studies* attests to the continuing, perhaps burgeoning, importance of scientific paradigms to literary study. Where some literary critics, such as N. Katherine Hayles, have taken up cybernetics and information theory as scientific theories by which to critique 'postmodern' or 'posthuman' constructions of the subject, it has been more usual for the biological, rather than the physical sciences, to provide the apparatus for experiments in science-inflected literary criticism. More specifically, it is Darwinian or evolutionary theory that has, in the last ten years or so, been the source for several attempts to re-invigorate the literary academy, in a moment which is being viewed as increasingly 'after Theory'. It is my intention in this essay to consider several contemporary deployments of evolutionary thinking within the field of literary studies. I will analyse Franco Moretti's *Graphs, Maps, Trees* (2005), his attempt to construct different (scientific) models for literary history, and then apply his thinking to science fiction (SF), a major literary genre self-consciously set aside in *Graphs, Maps, Trees*. I will also consider the difference between Moretti's evolutionary paradigm and that used by the sociobiology-influenced critic Joseph Carroll, whose work, as will be seen, propagandizes for an evolutionary psychology but in fact masks a very traditional form of literary analysis.

In a series of three articles published in the *New Left Review*, and collected in *Graphs, Maps, Trees*, Moretti provides three different (though connected conceptually) 'abstract' models for understanding literary history. In *Atlas of the European Novel* (1998) Moretti had used a 'mapping' technique for spatially laying out certain elements from fictional texts in order to reveal underlying ideological or structural emphases. In the second article/chapter, on maps, Moretti expands upon and rethinks his cartographic methods from his *Atlas*. He notes a criticism made by the Italian geographer Claudio Cerreti, who pointed out:

> how patterns entail a Cartesian reduction of space to extension, where 'objects are analysed in terms of reciprocal positions and distances ... whether they are close or far from each other is something else.' This however is not really geography, Ceretti goes on, but rather *geometry*; and the figures of the *Atlas*, for their part, are not really maps, but diagrams. The diagrams *look* like maps, yes, because they have been 'superimposed on a cartographic plane': but their true nature emerges unmistakeably from the way I analyse them, which disregards the specificity of the various locations, to focus almost entirely on their mutual relations. (Moretti 2005, 54)

A diagram, in Moretti's terms, is then a 'matrix of relations', whereas a map is a 'cluster of individual locations' (Moretti 2005, 54). Moretti is attracted to diagrams, he confesses, 'because for me *geometry* 'signifies' *more than geography*' (Moretti's emphasis, 2005, 56). Unapologetically, Moretti emphasizes the reductive nature of his models, the very abstraction which reveals significance, a reduction which does not distort but 'explains'. This word is very important to Moretti's project in the book, for it indicates his emphasis not on literary *analysis* but on literary *history*.

The form that this history takes is also very important. Moretti is concerned to widen the scope of literary history beyond the canonical texts that have made up narrative forms of literary histories, inevitably selective (and therefore possibly distorted). If, Moretti suggests, the canon for the British nineteenth-century novel consists of two hundred texts, this is still 'less than one per cent of the novels that were actually published: twenty thousand, thirty, more, no one really knows – and close reading won't help here, a novel a day every day of the year would take a century or so' (Moretti 2005, 4). Moretti instead advocates a 'quantitative' mode, the empirical collating and sifting of *data* (such as numbers of novels published analysed comparatively across national markets) extracted from the work of other critics to enable a 'more rational literary history' (Moretti 2005, 4), one that does not consign ninety-nine per cent of literary production to the dustbin. We will return to the implications of the word 'rational' later, but I would like to first emphasize the very material basis of Moretti's modelling here. Although he foregrounds the explanatory power of abstract and reductive models, these models are constructed from data compiled from lists of publication dates, not from literary 'analysis' of texts themselves.

Why is this important? I think it helps to make sense of the reasoning behind Moretti's turn to such quantitative modelling to arrive at a more 'rational' history. One might otherwise wonder why a critic (published in the *New Left Review* and by Verso) with a self-confessedly 'Marxist formation' turns to the methods of statisticians; Moretti himself, in the introductory section to *Graphs, Maps, Trees* writes:

> From texts to models, then; and models drawn from three disciplines with which literary studies have had little or no interaction: graphs from quantitative history; maps from geography, and trees from evolutionary theory. The distant reason for these choices lies in my Marxist formation, which was profoundly influenced by Galvano DellaVolpe, and entailed therefore (in principle, if not always in practice) a great respect for the scientific spirit. (Moretti 2005, 1–2)

The recourse to 'scientific' analysis of course echoes a long history of Marxist thinking and writing, but Moretti here confesses an alignment much closer to a more common usage of the 'scientific spirit', particularly in his adoption of 'evolutionary trees' to theorize genre history in his third model. I think it is the materialism, the empirical method, of 'science' that is of profound importance to *Graphs, Maps, Trees*. Christopher Prendergast, in his bracing and somewhat sceptical 'Response to Moretti' published also in the *New Left Review*, identifies an unacknowledged connection of Moretti's method with nineteenth-century Positivism and particularly the work of Gustave Lanson who tried to 'replace the history of literature (as the study of a disembodied procession of high-canonical names) with a scientifically grounded literary history' (Prendergast 2005, 43). Not only that, but Prendergast somewhat dismisses DellaVolpe's 'biological analogies' (between 'genus' and 'genre'), describing his efforts as 'neither conspicuously successful nor noticeably influential' (Prendergast 2005, 42 n. 6). The question we must ask is: why (biological) science, and why now?

While Prendergast acknowledges that Moretti 'renounc[es] the belief in the availability of "a single explanatory framework" ' (Prendergast 2005, 45), we can find the connection between the moment in literary studies 'after Theory', the desire for a materialist or empiricist method, and the attraction to models derived from the biological sciences, in a literary critic whose emphases and analyses could hardly be more different to Moretti: Joseph Carroll, author of *Evolution and Literary Theory* (1995) and *Literary Darwinism* (2004), self-appointed scourge of the 'impostures' of poststructuralism and highest-profile exponent of a mode of literary criticism strongly influenced by sociobiology and evolutionary psychology.

Carroll, in a series of articles and book chapters from the mid-1990s, inveighs against what he sees as 'the irrationalism that for over two decades has dominated the field of literary study' (Carroll 1996, 43) under the rubric of what he takes together as ' "poststructuralism", "postmodernism", "deconstruction", "reader-response theory", "New Historicism" and "cultural studies" ' (Carroll 1996, 43), eliding (or perhaps insufficiently understanding) the differences between these literary and critical theories. Note the 'irrationalism' that is emphasized here and elsewhere in Carroll's writings to characterize 'poststructuralist' theory; we might remember that Moretti called for a 'more rational literary history'. Carroll argues that all these conceptual frameworks can be brought under the term 'textualism', by which he means that 'language or culture constitutes or constructs the world according to its own internal principles' (Carroll 1996, 46), or, in a slogan derived from Derrida, 'there is nothing outside of the text'. Carroll's reaction against this mode of thinking is based on his belief that 'perception, thoughts, and emotional responses are themselves not exclusively linguistic in character, though it is of course true that perceptions, thoughts and emotional responses can be linguistically formulated only in linguistic formations' (Carroll 1996, 48). Carroll proposes a subject (perhaps here 'being' might be more appropriate) whose sensory perceptions exist in an experiential continuum that is *prior to* language, but which can only be understood and communicated through language. He affirms what would be called a 'realist' position in scientific discussion: the belief that there *is* a pre-existing 'reality' prior to human experience, culture, discourse; that the world is *not* constructed through (or human experience is only available through the mediating and constructing presence of) discursive or ideological formations.

The 'realist' position is one more suited to those inside the biological sciences rather than the physical, for particularly in the world of quantum mechanics, there is no such concretely material 'real' to rely upon. Werner Heisenberg's Uncertainty Theory, which stated that the very act of trying to determine the velocity and position of the particle will cause a change in both velocity and position, implied that measurement, or experimentation, is not a neutral process; in observing, the observer changes what is observed. As a non-scientist, I should presume too far if I were to press the difference between the physical sciences (as analogous to a 'social constructivist' model in its insistence on the implication between the act of experimentation and the results of that experiment) and the biological sciences (as 'realist' believers in a verifiable, concrete, prior reality that science sets out to understand and describe).

However, I think it is fair to suggest that a critic like Carroll is attracted to *biological* scientific models because it seems to provide an access to the possibility of 'truth' destabilized by the hegemony of the poststructuralist 'complex of ideas'. Carroll is a member of the 'Association of Literary Scholars and Critics', an offshoot of the National Association of Scholars in the USA, which even Carroll describes as an 'intellectually conservative academic organization' (Carroll 1995, 140). In his review of Carroll's *Evolution and Literary Theory* (1995) in *Novel: A Forum on Fiction*, Jonathan Greenberg suggests that despite Carroll's attraction to evolutionary psychology, he is in fact a traditional literary critic whose mentor is M. H. Abrams (a source Carroll draws from liberally in his *Literary Darwinism*, particularly in chapter 5).[1]

Carroll's own literary analysis, when he is not rather crudely vilifying what he would see as the sophistry, absurdity or even fraudulence of 'poststructuralist theory', tends towards the traditional: one of his chapters in *Literary Darwinism* even evaluates three texts (two 'pop' cultural, one 'high' cultural) in terms of literary *value*, a strategy I have not come across in some time and a somewhat dubious exercise in finding strictly what one was looking for: that Golding's *The Inheritors* is better than Auel's *Clan of the Cave Bear*.[2] In ' "Theory", Anti-Theory, and Empirical Criticism', his contribution to the collection *Biopoetics: Evolutionary Explorations in the Arts* (1999), Carroll identifies with a tradition of Arnoldian humanism that offers a 'pragmatic' or practical criticism, that understands the 'precious heritage' of 'the canonical texts of Western culture' to 'embody a normative set of values and imaginative experiences', and that suffers a 'revulsion against the subversive or anti-normative spirit of the postmodern paradigm' (Carroll 1999, 142). Further, in his article 'Evolution and Literary Theory' (1995b), Carroll

1   Meyer (M. H.) Abrams was a Professor of English at Cornell University, and the author of such well-known critical texts as *The Mirror and the Lamp* (1954) and *A Glossary of Literary Terms* (1957) as well as editing the *Norton Anthology of English Literature* (itself a means by which to effect major changes on literary history – but that is another matter). Abrams' work is characterized by a profound engagement with the ideas and movements of English literary history (particularly Romanticism), and with a long tradition of humanist scholarship and critical practice.
2   An instance of Carroll's rhetoric is as follows: 'From the outside, as seen by practitioners in other disciplines, one might characterise [the attitude of contemporary literary academics] as arrogance, a certain narrow and overweening vanity, a provincial complacency that is protected by the general laxity of intellectual standards in the humanities' (1999, 140).

praises Arnold and Samuel Johnson for 'integrating genuinely personal judgments with genuine cultivation, [by which] criticism achieves the large, general validity that we designate by the word "authority" ' (Carroll 1995b, 131). I think it is clear in what tradition he sees himself as a literary critic. Carroll seems worried by what he sees as the undermining of authority in the contemporary academy brought about by 'poststructuralist theory', an authority that perhaps the biological sciences could return to humanities scholars. In effect, Carroll's plea for 'newness' (the embracing of a Darwinian mode of literary criticism) is largely a call to return to traditional, prestructuralist, pre-'theory' close reading or 'practical criticism', a return also to rather less troubled understandings of the 'truth' and the importance (or otherwise, in Auel's case) of literature.

This can be seen in a chapter from *Literary Darwinism* called 'Human Nature and Literary Meaning' in which he offers a reading of *Pride and Prejudice* in 'Darwinian' terms. Throughout this text Carroll locates a 'humanistic paradigm' that is in a continuum with 'adaptationist theory', drawing once again on Abrams to assert:

> Within this paradigm, 'the site of literature is the human world, and a work of literature is the product of a purposive human author addressing human recipients in an environing world'
> (Carroll 2004, 164).

The word 'environing' here looks like a nod from Abrams towards evolutionary discourse, and is certainly presented by Carroll as such. Carroll is able to assert continuity between Abrams' 'humanisitic paradigm' and adaptationist theories because he sees them both to be fundamentally *right* about 'human nature' and, one must assume, human culture. In Carroll's rhetoric, evolutionary psychology *is* 'common sense'. Carroll assumes an unproblematic fit between humanist scholarship and evolutionary psychology because both are *correct*. Abrams foregrounds 'common sense' as the bedrock upon which all literary investigation must rest (and which it cannot penetrate); Carroll asserts that 'authors, like people in general, are instinctively attuned to evolutionary psychology. It is the psychology by which they actually operate' (Carroll 1999, 151). According to Carroll, authors are intuitive evolutionary psychologists, their fictional explorations of human psychology fitting perfectly with the approach of evolutionary psychology. The tools of evolutionary psychology, it follows, are best suited to correctly analysing the workings of literary texts. The case seems conclusive, although it is somewhat circular. Little wonder that Carroll excoriates the 'coun-ter-intuitive' concepts of Jacques Derrida, and believes that they are simply *wrong*.

Irony attends this location of Darwinian evolutionary ideas as 'common sense', of course. As George Levine, in *Darwin and the Novelists* (1988), suggests, the Darwinian 'revolution' was itself a challenge to assumptions about human beings and their 'nature':

> Darwin's theory thrust the human into nature and time, and subjects it to the same dispassionate and material investigations hitherto reserved for rocks and stars. His history of the development of species gave authoritative form to a new narrative – or set of narratives – that has permanently reshaped the Western imagination.
>
> (Levine 1988, 1)

Gillian Beer, in *Darwin's Plots* (1983), goes even further. She argues:

> Most major scientific theories rebuff common sense. They call on evidence beyond the reach of the senses and overturn the observable world. They disturb assumed relationships and shift what has been substantial into metaphor. The earth only now *seems* immovable. Such major theories tax, affront, and exhilarate those who first encounter them, although in fifty years or so they will be taken for granted, part of the apparently common sense set of beliefs which instructs us that the earth revolves around the sun whatever our eyes may suggest. When it is first advanced, theory is at its most fictive. (Beer 1983, 3)

According to Beer, not only was Darwinian theory, when first proposed, counterintuitive, then; it subsequently displaced former versions of 'common sense' and *became* our set of 'common sense' assumptions about what (and who) human beings are. Levine goes on to argue that although Darwin 'presented himself as the genial empiricist', he had in fact 'seized it imaginatively before he could prove it inductively' (Levine 1988, 1): theory *preceded* empirical observation. Levine, who follows Michel Serres in placing science not as a metadiscourse but as a 'cultural formation' (Levine 1988, 3) then implicates theory *in* observation, the abstract and counterintuitive in the 'common sensical', rather than turning them into a binary opposition (to explicitly denigrate one term) as Carroll does – a neatly ironic Derridean twist.

In asserting that 'Literary works can be understood as products of an adaptive need to make sense of the world in emotionally and imaginatively meaningful ways – to produce cognitive order' (Carroll 2004, 164), Carroll proposes to use Darwinian theories – more properly, an assertion that environment and innate biological traits are central to understanding human social behaviour – to analyse literary texts, to produce 'true', 'verifiable', empirical scientific knowledge.[3] When he gets down to analysing *Pride and Prejudice*, however, the results are not really very radical. Although the chapter deploys adaptationist concepts such as 'human universals' as a frame for understanding individual actions, 'categories for analyzing individual difference in identity', and the importance of environmental factors (Carroll 2004, 188), the actual reading of Austen's text does not stray too far from traditional concepts of character, 'mind' or personality. Moreover, the concerns of the chapter are largely on property, society and the role of marriage, for which one does not really need the Darwinian apparatus at all. Instead of writing of 'resources' in a competitive environment, one could consider the importance of property; for 'mate selection' one can write of marriage and its societal codes. When Carroll, at the end of the chapter, criticizes 'theoretical' critics of Austen for shading into 'the thematic, tonal and formal analyses of the traditional criticism' (Carroll 2004, 215) he misses that his own text demonstrates this *inevitable* hybridity, that the properties of 'theoretical' and 'traditional' critical forms are not separated by the clear blue water he assumes.

In this way, then, critical discourse itself, in its 'adaptive' variations in response to environmental stimuli, such as the changing institutional, economic and discursive patterns of the academy, could, at a stretch, be deemed 'evolutionary'. Levity aside, what Franco Moretti may be said to share with Carroll – an attraction to the 'scientific spirit', the use of evolutionary models, the desire to open what Moretti calls a 'new front of discussion' in literary studies (Moretti 2005, 2) – is balanced by what is markedly different. This is particularly evident in terms of politics, but also in the uses to which 'Darwinian' models are put. We will turn to Moretti's genre 'trees' in a moment, but worth mentioning first is the *focus* and the *analytical method* which are so divergent in the two critics.

---

[3]   This search for empirical knowledge does lead Carroll down some strange avenues. In ' "Theory", Anti-Theory, and Empirical Criticism', Carroll proposes an experiment in which one could 'take the opening chapter of Jane Austen's novel *Pride and Prejudice*, have an experimental subject read it while under a scanning machine, and find out about the way comedy actually alters the brain' (1999, 150). In a highly excited manner, Carroll here proposes a very different variant of 'reader-response' criticism, one that annexes literary study to a branch of neurology.

For Carroll, adaptationist theories in connection to a 'humanistic para-digm' are a means by which to return to the Western canon and the tools of 'practical criticism'; it is almost certainly no coincidence that Carroll turns to Austen for his example. For Moretti, Darwinian evolutionary trees are a means by which to offer a comparative, macrocosmic ('world') model of the development of literary genres, and to promote the aban-donment of literary 'analysis' *per se* in favour of data collection and quali-tative 'explanation' of developmental trends. If the contemporary (American) university, and particularly the field of English studies, is the adaptive environment, then we find responses here which can almost be said to be polar opposites.

Moretti also differs from well-known critics such as Gillian Beer and George Levine whose focus is upon the importance of Darwinism to nineteenth-century literary culture, and of literary discourse to Darwin and his writings. Their discursive, historicizing method is at odds with Moretti's abstract, reductive (but no less material) approach which, as I have stated earlier, proposes to do away with literary *analysis* entirely. Christopher Prendergast in fact critiques Moretti for his failure to prop-erly attend to his own prescription: ' "interpretation" plays – and *has* to play – a major part in Moretti's undertaking', argues Prendergast (2005, 45). There are interesting echoes here of Carroll's criticism of literary analysis that shades from 'theory' into 'traditional' modes of analytical discourse: the practice of criticism always slips, it seems, towards hybrid approaches. A more penetrating argument is that Moretti's speculations are simply analogies:

> if not meant literally, if you strip from the evolutionary paradigm its at once defining and delimiting genetic processes, then all you are left with is the husk of an analogy. ... In fact Moretti's entire project rests on the extended tracing of an analogy. Analogical reasoning from a base of scientific terms is not the same as scientific reasoning itself. (Prendergast 2005, 59)

Curiously, this chimes with Carroll's own criticism of 'evolution taken as an analogical model' in his 'Adaptationist Literary Study: An Emerging Research Program' (2003), which predates Moretti's articles in the *New Left Review*. Carroll writes:

> [A] misconceived way to adapt evolutionary theory to literary purposes is to take evolution as an analogical model – to use a meta-phor as a conceptual framework. This is a shortcut to causal thinking,

and it is another version of formalism. The analogical theorist takes it for granted that the causal processes in one field will provide a neat and reliable pattern for processes in other fields.

(Carroll 2003, 601–02)

While Moretti's own description of his methods in *Graphs, Maps, Trees* as '*a materialist conception of form*' (Moretti's emphasis, 2005, 92) seems to confirm Carroll's diagnosis, it is the *difference* between an evolutionary process in nature (that as both Prendergast and Carroll point out, is reliant upon genetics and environment) and one in culture that not only threatens to undermine Moretti's proposals, but the critical acuity of Carroll's own mapping of 'environment' onto 'society' in his analysis of *Pride and Prejudice* in *Literary Darwinism*. In a sense, both critics apply analogical thinking, but in the service of very different applications of the 'evolutionary' dynamic. Where, for Carroll, 'environment' is aligned with society, in Moretti's work 'environment' becomes the literary marketplace, and this is the site of another of Prendergast's points of attack: 'the equation of market and nature under the aegis of evolutionary biology is exactly the move of social Darwinism', he argues (Prendergast 2005, 61). Not surprisingly, Moretti, in his 'Reply' to Prendergast, balks at such a critique: Prendergast's 'strong words' are 'mistaken', he declares, because of the underlying logic 'behind literary survival and oblivion' (Moretti 2006, 76). Moretti defends himself by emphasizing his own empirical methods: he reports what he found, and the criticism (from a 'libertarian spirit') is erroneous because it is, to Prendergast, politically inconvenient.

The question begged, of course, concerns the very underlying structure of 'survival and oblivion', the logic of natural selection that emphasizes not only selection, adaptation and divergence, but also extinction. Prendergast several times highlights the circular logic sometimes at work in Moretti's argument with regard to literary 'survival': that a reliance upon the 'alleged' preferences of readers to explain the continuing popularity of the Sherlock Holmes stories 'is imply tantamount to saying that Doyle survived because he survived' (Prendergast 2005, 52). This argument could be extended here to suggest that Moretti's work in *Graphs, Maps, Trees* mainly 'proves' the underlying assumptions about literary survival that he starts off with. The case of science fiction, for instance, which does *not* become extinct, is set to one side. It this very emphasis on 'extinction' that I find most troubling.

Moretti, in both his 'Graphs' and 'Maps' chapters, uses abstract models to try to understand the development and 'extinction' of literary genres.

His central chapter, 'Maps', is much more akin to Moretti's former method in the *Atlas*, much more attuned to the textual and to the contextual, and it is perhaps symptomatic of his own unease with the thrust of the other two chapters at the end of his 'Reply' to Prendergast that he declares his intention to 'bid farewell to the ethereal elegance of methodological abstractions, and return to the messy realities of social history' (Moretti 2006, 86) in his future work. In 'Graphs' and 'Trees', which use different abstract models but are complementary (and are based on similar underlying assumptions about literary survival and extinction), Moretti abjures the 'interpretation' of literary analysis for a form of data analysis. In 'Graphs', he compares, among other things, the 'rise' of the novel in Britain, Italy and Nigeria; the 'fall' of the novel in Japan, India, and France and Italy; and then the sequential hegemonic forms (epistolary, Gothic, historical) in the British novel between 1760 and 1850. The use of the visual 'graphing' techniques are illuminating and do indeed offer fresh insights into literary history, recovering a sense of the non-canonical, the 'lost' ninety-nine per cent. With his figure nine, however, 'British novelistic genres, 1740–1900' (Moretti 2005, 19), the emphasis upon survival and extinction is made most explicit. Sampling a range of previous literary histories, Moretti develops a graph which charts the periods of longevity of forty-four subgenres of the novel, from the 'courtship novel' (from c. 1740 to c. 1825) to the 'Kailyard school' (c. 1880 to c. 1900). Again, the reductive, abstracting method seems to provide a penetrating insight into the development of these subgenres, though of course it requires the reader to fill in the historical and cultural context. As we look, however, we might wonder that the Gothic runs from around 1770 to around 1830. This is fine for the 'first wave', but where is the late nineteenth-century flowering that has provided some of the most iconic figures and texts of that mode (Dracula, Jekyll and Hyde)? There seem to be gaps in the development of some genres, and some are missing entirely. Where is science fiction, for instance? One wonders, then, if these absences are caused by the form of the graph itself. This bar chart does not have segmented bars; all bars have simply a beginning and an end. Are some genres not present because they do not 'fit'? Then we also find, at the bottom of this graph, a reference to a 'Note on the Taxonomy of the Forms' to be found at the end of the chapter.

It is here that some of the worrying implications for the results of Moretti's abstraction and necessary reduction in the form of graphs (or later, Darwinian trees) come to the fore. Moretti notes that his chart is based on 'dates of beginning and end' (Moretti 2005, 31), then confesses:

A few genres experience brief but intense revivals decades after their original peak, like the oriental tale in 1819–25, or the gothic after 1885, or the historical novel (more than once). How to account for these Draculaesque reawakenings is a fascinating topic, which however will have to wait for another occasion. (Moretti 2005, 31)

The putting aside of such concerns at this point is, I think, intensely problematic for Moretti's project, for the very idea of 'survival and extinction' is compromised by these revivals. The joking dismissal of the genre revivals as somehow occult revenants ill-serves their importance: if genres become 'extinct', how can they return? If historical and cultural contexts are the main causal factor, is this kind of literary 'history' well served by bracketing off the literary marketplace (the 'environment') from the wider contextual landscape? At the bottom of the 'Note' is a further revelation, which seems to answer some of the questions I put in the paragraph above, but in a rather disquieting way:

> The chart shows neither detective fiction nor science fiction; although both genres achieve their modern form around 1890 (Doyle and Wells), and undergo a major change in the 1920s, in step with the overall pattern, their peculiar long duration seems to require a different approach. (Moretti 2005, 31)

What this approach might be is also left until another occasion. The absence of the two genres does appear to knock a rather large hole in Moretti's conceptual edifice, and the reason for their omission – their 'long duration' – is an issue that simply cannot be left aside in this way. Does the longevity of science fiction suggest that it is outside the 'environmental' pressures (i.e. the market) that seem to regulate the rise and 'extinction' of all the others? How so? Why does it *not* become 'extinct'? As Prendergast argues, the issue of timescales – the fundamental incompatibility of evolutionary timescales, the *longue durée* of biological time, to the 'far speedier' developmental spans of cultural forms (Prendergast 2005, 57) – is so central to the thrust of Moretti's argument that his punning disposal of genres that do not fit the analogous developmental structures seems insufficient.

Part of my own response to Moretti's articles and book was to try to conceptualize a history of science fiction (SF) on his own terms: to sample critical histories of SF to try to come up with a generic 'tree' for science fiction, one that took full account of the genre's own subgeneric developments. To this end, I consulted texts from the critical history of SF, from Brian Aldiss's *Billion Year Spree* (1973), to Darko Suvin's *Meta-*

morphoses of Science Fiction: On the Poetics and History of a Literary Genre (1979), to Adam Roberts' *Science Fiction* (2000), to Roger Luckhurst's *Science Fiction* (2005). I also consulted John Clute and Peter Nicholls' authoritative (and award-winning) *Encyclopaedia of Science Fiction* (1999). From Roberts, I also took a schematic list of fifteen subgeneric SF narratives, which are as follows:

1. Time-travel story.
2. First encounter with alien life.
3. Novum story (new piece of technology).
4. Interplanetary/interstellar travel story.
5. Robot story.
6. Virtual Reality story.
7. 'Philosophical' story.
8. Post nuclear war mutation story.
9. Scientist story.
10. Alternative History.
11. Magic Realism.
12. Utopia/Dystopia.
13. Sword and Sorcery.
14. Thundering good old-fashioned space opera story.
15. The End of the World.

To these one might want to add others: the Future War story; the ESP narrative; and Cyberpunk. These I placed on a time line, and attempted to work out formal connections which might provide an 'evolutionary' model of SF's development.

Several things became apparent during this process. The first was how rigorously the SF historians I have mentioned avoid evolutionary discourse in their texts: only Aldiss, at the very beginning of his text, invokes Darwin, his first chapter being called 'The Origins of the Species' (Aldiss 1973, 7–39). The other texts use 'history', or 'development', but *not* 'evolution'. Aldiss's chapter title itself opens up another telling discovery: to these literary historians, there is no single origin point that can be agreed upon. Their definitions of SF are themselves divergent, and the narratives they offer, while producing some consensus on key textual waystations, differ widely in assumptions and approaches. Aldiss and Suvin, the earlier histories consulted, are the most inclusive, placing SF in a very long literary tradition that, for Suvin at least, can be traced back to classical times. Roberts and Luckhurst concentrate much more closely on what the *Encyclopaedia* would call 'generic' SF, published in SF magazines and in publishing imprints dedicated to the genre.[4] Aldiss's 'history' begins with Mary Shelley's *Frankenstein* in 1818, SF being produced out of 'first wave' Gothic; his narrative encompasses 'canonical' SF writers such as Jules Verne and H. G. Wells, while always looking to more 'literary' examples (Stevenson, Jack London, Orwell, the utopian tradition) in order to situate SF in a wider sense of the literary fantastic. This strategy tends to blur the direct generic connections which would be emphasized by an evolutionary model which emphasizes formal (or narrative) developments and variations, as does Aldiss's concentration on authors, editors and SF magazines rather than subgeneric narrative tropes. Suvin's scope is even wider, though he offers a very famous formal definition of SF which runs as follows:

> *SF is, then, a literary genre whose necessary and sufficient conditions are the presence and interaction of estrangement and cognition, and whose main formal device is an imaginative framework alternative to the author's empirical environment.* (Suvin's emphasis; 1979, 8–9)

The centrality of 'estrangement' in this formulation indicates the political or ideological thrust of Suvin's approach to the genre; the foregrounding of 'environment' signifies the connection of the genre to the conditions of social reality. Elsewhere, Suvin offers a definition of Utopia which is not dissimilar to this, and it is no surprise that he places the Utopian tradition at the heart of his history of SF.[5] His definition of SF as a 'literature of cognitive estrangement' allows the broadest possible scope to include texts which have only a slight connection to 'genre SF', under the rubric of a shared concern with fabulation and the alternative

---

[4]   Perhaps this indicates something about their own 'conditions of emergence', in Luckhurst's phrase: Aldiss is a postwar British SF writer of considerable importance and longevity, while Suvin, a Canadian SF critic and scholar, was a pioneer for the genre in an academic context. Both of these texts were published in the 1970s. Roberts – a published author of SF himself – and Luckhurst wrote their own texts from within a British academia which has embraced SF as a quasilegitimate field of literary study, and certainly offers the genre as a long-standing element of undergraduate English degree programmes, albeit one often offered outside – or alongside – more canonical period or 'survey' courses.

[5]   The definition runs thus: 'Utopia is, then, a literary genre or verbal construction whose necessary and sufficient conditions are *the presence of a particular quasi-human community where socio-political institutions, norms and individual relationships are organized on a more perfect principle than the author's community, this construction being based on estrangement rising out of an alternative historical hypothesis*' (Suvin's italics; 1988, 35).

imaginative framework. Suvin suggests six 'temporal clusters' – Hellenic, Hellenic-cum-Roman, Renaissance-Baroque, the 'cluster of democratic revolution 1770–1820', the *fin-de-siècle*, and modern SF proper – along his historical continuum, although Suvin himself proposes a spatial rather than temporal metaphor: 'an ideal history [of SF] … would have to be a geology … or a geography', he writes (Suvin 1979, 88).

Adam Roberts, by way of contrast, begins his history with Milton's *Paradise Lost*, in the 1660s. This divergent connection to the Epic form rather than the Gothic is ameliorated by his tracing of a path through Shelley's *Frankenstein* to Verne and Wells. The Miltonic inheritance helps Roberts propose a defining characteristic of SF as a response to the 'Age of Empires', in its foregrounding of encounters with the Other (in racial, gender, technological, cultural, or species terms). Roberts takes a historical overview up to the end of the 1960s; his chapters after the 'New Wave SF' of that decade are thematic rather than period based. I will suggest a reason for this shortly. By contrast, Luckhurst's narrative is foreshortened: he concentrates on SF as a response to modernity, and begins in the 1880s. His is most concerned of all the sampled SF histories with the connections to the social and cultural; it may be concluded that his decision (on sound formal grounds) to concentrate on the 1880s and afterwards allows him so to do, unlike (particularly) Aldiss and Suvin. Luckhurst's rootedness in the historically material 'conditions of emergence' (Luckhurst 2005, 16) of the genre lends his text a particular weight and authority, and throws rather different light on the connection between SF and the literary mainstream: the exclusion from the English literary canon of H. G. Wells, for instance, Luckhurst attributes to Wells' difficult relationship with influential late nineteenth-century literati, notably Professor Walter Raleigh, at a crucial time in canon- and discipline-formation for English as a university subject.

The differences I have pointed out should be balanced by what assumptions and emphases these histories share. Aldiss, Roberts and Luckhurst agree on the importance of magazines and editors to the development of SF as a genre: Hugo Gernsback at *Amazing Stories* from 1926, John W. Campbell at *Astounding Science Fiction* from 1937, and Herbert L. Gold at *Galaxy Science Fiction* from 1950 in the United States (to which we might add Michael Moorcock's editorship of *New Worlds* in the UK in the 1960s). Aldiss, Luckhurst and *The Encyclopaedia of Science Fiction* also point to a twin or double tradition in Anglo-American SF, 'parallel but separate' developments of an English SF born of the Wellsian 'scientific romance' and much closer to the literary mainstream; and an American SF born of the 'pulp' magazines mentioned above, crucial paperback imprints such as Ace, Pocket Books and DAW, and later anthologies edited by Judith Merrill and Damon Knight, among others. It is the 1960s, in this version of SF's double history, which brings the two strands back into dialogue, and also recombines generic SF with the literary mainstream through the New Wave's experiments with form and content.

To my surprise, considering my misgivings concerning Moretti's arguments, I discovered that it *was* possible to construct an evolutionary 'tree' of SF history from the materials I had gathered. With no agreement as to the genre's origins, I drew from the *Encyclopaedia* five main 'roots': the Fantastic Voyage (of the seventeenth and eighteenth centuries); the Gothic (the late eighteenth); the Philosophical Story or Satire (also the eighteenth century); the tale of 'Anticipation'; and the Utopian/ Dystopian tradition, dating from More's *Utopia* of 1516. These I traced to Roberts' list of fifteen SF narratives, with my own suggested three additions. A reordered chronological list would run as follows:

1. Utopia/Dystopia (More, 1516).
2. 'Philosophical' story or Satire (Swift, 1726).
3. Scientist story (*Frankenstein*, 1818; then Edisonade, 1880s).
4. The End of the World (Shelley's *The Last Man*, 1826).
5. Interplanetary/interstellar travel story (Verne, 1860s).
6. First encounter with alien life (mid-nineteenth century).
7. Novum story, based on a new piece of technology (Verne, 1860s).
8. Future War (Invasion) story (Chesney, 1871).
9. Time-travel story (Wells' *The Time Machine*, 1895).
10. Sword and Sorcery (Edgar Rice Burroughs, 1920s).
11. Robot story (Karel Capek, 1920).
12. Thundering good old-fashioned space opera story (E. E. 'Doc' Smith, 1927).
13. Alternative History (L. Sprague De Camp, 1941).
14. Post nuclear war mutation story (PostWorld War 2).
15. ESP narrative (1940s and 1950s).
16. Magic Realism (1960s and 1970s).
17. Virtual Reality story (1980s).
18. Cyberpunk (Gibson, 1982).

'Evolutionary' lines are not often clear, however. What can be concluded is that subgeneric 'extinction' is, for SF, rare; of the above list, only the 'Edisonade' or Gernsback-style 'Scientist story' (c.1890–c.1935) and the 'Invasion' story (1871–c.1914) can be said to have come to a definite end, and the traces of the latter can still be found in the 'Future War' variant. The British 'Scientific Romance' can also be seen to have largely expired some time in the 1950s, when the changes in generic SF that would lead to the New Wave were beginning to come into effect. However, every other form can be identified in current SF (although the mode of Magic Realism, never SF proper, may also have passed its period of influence). Even 'Space Opera', a mode once thought to be the most tired and cliché-ridden of all, has been revived by writers such as Iain M. Banks in his 'Culture' series of novels. For SF, then, to diagnose the 'extinction' of certain subgeneric modes caused by what readers like is almost impossible.

Other issues do present themselves, however, from this abstracted and schematic model. Perhaps the most striking is what seems to be a slowing of generic diversification: only five identified 'new' subgeneric modes since World War Two, and only two in the last twenty-five years (and even the 'Virtual Reality' story can be seen to have its antecedents in stories such as Frederik Pohl's 'The Tunnel Under the World' (1954) or the 1950s and 1960s narratives of Philip K. Dick). Cyberpunk can be seen as the only real innovation in the SF genre since 1980 (along with its offshoots 'splatterpunk' and 'steampunk'); Roger Luckhurst characterizes the 1990s and after as being the period of New Space Opera, Children's Fantasy, and the 'SF thriller', for instance. A cursory look at the SF shelves of a contemporary bookstore would certainly reveal a preponderance of Fantasy (or SF/ Fantasy hybrids), often written for the teenage or children's market. How to explain this seeming exhaustion of generic diversity? One can certainly turn to the marketplace as a crucial causal index for evidence. Perhaps the crucial element in the history of SF in the decades after World War Two is the slow, then increasingly rapid decline of the market for magazine publication of SF stories. The SF short story had always been the lifeblood of the genre, and the importance attached to *Amazing*, *Astounding*, *Galaxy* and *New Worlds* in the SF histories I have consulted signifies that it is this marketplace, rather than the paperback novel, that is the crucial environment until about 1970. According to Clute and Nicholls' *Encyclopaedia*, until around 1970 most SF narratives (including novels) would still be published first in the magazines, in serial format for longer stories. Since 1970, the market for SF has shifted to the dominance of the book: *Galaxy* finished publication in 1980. This era has become one not of divergence but convergence, of an increasing hybridity, and a blurring of the boundary between the mainstream and SF, perhaps precipitated by the experimental, late Modernist fictions published under the aegis of the New Wave in the 1960s. The *Encyclopaedia* notes that SF, fantasy and horror are now generically very close, to the extent that authors may publish in all three genres. The professional body for SF writers in the United States, it also notes, stopped being SF-only and embraced fantasy and horror writers in 1992, an important index of industry change.

The market for SF has also changed. The *Encyclopaedia* laments the increasing domination of commercial spin-offs, film and television tie-ins, and 'sharecrops' (novels written by lesser-known or apprentice writers in the idiom and 'world' of a much more commercially important author), resulting in a deluge of 'hack work' and 'product'. The 'midlist' writers, the SF authors who have steady but not spectacular sales, often over a career spanning decades, the kind of writers crucial to the history of SF, become pressurized by this increasingly commercial environment. Some cease publishing altogether. In his acceptance speech for the 1994 Pilgrim Award from the Science Fiction Research Association, published in 1995, John Clute offers a rather looser periodization but his sense of the change in SF in the postwar period is comparable. Clute suggests that 'First SF' (by which he means American genre SF) ended in 1957 at the launch of Sputnik, and thereafter, 'new versions of sf, new conversations' becomes a kind of 'teeming, immensely fruitful squabble' (Clute 1995, 10). Clute's insistence that contemporary SF is character-ized by 'exogamy' (loosely defined as 'marrying out': generic hybridity, a blurring of the boundary between SF and mainstream), where lines of development are much less easily identifiable, is borne out in the later chapters of Adam Roberts' text, which adopt a thematic rather than temporal organization, a mapping of the 'conversations' rather than exhibiting the ordering dynamic (or even narrative) of a history.[6] The literary history of SF has, in a sense, broken down; Clute confesses in his 1994 speech that on contributing to the *Encyclopaedia of Science Fiction*, 'I felt, and I think my partners may have felt, that a large and deeply loved part of what we were calling sf was, by 1993, a completed topic' (Clute 1995, 10–11). Clearly, however, it has not become extinct. Neither, it might be remembered, have the majority of SF subgenres. The model of 'survival and extinction', the underlying logic of Moretti's

---

[6]   In Clute and Nicholls' *Encyclopaedia of Science Fiction*, Clute is quoted as offering the following rough periodization for twentieth-century SF: 'in 1942 ... the inner tale of sf was a tale of empire ... in 1952, it was hubris ... in 1972, retri-bution ... in 1982, memory ... in 1992, the inner tale of sf is a tale of exogamy' (1999, 571).

'Graphs' and 'Trees', does not seem to pertain. The longevity of SF does, as Moretti admits, seem to require a different approach.

To conclude, then, my response to Moretti's abstract models, as an academic who partly works in the research field of science fiction, is ambivalent. There are clear methodological difficulties associated with this work, acutely probed by Christopher Prendergast, and, I hope, further outlined here. As Moretti also seems to acknowledge in his 'Reply' to Prendergast, 'abstract models' decouple the critical project from the urgent and material concerns of social reality, and that is perhaps too costly a loss. But my experiments in following Moretti's method have revealed something about the development of SF: that magazine publication and paperback book publication are indeed different 'environments', and have indeed produced different 'adaptive' strategies among the producers of SF. (One might also note that the decline of magazine publication after 1970 is concurrent with the explosion of SF as a cinematic genre to become a crucial part of the Hollywood industrial economy of the 'blockbuster' or the 'tentpole' summer hit. This can also be felt in the plethora of commercial, 'sharecrop', cross-media tie-in SF currently dominating bookstore shelves.) The increasing divergence of SF subgenre narratives between 1880 and 1970, the era dominated by magazine publication, can perhaps be explained by the need for novelty in competitive markets; or by the influence of crucial editors whose commissioning policy may have been deliberately plural, innovative or progressive; or even by the rapidity of technological, social and cultural change in the period, which drove SF to respond in increasingly diverse ways. By comparison, the economies of paperback book publication and distribution, in a less diverse and more monopolized retail environment, may produce an increased conservatism in SF commissioning editors. It is almost certainly too soon to gauge the impact of online booksellers, print-on-demand, or even online publication, but they too will affect the way in which SF develops in the future. I would hope that historical and cultural context will always enrich discussions, or 'explanations', of literary and generic history, even if 'evolutionary' models are used to structure them; but who will write that history, and what methods they will choose, remains to be seen.

Works Cited

Aldiss, Brian W., 1973. *Billion Year Spree: The History of Science Fiction*. London: Weidenfeld and Nicolson.

Beer, Gillian, 1983. *Darwin's Plots: Evolutionary Narrative in Darwin, George Eliot and Nineteenth-Century Fiction*. London: Routledge & Kegan Paul.

Carroll, Joseph, 1995a. *Evolution and Literary Theory*. Columbia: University of Missouri Press.

———, 1995b. 'Evolution and Literary History', *Human Nature* 6: 119–34.

———, 1996. 'Pluralism, Poststructuralism and Evolutionary Theory', *Academic Questions* 9, 3 (Summer): 43–57.

———, 1999. ' "Theory", Anti-Theory, and Empirical Criticism', in *Biopoetics: Evolutionary Explorations in the Arts*, ed. Brett Cooke and Frederick Turner. Lexington, KY: ICUS: 139–54.

———, 2003. 'Adaptationist Literary Study: An Emerging Research Program', *Style* 36, 4 (Winter): 596–617.

———, 2004. *Literary Darwinism: Evolution, Human Nature and Literature*. London: Routledge.

Clute, John, 1995. *Look at the Evidence: Essays and Reviews*. Liverpool: Liverpool University Press.

———, John and Peter Nicholls, 1999 (1993). *The Encyclopaedia of Science Fiction*. London: Orbit.

Greenberg, Jonathan, 2004. 'The Descent of Theory' [review of Carroll, *Literary Darwinism*], *Novel: A Forum on Fiction* 83, 1 (Fall): 117–20.

Levine, George, 1988. *Darwin and the Novelists: Patterns of Science in Victorian Fiction*. Cambridge, MA, and London: Harvard University Press.

Luckhurst, Roger, 2005. *Science Fiction*. Cambridge: Polity.

Moretti, Franco, 1998. *Atlas of the European Novel 1800–1900*. London: Verso.

———, 2005. *Graphs, Maps, Trees: Abstract Models for a Literary Theory*. London and New York: Verso.

———, 2006. 'Reply to Christopher Prendergast', *New Left Review* 41 (September/October): 71–87.

Pohl, Frederik, 1977 (1954). 'The Tunnel Under the World'. Reprint in *The Best of Frederik Pohl*, ed. Lester del Rey. New York: Taplinger: 8–35.

Prendergast, Christopher, 2005. 'On the Roots of Moretti's "Trees" ', *New Left Review* 34 (July/August): 40–65.

Roberts, Adam, 2000. *Science Fiction*. London and New York: Routledge.

Suvin, Darko, 1979. *Metamorphoses of Science Fiction: On the Poetics and History of a Literary Genre*. New Haven and London: Yale University Press.

———, 1988. 'Science Fiction and Utopian Fiction: Degrees of Kinship', in *Positions and Presuppositions in Science Fiction*, idem. Basingstoke: Macmillan: 33–43.

'The luxury of storytelling':
Science, Literature and Cultural Contest in
Ian McEwan's Narrative Practice

DAVID AMIGONI

IN IAN MCEWAN's *Enduring Love*, Joe Rose, the narrator of the story and a science journalist by profession, undertakes some research towards his next project, about 'the death of anecdote and narrative in science' (McEwan 1998, 41).[1] In doing this, he ventures to the London Library, a place that the philosopher of neo-Darwinism, Daniel C. Dennett, might refer to as a branch of 'the library of Babel'.[2] Rose is more at home in the harder edged world of Babel's analogue and antithesis – what Dennett referred to as 'the library of Mendel', or the DNA holdings of letter sequences, codes and 'paragraphs' that compose the genomic templates organizing life. Rose despises the Victorian London Library for the paucity of its scientific collections, and bemoans the library's 'assumption ... that the world could be sufficiently understood through fictions, histories and biographies. Did the scientific illiterates who ran this place, and who dared to call themselves educated individuals, really believe that literature was the greatest intellectual achievement of our civilisation?' (42). The question of literature's role in generating and enhancing 'civilization' remains, for intellectuals trained in science, a contested one.

Rose's purpose is to locate scientific writing on the edge of extinction: he peruses a key nineteenth-century source of scientific inquiry and debate, the journal *Nature*, established by T. H. Huxley in the late 1860s. The narrator locates an anecdote from a correspondent about a dog which appears, through its actions in relation to its human masters,

---

[1] Where the context indicates clearly that I am citing from either *Enduring Love* or *Saturday*, after the first full citation I shall supply just a page reference.

[2] For this terminology, see Dennett 1995, 113–15. Patricia Waugh has employed this terminology in her excellent account of the relationship between fiction and scientific thought in the 1990s, which includes an insightful reading of *Enduring Love*; see Waugh 2005.

to display some strikingly human traits: having been ordered off its favourite spot, it seems to dupe its master into a course of action that permits the dog to return, triumphantly, to the spot from which it has been removed: for the correspondent of 1904 this demonstrates canine memory, foresight and cunning. Of course, to the modern scientific journalist this merely represents a tendency of thought among 'Darwin's generation' which 'was the last to permit itself the luxury of storytelling in published articles'. What draws the narrator's attention to this anecdote is 'how the power and attractions of narrative had clouded judgment … No theory evinced, no terms defined, a meaningless sample of one, a laughable anthropomorphism' (41). As this chapter will argue, narrative in science is far from dead. It has an insistent power that McEwan's fictions interrogate at the same time as they explore a complex public culture saturated with the effects of science, technology – and literature.

McEwan is a master of narrative art; but his capacity for generating sensational effects is matched by his ability simultaneously to pose cognitive and intellectual challenges. Of course, *Enduring Love* is, as one of its back-cover blurbs tells us, 'a page turner'. Joe Rose tells a sensational story which begins with a meeting at an airport, and a picnic in the Cotswolds for his returning lover, Clarissa. McEwan is drawn to fictive relationships that dramatize the differences between literature and science: Clarissa is an academic who is undertaking literary historical research into the love letters of John Keats and Fanny Brawne. The picnic is disrupted by a fateful ballooning accident, in which a doctor, John Logan, who seeks with other bystanders including Rose to rescue the balloon's hapless occupants, falls to his death. The ballooning accident and Logan's death is at once a source of the self-preserver's guilt (Rose and the other helpers let go of the balloon at a crucial point, Logan does not), and the cause of Rose's initial encounter with Jed Parry. Parry has been another arbitrary helper, and witness to Logan's death. Parry also suffers from de Clérembault's syndrome, and goes on to stalk and reveal an obsessive love for Rose. This 'enduring love' – a love that has, precisely, to be endured – wrecks Rose's relationship with Clarissa.

It is Parry, indeed, who brings Rose's reflections on 'the luxury of storytelling' in nineteenth-century science to an abrupt end: Rose realizes that he is being stalked by Parry in the Library, and his note taking on the dog anecdote is brought to a halt at the words ' *"intentionality, intention, tries to assert control over the future"* ' (43). He realizes that the words referred first to a dog when he first transcribed them, but that now, their source of reference is split, and that they refer as much to him as the dog. References that can be split between more than one referent are important to the 'entanglements' that McEwan's fiction weaves and invites the reader to un-weave. Rose's attempts to narrate an account of the shock that his body undergoes may eschew post-Saussurean linguistic orthodoxy – 'It is clearly not true that without language there is no thought' – but the challenge of representing a material 'sensation' registered in the body is no simple task of fitting the word to the thought: 'Unclean, contaminated, crazy, physical but somehow moral … It wasn't fear exactly. Fear was too focused, it had an object … Apprehension then. Yes, there it was, approximately. It was apprehension' (43).

Apprehension is born of tension and anxiety: it also means to 'grasp', and this is something that we seek when we read, in an effort to understand. But what we grasp from the 'luxury of storytelling' may not be comforting. In fact, the matter of what we can apprehend or grasp is what McEwan explores through his fictions. 'The act of reading and understanding' is also something that Rose reflects upon as he recollects a moment in which he managed to indulge 'simultaneously … two of life's central, antithetical pleasures, reading and fucking'; as Clarissa makes love to him, he reads in a newspaper of the death of an entire football team in Canada, exterminated randomly by nature in a freak and devastating snow storm (161). It enables Rose to be, as he puts it, 'in two places at once' (158). If storytelling as 'luxury' connotes both amateurism and the leisure to craft a literary form and humanistic discourse of subjectivity that it might privilege (a conscious, intending agent in time and an intelligible world), then the relationship between its luxurious moments in prestigious sites of publication and the baser forces that drive our need both to produce and consume narrative – 'an unreliable urge to crap' (40), or the desire to fuck – is what McEwan's fiction perhaps seeks to expose. But it may also, in exposing something of the reductive drives that generate narration, articulate a more complex view of the human capacity for 'being in two places at once', in a world conditioned by both biological determinism and indeterminate, proliferating social and cultural meanings. And that takes us into critical debates within the contemporary study of literature and science.

One strand in the recent study of literature and science in Anglo-American literary studies has been dominated by an historicism focused predominantly on the seventeenth and nineteenth centuries, an historicism that has foregrounded, moreover, the importance of narrative and anecdote: in the case of nineteenth-century science studies, Gillian Beer's seminal *Darwin's Plots* (Beer 2000) was premised on the insight into the structuring role of the narrative imagination in Darwin's theories of natural and sexual selection, and the complex 'two way traffic' that moved between scientific writing and novelistic fiction, particularly in the writings of George Eliot and Hardy. Beer is no card-carrying New Historicist, but her later work takes something of a lead from this method of criticism in the way in which it examines, for instance, the relationship between nineteenth-century anecdotal ethnographic reportage in one domain, and an artistic rendering and interrogation of that narrative in another: for instance, the story of exile and return experienced by the Fuegian 'Jemmy Button' from Darwin's *Beagle* narrative, and Hardy's story of exile, return and alienation in his novel *The Return of the Native* (see 'Can the Native Return?' Beer 1996). Thus, McEwan's interest in the authority of narrative and anecdote finds resonances in contemporary critical methods for analysing the linguistic materials common to literature and science, a feature shared with poststructuralist accounts of the literature-science relation (of which more in due course). Moreover, as I have indicated in my initial discussion of *Enduring Love*, McEwan's reflections on narrative incorporate a sense of the nineteenth-century history of science. And an awareness of nineteenth- and indeed seventeenth-century traditions of scientific thought also figure in the other novel that I shall discuss, *Saturday* (2005a), McEwan's recent novel about a traumatic day in the life of Henry Perowne, a consultant neurosurgeon. McEwan's fiction interrogates what science may mean in the lives of western subjects at a time of both great material comfort, and multiple threats (terrorism, warfare between states, urban criminal violence). It acknowledges a broader cultural narrative of which scientific discourses are an insistent, authoritative and in some sense contested component. McEwan's fiction contributes subtly, intelligently and imaginatively to that process of contestation.

On the face of it, McEwan seems to participate in and extend C. P. Snow's 'two cultures' perspective on science, the humanities and the cultural contest in which they are involved (Snow 1964). In a recent interview McEwan explained to Boyd Tonkin that he likes the company and outlook of scientists as an antidote to 'lazy arts-faculty despair'. 'Among cultural intellectuals, pessimism is the style' [McEwan] says with a tinge of scorn. 'You're not a paid-up member unless you're gloomy' (McEwan 2007a). This pessimistic despair is embodied in characters in his novels: John Grammaticus, the eminent poet and father-in-law to the neurosurgeon Henry Perowne in *Saturday*, rails against the dominant presence of the Telecom Tower in London (Henry, a child of the sixties, continues to refer to it as 'the Post Office Tower'), and he imagines how it would be seen by the eighteenth-century architect Robert Adam who built the square of elegant houses in which his son-in-law resides. ' "He was bound to think of it as a religious building of some kind – why else build so high? He'd have to assume those dishes were ornamental, or used in rites. A religion of the future ... Adam would have been stunned by the ugliness of that glass thing ... If that's going to be our religion, he'd have said to himself, then we're truly fucked" ' (McEwan 2005a, 197). Perowne quietly replies that Grammaticus's degenerative satire may be 'not far out' in its rendering of the Tower's communication dishes as ritual symbols of a 'religion of the future'. This raises a vital context for contemporary understanding of science: the place of communicative media, and technological innovation itself, in the dissemination of scientific discourse by intellectuals, a process which complicates a simple invocation of the 'two cultures' debate.

The 'two cultures' debate is now held no longer adequate to define the horizon of the contemporary relationship between literature and science. In 1991, the publisher and writer John Brockman referred to C. P. Snow when elaborating what he called 'The Third Culture', a concept which Brockman borrowed from Snow's lecture 'The Two Cultures: A Second Look' (1961) (Snow 1964). 'The third culture' was a space in which Snow imagined that humanities intellectuals and scientists would begin to talk to each other in a more equal dialogue, once the barrier that had been erected to divide the 'two cultures' had started productively to dissolve. However, Brockman was at once less sanguine about this possibility, and more aggressive in promoting the peculiar claims of science as the millennium approached. Brockman argued that 'what traditionally has been called "science" has today become "public culture" ' (Brockman 1991). In some sense, Brockman's historical thesis dramatically illuminates the exchange between Perowne and Grammaticus in McEwan's *Saturday*: Christianity, with its traditions of theological refinement and literary sensibility, as well as its command of the built environment, once constituted public culture, with 'science' and its arguments from design as one of its subdepartments. Now 'science' has become public culture itself, symbolized by the Telecom Tower, as both medium (beaming digitized information around the world by microwave), and iconic message built in glass, steel and neon light. For Brockman, this new configuration of public culture, the 'third culture', constitutes the major challenge for intellectuals as disputants and public communicators:

There is no canon or accredited list of acceptable ideas. The strength
of the third culture is precisely that it can tolerate disagreements
about which ideas are to be taken seriously. Unlike previous intellectual pursuits, the achievements of the third culture are not the
marginal disputes of a quarrelsome mandarin class: they will affect the
lives of everybody on the planet. ... The role of the intellectual
includes communicating. Intellectuals are not just people who know
things but people who shape the thoughts of their generation. An
intellectual is a synthesizer, a publicist, a communicator ... The
third-culture thinkers are the new public intellectuals.

(Brockman 1991)

Brockman has responded to the new challenge of science as public
culture itself by developing first, in the late 1980s, the 'Reality Club', a
discussion society self-consciously modelled on Erasmus Darwin's late
eighteenth-century 'Lunar Society' (and though he does not cite this,
presumably T. H. Huxley's famous 'X Club'); and, since 1997, a major
website, *Edge*, to disseminate the thinking of 'Third Culture intellectuals'. These include such major figures as the scientist Richard Dawkins,
the philosopher Daniel C. Dennett, and the psychologist Steven Pinker.
These thinkers are committed Darwinians, a theoretical paradigm that is
shared with a new movement in literary criticism that seeks to promote
the authority of an evolutionary explanation of literature itself; the
literary critic Joseph Carroll is a major figure here, and the controversial
biologist and proponent of 'socio-biology' E. O. Wilson is an influential
sponsor (Gottschall and Sloan Wilson 2005). While Brockman says that
there is no 'accredited canon' of ideas, and that 'Third Culture' discussion thrives on disagreement, it is still the case that as the title 'Reality
Club' suggests, there is a core of truth that 'Third Culture' intellectuals
defend and aggressively promote. The truth is embodied in the 'modern
synthesis' of evolutionary biology, that is to say biochemical genetics
and Darwinian natural selection, which also sets the prevailing intellectual tone for evolutionary literary criticism. The common enemy of the
'Third Culture' and Darwinian literary criticism as its offshoot is 'social
constructivism'. If this 'blank slate' approach to human character origi-
nates in many classical Enlightenment and post Enlightenment sources,
from Locke and Hume to the behaviourism of B. F. Skinner, it perhaps
reaches its apogee in the broadly poststructuralist account of scientific
discourse that would see it precisely as linguistically determined and
'constructed' according to ideological predilection and social conven-
tion (witness again Joe Rose in *Enduring Love* contesting the poststructuralist axiom that there can be no thought without language).

Hostility to 'social constructivism' was intensified by the 'Sokal affair': in 1996 an article offering a 'cultural' reading of quantum gravity that proclaimed itself to be both 'transgressive' and 'liberationist', was submitted to the US journal *Social Text* by Alan Sokal, a US Professor of Physics (Sokal 1996). When published, Sokal declared it to be a hoax: the article turned out to be a randomly stitched together tissue of quotations from a range of sources (cultural studies, postmodernist, deconstructionist) that are deemed to be 'social constructivist'. 'Third Culture' intellectuals and evolutionary literary critics see their mission as rescuing literary studies from 'social constructivism' and restoring the field to the standards of truth and clarity expected by a new, scientifically driven public culture; Dawkins' review of Sokal's book certainly puts it in these terms (Dawkins 1998). Though different to the historicist model of literature and science outlined earlier, poststructuralist critiques of scientific discourse and its social authority have been especially influential in America, where the so-called 'Science Wars' prevail; and in France as the home of the structuralist and poststructuralist revolution. The Sokal affair has been lively in both contexts. We come then to another version of what McEwan has critically styled literary-theoretical 'pessimism' which rejects a world of inequality allegedly constructed in the 'objective' name of Enlightenment science, and seeks, in utopian impulse, to 'exult in another well out of … reach' (McEwan 2005a, 197). Yet, McEwan does not, cannot, repudiate literature's role in constructing and interrogating social meanings.

McEwan has himself become an intellectual who has contributed to shaping the discussion of scientific public culture, and the contemporary novelist that scientific intellectuals like to lionize. He has contributed to discussions in Brockman's *Edge*. For instance, invited to reflect on the conundrum of what you believe though you cannot prove it, McEwan, reminds us, paradoxically, that his belief in the false promise of an after life remains just that, as an after life cannot actually be disproved (Brockman 1997–2007, McEwan 2005b). McEwan has also contributed to major discussion platforms sponsored by the 'Third Culture'; in 2006, he contributed a talk for the event (at the London School of Economics) marking thirty years since the publication of Dawkins' hugely influential book, *The Selfish Gene* (McEwan 2006). McEwan has also published a chapter in the book edited by Jonathan Gottschall and David Sloan Wilson on evolutionary approaches to literary narrative, *The Literary Animal* (McEwan 2005c). I shall discuss these contributions as literary

exercises and reflections on narrative in their own right. They contain
striking echoes of ideas and motifs that are pursued in *Enduring Love* and
Saturday. The connection with the fiction is important to stress, but not
because the fiction in some passive way 'reflects' McEwan's views. At the
same time as it important to claim the fictional writings as in some sense
a distinctive, 'literary' space for thought, it is equally important to stress
that while McEwan adopts the position of the 'Third Culture' intellectual in public culture, his affiliations are harder to measure as he explores
the implications of narrative and literary practice in the dissemination of
science.

When McEwan addressed the event celebrating the thirtieth anniversary of Dawkins' *The Selfish Gene* he spoke of the 'need [for] a stronger
sense of a scientific literary tradition. Those of us educated in a literary
tradition take for granted a kind of mental map – a temporal map, really
– of a literary history, a canon, a hierarchy if you like' (McEwan 2006).
In speaking up for a canon and hierarchy, McEwan seems somewhat at
odds with Brockman's 1991 manifesto on 'Third Culture' intellectual
practice, with its self-conscious refusal of a 'canon or accredited list of
acceptable ideas'. In invoking some sense of scientific writing as a custo-
dian of the best that has been thought and said, McEwan was not merely
'speaking' for literature as though through the 'Two Cultures' debate
shaped by Snow, but in turn invoking its precursor, the debate about
science, literature and 'culture' conducted between T. H. Huxley and
Matthew Arnold in the 1880s. But McEwan's writings do not simply
invoke a canonical tradition to glorify it; rather, they ask what place
such canonical discourse occupies in contemporary culture. For McEwan
sees tradition and innovation at work in writerly voices of scientists –
narrative voices – from his praise for Dawkins' prose ('I raise my hat to
the phrase "shuffled into oblivion" ') to his awareness that Watson and
Crick's groundbreaking essay announcing the structure of DNA in
Nature (1953) employs the 'drawing-room politesse of the double negative': ' "It has not escaped our notice that the specific pairing we have
postulated immediately suggests a possible copying mechanism for the
genetic material" ' (McEwan 2005c, 6). McEwan notes a later echoing of
this politesse from the report of the Human Genome Sequencing
Consortium, published in *Nature* in 2000; 'it has not escaped our notice
that the more we learn about the human genome, the more there is to
explore'. As McEwan observes, 'This form of respectful echoing within
the tradition must surely appeal to those who admire literary modernism'
(McEwan 2005c, 19).

These reflections on the presence of self-conscious echoing in scientific writing occur in McEwan's essay for *The Literary Animal*. In a collection that is otherwise dominated by readings of literary works from the perspective of evolutionary psychology and neuroscience, McEwan's 'Literature, Science and Human Nature' is a deeply literate understanding of canonical scientific writing which is aware of its dependence on literary form and texture. At the centre of his essay is a biographical sketch of the life of Charles Darwin, and his complex and disturbing discovery of human and animal 'brotherhood' from the voyage of the *Beagle* through to the writing of the *Expression of the Emotions in Man and Animals*. In one sense, this latter text can be seen as McEwan's 'source' for Joe Rose's reactions to the expressions of emotions that he sees at multicultural Heathrow Airport as he meets Clarissa: reactions that point to a universal human nature that is 'genetically inscribed' in ways that indicate both the inheritance of instinct, and brotherhood with animals (McEwan 1998, 4). However, McEwan does not want us to read Darwin's life as a biography that 'sources' ideas for his novel – instead, we are asked 'to read his life as a novel ... driving forwards towards a great reckoning' (McEwan 2005c, 7). To read Darwin's life *as* a novel is in some sense to participate in the 'luxury' of storytelling. Except that McEwan does not present the apprehension of Darwin through reading as an unmitigated luxury. Rather, he explores, through his own fictional narrative practices, the place of narrative and the texture of scientific discourse – the voices that inscribe science as a tradition of discourse – in lives that, if not luxurious, are at least comfortable due substantially to the benefits of a culture shaped and defined by science.

Saturday is about a day in a comfortable life that is brought to the brink of a catastrophe. It reaches its dramatic peak in a somewhat similar scene to the end of *Enduring Love*: while Joe Rose 'rescues' Clarissa from the stalking, knife-wielding, home-invading Jed Parry, Henry Perowne finds himself in his own luxurious living room, watching on as an unstable petty criminal with Huntington's disease, and whom he has humiliated earlier in the day, holds a knife to his wife's throat, and threatens his pregnant daughter with rape. In both situations, professional middle-class men have to resort to desperate measures to protect their loved ones (shooting in *Enduring Love*, deception and a shove down the stairs in *Saturday*). And *Saturday* begins with McEwan's characteristic (but now 'Post 9/11') sense of brooding tension, as Perowne is drawn inexplicably from his bed in the early hours of Saturday, 15 February 2003 to witness – what? a burning plane in the night sky, certainly, but caused by an accident, or a terrorist attack? Twenty-four-hour news eventually informs Perowne that it is the former, there is a 'decent landing. Neither of the two man crew is hurt' (35). Having closed this alarming opening comfortingly, the keynote of what follows is Perowne's contentment, his comfort. In fact, McEwan has reflected on this in a recent interview, offering an analysis of the rather negative reaction to the character of Perowne: 'People felt very uncomfortable because I painted this exaggerated version of themselves, really. Henry is really the fat contented western man, they themselves are fat contented western people. And it was a mirror, in a sense, like Caliban's mirror, and it made people feel enraged' (McEwan 2007b, 26).

Enduring Love and Saturday also hold up the mirror to a public culture saturated by comforts born of scientific thought and innovation. In the character of Joe Rose, McEwan fashions a figure whose professional role is to mediate between scientific specialization and the public. Henry Perowne tends not to intellectualize his working life: a neurosurgeon whose specialisms are at once a biochemist's knowledge of the micro-composites of life, and the engineer's understanding of the body as a complex mechanism, McEwan nonetheless shows him striving to develop an understanding of, first, the affective dimensions of the culture that he inhabits, and second a history of the expertise that he contributes to it, through a kind of education orchestrated by his daughter, Daisy. Daisy has read English at Oxford, and is a young published poet: she is determined to educate her father in the literary canon (Flaubert, Tolstoy, Conrad), but also the greats of scientific writing. A recollected image of comfort frames the reader's first encounter with the education of Henry Perowne. As Perowne re-awakes on Saturday morning following his disrupted sleep in the early hours, a phrase passes through his mind: 'There is grandeur in this view of life.' Of course, as he himself comes gradually to realize, this is from Darwin, the closing paragraph of the Origin of Species, unconsciously recalled second-hand from the biography that Daisy has 'set' him to study (Daisy conducts her relationship with her father rather in the manner of a tutorial), and read sleepily in the bath the night before. The section of the biography he reads is about 'the dash to complete the Origin', and a 'summary of the concluding pages [of the Origin], amended in later editions' (55). As McEwan has observed in his 'novelistic' account of Darwin's life, 'the most frequently quoted passages [from the Origin] occur in the final paragraph' (McEwan 2005c, 8). It leads to Perowne's reflection on the creation story told by evolution, how out of war, death and destruction, life forms, morality is shaped, and even cities have evolved. If there is luxury in storytelling, the content of the story is not uniformly comforting. Darwin's canonized words will figure again in Perowne's consciousness, later in the story.

The evolution of the city, and the illustrious traditions of scientific enquiry that have forged the present, flash through Perowne's mind again as he becomes stuck in a traffic jam in London: McEwan sets *Saturday* on the day in February 2003 when up to a million people took to the streets of London to demonstrate against the impending invasion of Iraq. Perowne, comfortable again in his silver Mercedes S500 ('a sensuous part of what he regards as his overgenerous share of the world's goods' [75]) tries to take in the scene as it might have been seen by those 'curious men of the English Enlightenment' who gave birth to his world view, and the science that has shaped modern culture. But his attempt to do so is haunted, or in his case thwarted, by literary possibilities that Daisy understands only too well:

> He tries to see it, or feel it, in historical terms, this moment in the last decades of the petroleum age, when a nineteenth-century device is brought to final perfection in the early years of the twenty first; when the unprecedented wealth of masses at serious play in the unforgiving modern city makes for a sight that no previous age could have imagined. Ordinary people! Rivers of light! He wants to make himself see it as Newton might, or his contemporaries, Boyle, Hooke, Wren, Willis – those clever, curious men of the English Enlightenment who for a few years held in their minds nearly all the world's science. Surely, they would be awed ... But he can't quite trick himself into it. He can't feel his way past the iron weight of the actual to see beyond the boredom of a traffic tailback ... He doesn't have the lyric gift to see beyond it – he's a realist, and can never escape. (168)

McEwan brings literature and science into cultural contest: *Saturday* is an urban fiction, a day in the life of a professional man on his day off, a fiction that owes much to a modernist tradition exemplified by Virginia Woolf's *Mrs Dalloway*: 'this moment' is an intertextual echo of the earlier novel preoccupation with passing hours and fleeting moments of consciousness, but so too are Perowne's attempts at modernist epiphanies, 'Ordinary people! Rivers of light!' Perhaps less easy to spot though are echoes of T. H. Huxley's *Lay Sermons* from the mid- to late 1860s, and their promotion of a scientific culture through the celebration of the achievements of the Royal Society in the 1660s (see in particular 'On the Advisableness of Improving Scientific Knowledge', Huxley 1891). But it's a stand off, the realist surgeon cannot enter into the way of seeing mastered by his lyrical daughter. While *Saturday* is a novel in which texts that construct and enrich our literacy actually play a significant role, it still poses the question: what does literature do?

The question begins to be answered as Perowne steers his car away from the jam, and, accidentally, into the path of another car, dislodging its wing-mirror. The minor collision brings Perowne into the lower social orbit of Baxter and two other petty criminals who use the occasion as an attempt to extort money, and threaten Perowne with a beating when he resists. However, Perowne notes 'muscular restlessness' in Baxter's face and the biochemist and engineer in him immediately reaches this diagnosis:

> Chromosome four. The misfortune lies within a single gene, in an excessive repeat of a single sequence – CAG. Here's biological determinism in its purest form. More than forty repeats of that one little codon and you're doomed. Your future is fixed and easily foretold … nightmarish hallucinations and a meaningless end. This is how the brilliant machinery of being is undone by the tiniest of faulty cogs. (94)

Perowne offers his expert diagnosis, and it turns the situation, exploiting the magical thinking that hovers below the surface of the patient-doctor relationship, and which continues, as McEwan recognizes while many 'Third Culture' intellectuals do not, to haunt the legitimating strategies of modern science: 'They are together … in a world not of the medical, but of the magical. When you are diseased, it is unwise to abuse the shaman' (95). But it is borrowed time, and the episode ends in Baxter's humiliation as he loses command of his semi-detached henchmen, and the moment for violence. Perowne drives off, to a squash match, but will be made to pay. He does so later in the day as the family dinner with Grammaticus, Daisy and his son, is shattered when Rosalind Perowne returns from work with Baxter, his henchmen, and a knife threatening her. It is in this context that McEwan finally 'answers' the question of what literature does. If Perowne's 'magical' knowledge of 'biological determinism' shapes the first reversal of Baxter's behaviour, then it is a literary recital that shapes the second. Daisy refuses the invaders' sexual taunts to read one of her 'dirty' poems from the set of proofs (entitled *My Saucy Bark*) that sit upon the table; she follows instead Grammaticus's cue and recites Arnold's 'Dover Beach', passing it off as her own. What McEwan produces here is a curious kind of parody of literature's civilizing mission, so frequently rehearsed in the nineteenth century and since. The twitching, 'simian'-like Baxter, wracked by mood swings triggered by faulty genes, becomes a kind of Arnoldian best self, transformed by a literary conversion. All thoughts of rape dissipate as he says 'You wrote that … it's beautiful. You know that, don't you. It's beautiful. And you wrote it.' (222). The episode is especially rich because of the way in which McEwan translates a lyrical moment into the stuff of storytelling. In narrating the episode, he does not 'tell' that the poem being recited is 'Dover Beach'. The reader oversees fragmented images grasped during the recital from Perowne's perspective; Perowne does not know and cannot identify the poem as Arnold's (a further parody perhaps of I. A. Richards' 'experiments' with Cambridge undergraduates in the 1920s, exposing them to unidentified poems which they were asked to close-read). Perowne finds many associations, many 'subject positions' from his life and his sense of Daisy's life, in the discourse that is recited. McEwan seems to be suggesting that the civilizing process that the poem effects upon Baxter is only one kind of affective response, and ironically it works on the most deranged person present. If the Library of Mendel has inscribed an irrevocable genetic script for Baxter – '*It is written*' (210) – the Library of Babel is characterized by indeterminacy. Literature multiplies the positions available for judgment and response.

That resonantly literary phrase from the canon of scientific writing, '*There is grandeur in this view of life*', apprehended from a narrative about the life of Darwin, occurs to Perowne again, only at this point, Perowne the neurosurgeon is operating on the damaged brain of Baxter. The eventual struggle to overcome Baxter ends in further damage to his brain: Perowne and his son exploit a mood swing in Baxter, encourage him upstairs to Perowne's study to look at the latest treatment protocol for his disease, only to push him down the stairs. In a narrative reversal, it is Perowne in his domain of expertise, the operating theatre, who ends up wielding the knife to restore and repair the immediate damage to Baxter's otherwise hopeless brain. As he operates, he reflects on the origins and workings of 'the brief privilege of consciousness', (56) or how matter evolves into the brain's 'unknown codes, this dense and brilliant circuitry' that produces consciousness: Perowne's humility reminds him that the best work that he and his surgeon colleagues can perform amounts to 'brilliant plumbing', but he comforts himself with the faith that 'as long as the scientists and the institutions remain in place, the explanations will refine themselves … That's the only kind of faith he has. There's grandeur in this view of life' (255). Darwin's vision of grandeur provides Perowne with a degree of comfort. A faith in scientists and institutions enables the surgeon to construct a forward-looking narrative promising salvation in 'refinement'. This goes hand in hand with a sense of sublime complexity that has to be refined: there is, under Perowne's immediate gaze, the 'brilliant circuitry' at work in the brain, and we should remember that Darwin's assertion of 'grandeur' occurs in the famous 'entangled bank' paragraph outlining the different and yet interdependent organisms and forces at play in the evolutionary process (Darwin 1982, 459). We might say that the novel itself is a complex, entangled weave of discourses.

Clifford Geertz, the anthropologist, argued in his famous essay on 'Thick Description' that anthropological interpretation could be enhanced through borrowing from literary criticism. He called this 'sorting out the structures of signification' (Geertz 1993, 10). Addressing *Saturday* from the perspective of evolutionary literary criticism – as we have seen, a development shaped by 'Third Culture' thinking – could lead us to reduce the novel's concerns to some kind of primary evolutionary logic, vested in, for example, rituals of primitive male rivalry (Baxter and Perowne fight, and Baxter exudes a general 'simian air' [88]). But structures of signification are entangled, and pull in semantic directions that resist a reductive logic. With some structures, we are confronted by something altogether uncanny. During the scene of Perowne's surgical intervention on Baxter, he reflects that he is in a terrain that feels like a kind of 'homeland', consisting of a map of the routeways conducting the circuitry of the brain:

> just to the left of the midline, running laterally away out of sight under the bone, is the motor strip. Behind it, running parallel, is the sensory strip. So easy to damage, with such terrible, lifelong consequences. How much time he has spent making routes to avoid these areas, like bad neighbourhoods in an American city. (254)

Paradoxically, the region of the brain that must be most protected is to be most scrupulously avoided in an image of fear and threat that names the degenerate city, the city that has brought, not aeroplanes aflame as a result of terrorist action, but instead the damaged Baxter into Perowne's path. Evolution is a vision of 'grandeur': but it is one driven by the 'blind furies of random mutation' (56). Evolution may have created the brain, morality, cities: it also creates spaces of degeneracy in Perowne's 'homelands', at one and the same time the human tissue in which he lives and works, and the city which he inhabits. Perowne, with the canonical words of Darwin flashing through his 'brief privilege of consciousness', finds that literature and anecdote ('How much time he has spent making routes to avoid these areas …') can enable him to be in two places at once.

This returns me, in conclusion, to McEwan's earlier fiction, *Enduring Love*, and Joe Rose's speculation that, because of his ability to engage simultaneously in two of human life's antithetical pleasures, reading and fucking, he can be in two places at the same time, and that this may make him an evolutionary 'throw forward'. In response, Clarissa mimics Joe in his 'know-all' voice that she hears on the radio (another instance of the mission of the Third Culture intellectual), replying that 'speciation is an event that can only be known in retrospect' (161). In other words, far from being 'dead', there is no escaping the organizing power of narrative in natural history, and the history of science itself. This is confirmed by the chilling episode of the botched attempted contract shooting of Joe in the restaurant, during Clarissa's birthday celebrations (chapter nineteen), an event narrated in self-consciously slow motion, accompanied by recollections of the anecdotes delivered at the dinner table, from two different disciplinary domains – Clarissa's account of the meeting between Keats and Wordsworth, and her geneticist uncle's narrative about the ambitions and conflicts that led to the discovery of DNA. In the same way that Joe Rose fails to acknowledge his own role in inflaming and perpetuating Jed Parry's obsessions – a role that Clarissa is more aware of – and strives to deny the persistent presence of narrative in science, he perhaps fails to appreciate the true significance of his own insight into 'being in two places at once'.

Having resolved to meet the threat of Parry with violence, and having acquired a gun, farcically, from a group of former criminals with intellectual aspirations, Joe Rose finds himself in woods, practising with the death tool that is quite alien to him. Of course, his 'bowels had gone watery' (206) – another 'unreliable urge to crap'. As he retires into the wood and digs a trench to relieve himself, he engages in a kind of evolutionary reverie, inspired of course by Darwin's vision of an 'entangled bank' of living co-dependencies in the mulch and soil, from the ants and worms ('rumbling giants of this lower world'), to the microscopic bacteria ('perhaps ten million of them in this handful of soil'). Joe seeks comfort, if not luxury, from the story he tells himself: 'What I thought might calm me was the reminder that, for all our concerns, we were still part of this natural dependency.' Yet he pulls back from this position and, reflecting on the destructive technology that he controls (car, gun), and the city for which he heads, concludes that 'We were no longer in the great chain. It was our own complexity that had expelled us from the Garden' (207).

This is a wonderfully resonant passage, rich in intertextual echoes from the literary canon of science that McEwan has taken recently to celebrating. We have noted the presence of Darwin's voice. But other voices are present too. In his plea for the recovery of a tradition, delivered at the event marking thirty years since the publication of Dawkins' *Selfish Gene*, McEwan spoke of the clerk, natural philosopher and microscopist Antonie van Leeuwenhoek who, in 1674, wrote to the Royal Society, observing for the first time spirogyra through his microscope. McEwan describes the Royal Society as a repository of tradition, 'the core of our library – its classical moment if you like' (McEwan 2006). The passage from Leeuwenhoek that McEwan cites is of course the precursor of the vision that Joe Rose espouses as he defecates in the woods. The microscopic perspective that opens up the relativity of scale, and issues challenges to ideas about human centrality, connects with other writings cited by McEwan in his talk – Huxley's 'A Piece of Chalk', for instance, which is one of the first to narrate the move from the micro-object to cosmic vision. And Joe Rose's conclusion – that humans have been expelled from the natural order, the Garden, because of their complexity – echoes Huxley's other great lecture and essay, 'Evolution and Ethics'.

The question that remains, however, is how one reads or apprehends the classical library of scientific writings. Arguably, the narrator of *Enduring Love* overstates the extent of the expulsion of humans from the natural order, as Huxley did before him (McEwan, I suspect, does not agree with the conclusion his character reaches). The crucial point about humans is that they *are necessarily* in two places at the same time – the order of nature, and the fields of inherited social practice and culture, and much of the most exciting work currently is concerned to break down the conceptual divide between the two (Ridley 2003). Even so, the orders and branchings of biogenetic evolution and cultural-linguistic evolution will continue to work in different ways. If the Library of Mendel orders its codes and cataloguing in deterministic fashion, then the Library of Babel, to which the 'tradition' of scientific writing also belongs, works in ways that do not follow the same restrictions. Put simply, signifying material can be transferred between genres and practices of writing in inventive ways which are barred to established configurations of genes and their replicators (species) that might seek to move between genera. 'Textualist' interdisciplinary aspirations need to recognize this. What follows from this recognition, however, is a strengthened and continuing relevance of what is inclined to be dismissed by neo-Darwinists and others as 'social constructivism'. If the Third Culture contends that culture is now science, then McEwan's fiction subtly and respectfully contests this view by seeming to suggest that it is necessary to be in two places at the same time – literature and science – when reflecting on where, as a species, our narratives are taking us.

Works Cited

Beer, Gillian, 2000 (1983). *Darwin's Plots: Evolutionary Narrative in Darwin, George Eliot and Nineteenth-Century Fiction*. Cambridge: Cambridge University Press.

————, 1996. *Open Fields: Science in Cultural Encounter*. Oxford: Clarendon Press.

Brockman, John, 1991. 'The Third Culture', http://www.edge.org/3rd_culture/ <date accessed 8 August 2007>

————, 1997–2007. *Edge*. http://www.edge.org/ <date accessed 24 August 2007>

Darwin, Charles, 1982 (1859). *The Origin of Species*, ed. J. W. Burrow. Penguin English Library. Harmondsworth: Penguin.

Dawkins, Richard, 1998. 'Postmodernism Disrobed', *Nature* 394 (9 July): 141–43.

Dennett, Daniel. C., 1995. *Darwin's Dangerous Idea: Evolution and the Meanings of Life*. Harmondsworth: Penguin.

Geertz, Clifford, 1993 (1973). *The Interpretation of Cultures: Selected Essays*. London: Fontana.

Gottschall, Jonathan and David Sloan Wilson, eds., 2005. *The Literary Animal: Evolution and the Nature of Narrative*. Evanston, IL: Northwestern University Press.

Huxley, T. H, 1891 (1870). *Lay Sermons: Addresses and Reviews*. London: Macmillan.

McEwan, Ian, 1998 (1997). *Enduring Love*. London: Vintage.

————, 2005a. *Saturday*. London: Jonathan Cape.

————, 2005b. 'Contribution to *Edge* World Question Centre, 2005'. http:// www.edge.org/q2005/q05 <date accessed 24 August 2007>

————, 2005c. 'Literature, Science and Human Nature', in *The Literary Animal: Evolution and the Nature of Narrative*, ed. Jonathan Gottschall and David Sloan Wilson. Evanston, IL: Northwestern University Press: 5–19.

————, 2006. 'Science Writing: Towards a Literary Tradition?' in *The Selfish Gene: Thirty Years On*. http://www.edge.org/3rd_culture/selfish06/selfish06_ index.html <date accessed 24 August 2007>

————, 2007a. 'Ian McEwan: I hang on to hope in a tide of fear'. Interview with Boyd Tonkin, *Independent*, 6 April. http://www.independent.co.uk/ arts/books/features/article2424436.ece <date accessed 6 August 2007>

————, 2007b. 'Enduring Fame'. Interview with Aida Edemariam, *Guardian*, 18 August: 25–26.

Ridley, Matt, 2003. *Nature via Nurture: Genes, Experience and What Makes us Human*. London: Fourth Estate.

Snow, C. P., 1964. *The Two Cultures: And A Second Look*. Cambridge: Cambridge University Press.

Sokal, Alan, 1996. 'Transgressing the Boundaries: Towards a Transformative Hermeneutics of Quantum Gravity', *Social Text* 46/47 (Spring/Summer): 217–52.

Waugh, Patricia, 2005. 'Science and Fiction in the 1990s', in *British Fiction of the 1990s*, ed. Nick Bentley. London: Routledge: 57–77.

Index